CW01086216

1 MONTH OF
FREE
READING

at
www.ForgottenBooks.com

By purchasing this book you are eligible for one month membership to ForgottenBooks.com, giving you unlimited access to our entire collection of over 700,000 titles via our web site and mobile apps.

To claim your free month visit:
www.forgottenbooks.com/free286503

* Offer is valid for 45 days from date of purchase. Terms and conditions apply.

ISBN 978-0-260-28476-1
PIBN 10286503

This book is a reproduction of an important historical work. Forgotten Books uses
state-of-the-art technology to digitally reconstruct the work, preserving the original format
whilst repairing imperfections present in the aged copy. In rare cases, an imperfection in
the original, such as a blemish or missing page, may be replicated in our edition. We do,
however, repair the vast majority of imperfections successfully; any imperfections that
remain are intentionally left to preserve the state of such historical works.

Forgotten Books is a registered trademark of FB &c Ltd.
Copyright © 2017 FB &c Ltd.
FB &c Ltd, Dalton House, 60 Windsor Avenue, London, SW19 2RR.
Company number 08720141. Registered in England and Wales.

For support please visit www.forgottenbooks.com

THE

COINS AND TOKENS

OF THE

POSSESSIONS AND COLONIES

OF THE

BRITISH EMPIRE.

BY

JAMES ATKINS.

LONDON:

BERNARD QUARITCH, 15 PICCADILLY.

1889.

LONDON:
G NORMAN AND SON, PRINTERS, HART STREET,

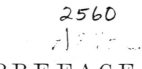

2560

PREFACE.

THE great and ever-increasing interest which is manifested in all that appertains to the Colonies and Dependencies of the British Empire, is a quite sufficient justification for the production, at this time, of a work devoted to a consideration of the Coins and Tokens which have, from time to time, been struck for, or been current in, these places.

In addition to this, all who at any time may have acquired any such coins (and most persons who are collectors must have done so), as well as systematic seekers after them, have felt the want of some work of reference, to which to turn for guidance and direction. Yet, notwithstanding the importance of the subject, to the best of my belief no attempt has, up to the present, been made to give as a whole, anything approaching a complete or comprehensive list of our Colonial Coins and Tokens. And so it has come to pass; whilst every other branch of Numismatic lore has been written upon, over and over again, this large and important section of the coins of our own Empire has been almost entirely neglected.

It is true that piecemeal attempts have been made to remedy this state of things. The Rev. H. Christmas, in articles contributed to the *Numismatic Chronicle*, has dealt with the copper coins of several of our Colonies and Dependencies. Boyne also, in his "Silver Tokens," notices a number of the silver pieces of this series; Clay's pamphlet (now so difficult to obtain), gives a considerable amount of information concerning the early American and Manx Coins, and several other contributors to the Numismatic press have touched on some portion of the ground

which I am now endeavouring to cover entirely. Nor must
I omit to mention Mr. C. Stainsfield, whose book on the
" Australian Tokens " is so thorough and painstaking that
I have no corrections to make in it, but only to supply
notices of some ten or twelve pieces, unknown to the author
at the time.

American writers have contributed several works upon
the coinage of their own country; amongst others it will
not be invidious to mention Dr. Crosby's " Early American
Coins," and Sandham's " Coins and Tokens of the Dominion
of Canada." Then again we have in German the excellent
catalogues of Neumann and Weyl, the former relating to
copper coins only; in addition to which, the cost of these
works, and the fact of their being in a foreign tongue,
prevent them being readily accessible to most collectors.

Having personally experienced the inconvenience of being
compelled to consult so many different works, whilst
endeavouring to make a collection of Colonial Coins, I
determined, so far as I might be able, to remedy this
deficiency by gathering into one volume the information
scattered in so many forms and directions, supplementing
with such additional knowledge as I have acquired during a
collecting experience of thirty years.

In preparing this list I would seek altogether to disarm
criticism by disclaiming at once any pretension to finality
or completeness. The vastness of the subject, embracing
as it does the British possessions scattered over the habit-
able world, together with the fact that no previous effort
has ever been made in this direction, are quite sufficient
grounds, if any such were requisite, for offering no apology
for any incompleteness in this the first attempt to produce
an entire view of the Coins and Tokens of our Colonial
Empire. Whatever the sins of omission or commission
may be, of the latter I trust there will be but few, as I have
carefully abstained, with rare exceptions, from describing
any coins but those I have myself seen.

Should, however, any such errors be discovered, I should be most obliged for such corrections or additions as might make a future edition (should one ever be called for) more perfect than the first.

Neither do I make any claim to literary style in the following pages, as this would be quite out of place in a work professing simply to give a plain, and, so far as may be, a reliable list of these pieces.

The making of this book has been a labour of love to me for several years past, and until recently no thought of its ever being published had occurred to me; but encouraged by the advice and assistance of many friends, I have at last brought it out. I do so in the hope that there may be some brother collectors to whom it will prove of assistance, and who may be spared by my research some of the difficulties and labours which I experienced during my early years as a collector.

Amongst so many who have kindly rendered me aid in this endeavour, it would perhaps be invidious to mention any in particular, but I cannot refrain from returning my thanks to J. B. Caldecott, Esq., for many valuable suggestions, especially in the East India section; to W. Carew Hazlitt, Esq., and R. A. Hoblyn, Esq.; to H. Montagu, Esq., for ready access to his unrivalled collection of proofs and patterns; and to J. G. Murdoch, Esq. I have also to thank Messrs. Lincoln & Son, Messrs. Spink & Sons, and Mr. F. E. Whelan, of London, and Messrs. R. Heaton & Sons, of The Mint, Birmingham, for the invariable kindness shown in giving me any information in their power; and last, but not least, to the authorities at the British Museum and the Royal Mint, for much assistance during the course of my researches in the National Collections at those places.

In conclusion, I have only to add that a short historical notice is prefaced to each section; that each division of the globe—Europe, Asia, Africa, America, and Australasia—is treated separately; and that an effort has been made, as far as possible, to arrange the colonies and dependencies of each division, and also the coins and tokens issued by them, in chronological as well as in geographical order. It may not be altogether out of place here also to state that to the European section I have added, what I believe to be the only attempt in this country to give, a complete account of the coins struck during the reign of the four Georges and William IV. for their German possessions, and which, although they cannot be strictly classed as Colonial Coins, have yet too intimate a relationship to them to be left out of a work of this kind.

JAMES ATKINS.

BROMLEY, KENT,
    October, 1888.

NOTE.

THE only abbreviations used in this work are—*O* : for obverse, and *R* : for reverse.

In many cases the distinctive application of obverse, or reverse, are purely arbitrary, and simply intended to distinguish one side from the other.

In the illustrations the obverse of the coin is usually found to the left, with the reverse to the right; but I am sorry to say that the artist in drawing some of the illustrations was pleased to take a different view of the subject to myself, and so it has come to pass in a few instances that the *O* : and *R* : of the description does not agree with those of the illustration. This was not discovered until it was too late to correct it.

I may also add that the illustrations will be found to immediately follow the description of the coin to which they refer.

TABLE OF CONTENTS.

COINS AND TOKENS

OF THE BRITISH POSSESSIONS

IN

EUROPE.

THE CHANNEL ISLANDS.	ISLE OF MAN.
GIBRALTAR.	MALTA.
IONIAN ISLANDS.	CYPRUS.

AND INCLUDING

HANOVER WITH BRUNSWICK-LUNEBERG.

EAST FRIESLAND AND BRUNSWICK-WOLFENBUTTEL.

THESE islands were captured by Rollo, and thus became an appanage of the Duchy of Normandy, and afterwards united to the Crown of England by his descendant William the Conqueror. The inhabitants preferred to remain subjects of John at the period of the invasion of Normandy by Philip Augustus, and, while retaining the laws, customs, and (until lately) the language of their continental ancestors, have always remained firm in their allegiance to England. The only coins struck for these islands have been copper and bronze, which will first be described, and afterwards the tokens, both silver and copper.

GUERNSEY.

COPPER COINS.

1. *O*:   Shield of arms, GUERNESEY above, and a laurel wreath below.

   R: **8** | DOUBLES | 1834, in three lines, within a wreath of laurel.

2.   Similar to last, excepting date, which is 1858.

3. *O*:   Shield as before, GUERNESEY under it, no wreath.

   R: **4** | DOUBLES | 1830 | in three lines.

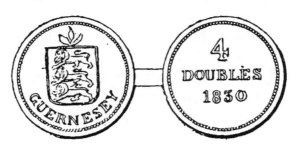

4.   Similar to last, excepting date, which is 1858.

5. *O* :   As No. 3.

    R :   **2** | DOUBLES | 1858, in three lines.

6. *O* :   Similar to last.

    R :   **1** | DOUBLE | 1830, in three lines.

There are bronzed and copper proofs of Nos. 1, 3, and 6, of this series.

Bronze Coins.

7. *O* :   Shield of arms, GUERNESEY above, and a laurel wreath below.

    R :   **8** | DOUBLES | 1861, in three lines, within a wreath of laurel.

8.   Similar to last, excepting date, which is 1864.

9.   Similar to last, excepting date, which is 1868.

10.   Similar to last, excepting date, which is 1874.

11.   Similar to last, excepting date, which is 1885.

12. *O* :   Shield as before, GUERNESEY under it, no wreath.

    R :   **4** | DOUBLES | 1864, in three lines.

13.   Similar to last, excepting date, which is 1868.

14.   Similar to last, excepting date, which is 1874.

15.   Similar to last, excepting date, which is 1885.

16. *O* :   Similar to No. 12.

    R :   **2** | DOUBLES | 1868, in three lines.

17.   Similar to last, excepting date, which is 1874.

18.   Similar to last, excepting date, which is 1885.

19. *O* :   Similar to No. 12.

    R :   **1** | DOUBLE | 1868, in three lines.

20.   Similar to last, excepting date, which is 1885.

JERSEY.

Copper Coins.

21. *O* :   Bust to left, the hair filleted. VICTORIA D:G: BRITANNIAR:REGINA F:D: 1841.

    R :   Shield of arms, STATES OF JERSEY, above, 1/13 OF A SHILLING, below.

22.   Similar to last, excepting date, which is 1844.

23.		Similar to last, excepting date, which is 1851.
24.		Similar to last, excepting date, which is 1858.
25.		Similar to last, excepting date, which is 1861.
26.		Similar to last, excepting date, which is 1865.

There are proofs of Nos. 21, 24, 25, and 26.

27. *O*: Bust as before, see No. 21, date 1841.

   R: Shield of arms as before, STATES OF JERSEY above, 1/26 OF A SHILLING below.

28. Similar to last, excepting date, which is 1844.

29. Similar to last, excepting date, which is 1851.

30. Similar to last, excepting date, which is 1858.

31. Similar to last, excepting date, which is 1861.

Proofs occur of Nos. 27, 30, and 31.

32. *O*: Similar to No. 21, excepting in size, date 1841.

   R: Shield as before. STATES OF JERSEY .above. 1/52 OF A SHILLING below.

33. Similar to last, excepting date, which is 1861.

Proofs exist of both these pieces, the latter rarely occurs in any other condition.

BRONZE COINS.

34. *O*: Coroneted bust to left, VICTORIA D.G. BRITANNIAR.REGINA F.D. 1866.

   R: Shield of arms, STATES OF JERSEY above, ONE THIRTEENTH OF A SHILLING below.

35. Similar to last, excepting date, which is 1870.

36. Similar to last, excepting date, which is 1871.

37. *O*: Similar to No. 34, excepting in size, date 1866.

   R: Shield as before, STATES OF JERSEY above, ONE TWENTY-SIXTH OF A SHILLING below.

38.   Similar to last, excepting date, which is 1870.
39.   Similar to last, excepting date, which is 1871.
          All these pieces are found as proofs.

40. *O*: Coroneted bust to left, a seven-pointed star under, and a small H (for Heaton,) VICTORIA D.G.BRITANNIAR.REGINA F.D.

     R: A pointed shield of arms divides the date 18— 77, STATES OF JERSEY above, ONE TWELFTH OF A SHILLING below.

41.   Similar to last, excepting in size and value, ONE TWENTY-FOURTH OF A SHILLING.

42.   Similar to last, excepting in size and value, ONE 48TH OF A SHILLING.
          These three also occur as proofs without the initial H. on obverse.

43.   Similar to No. 40, excepting date, which is 18-81.

SILVER TOKENS.

44. *O*: Arms of Jersey within a double circle, BISHOP DE JERSEY & Co. ✿

     R: TOKEN OF FIVE SHILLINGS in three lines within a wreath, BANK OF GUERNESEY. 1809.

45. *O*: Shield of arms, STATES OF JERSEY, 1813.

     R: THREE SHILLINGS TOKEN, in three lines, within a wreath.

46. *O* :   As last.

   R :   EIGHTEEN PENCE TOKEN, in three lines, within a wreath.

       All these tokens are found as proofs, No. 44 being exceedingly rare.

COPPER TOKENS.

All Penny size.

47. *O* :   Laureated bust of George III. JERSEY BANK TOKEN, 1812.

   R :   ELIAS NEEL, JERSEY. A BANK OF ENGLAND NOTE FOR 240 TOKENS.

48. *O* :   Draped bust of George III. JERSEY BANK, 1813.

   R :   Female seated, holding scales and cornucopia, ONE PENNY TOKEN.

49. *O* :   JERSEY. GUERNESEY AND ALDERNEY. ONE PENNY TOKEN.

   R :   Prince of Wales' plume and motto. TO FACILITATE TRADE. 1813.

50. *O* :   As last.

   R :   Bust of George III. in a thick wreath of oak.

51. *O* :   As last.

   R :   ONE PENNY TOKEN. Within a wreath.

52. *O* :   As last.

   R :   Druid's head. PURE COPPER PREFERABLE TO PAPER. PENNY TOKEN.

ISLE OF MAN.

THE Isle of Man was owned by the Earls of Derby from the year 1406 to 1735, who exercised all the rights of a sovereign even to the coining of money. The first issue of copper coins took place in 1709, and consisted of pennies and halfpennies. These coins are cast. There had been an issue of private tokens prior to this in 1668. In 1735 the island fell by inheritance to the Duke of Atholl who also exercised sovereign rights, and who in 1758 issued pennies and halfpennies. His rights were in 1765 purchased by the English Parliament for the sum of £70,000, and a further sum of £132,944 was given in January, 1829, for the purchase of his remaining interest in the revenues of the island. Copper pennies and halfpennies were issued in 1786, 1798 and 1813, and again, with the addition of farthings, in 1839. There are no silver coins, and in 1840 the separate issue for the island was stopped; since that time they have the ordinary coins such as are current in other parts of the kingdom. In addition to the seventeenth century token already mentioned, a considerable number of tokens, both silver and copper, were issued early in this present century.

COINS OF THE ISLE OF MAN.

Penny.

1. *O* : The Stanley crest, upon a cap of maintenance. ✽ SANS ✽ CHANGER ✽ 1709.

   R : The triune. QVOCVNQVE ✽ GESSERIS ✽ STABIT ✽

Halfpenny.

2.   Similar to last. Both these coins are cast.

Penny.

3. *O* : The Stanley crest, &c., as before. SANS . CHANGER . 1723.

   R : The triune. QVOCVNQVE . GESSERIS . STABIT ·:

4.   Similar to last excepting date, which is 1724.

Halfpenny.

5   Similar to No. 4.

There are silver proofs of Nos. 3, 4 and 5, and these, as well as the copper pieces, are all very rare.

Penny ?

6. *O :*   The Stanley crest, &c., as before. SANS . CHANGER . 1725.

   R :   The triune. QUOCUNQUE . GESSERIS . STABIT :·:

This piece is in silver and may be a pattern for a penny, but much more probably is a medal, as it is much larger than any of the pennies of this period. It is exceedingly rare.

Clay in his work on the Manx coinage erroneously gave the date as 1705. This was due to the fact that the specimen described by him, had the date so low down, that the bottom part of the figure 2 cannot be seen. The specimen in the British Museum is in the same condition.

7. *O :*   Similar to No. 4, excepting that the eagle has a sprig in its mouth, date 1732.

   R :   The triune dividing the initials $\begin{smallmatrix} I & D \\ & J \end{smallmatrix}$ QUOCUNQUE . IECERIS . STABIT.

8.   Similar to last but with a difference in the sprig. These also are patterns and very rare.

ſ 9. *O :*   The Stanley crest . SANS . CHANGER . 1733.

   R :   Triune dividing initials $\begin{smallmatrix} I & D \\ & J \end{smallmatrix}$ Legend as before.

This occurs in copper and in brass. There are also patterns in silver, and there are several minor variations of die.

Halfpenny.

10.   Similar to last ${}^{I}_{\frac{1}{2}}{}^{D}$. Also in silver, copper
and brass.

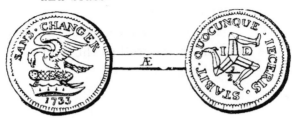

Æ

Penny.

11.   *O :*   𝒜.𝒟.—the monogram of the Duke of Atholl, a
crown above, and the date below, 1758.

    R :   The triune. QUOCUNQUE.JECERIS.STABIT.
There are silver and bronzed proofs of this,
and there are several slight variations of die,
as also of No. 12.

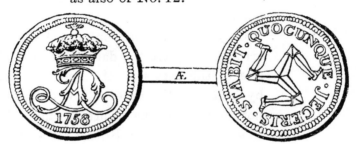

Æ

Halfpenny.

12.   Similar to No. 11, excepting in size and value.

Penny.

13.   *O :*   Laureated bust to right . GEORGIVS III DEI
GRATIA . 1786.

    R :   The triune. QVOCVNQUE IECERIS.STABIT.

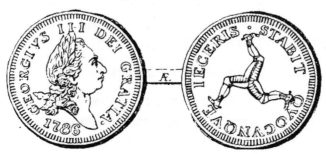

Æ

Halfpenny.

14.   Similar to last, excepting in size and value.

         Proofs occur of Nos. 13 and 14 with both plain and milled edges.

Penny.

15.   *O:*   Laureated bust to right.   GEORGIVS III. D : G . REX, 1798.

    R: The triune QVOCVNQVE IECERIS STABIT.

16.   Similar to last excepting date, which is 1813.

Halfpenny.

17.   Similar to No. 15, excepting in size and value. 179:

18.   Halfpenny similar to No. 16, excepting in size and value.

         These are broad rim coins with the legends in incuse letters on the rim.

         There are bronzed proofs of Nos. 15-18; also gilt bronze of Nos. 15 and 16.

Penny.

19.   *O:*   Bust to left . VICTORIA DEI GRATIA 1839

    R: . The triune. QVOCVNQVE IECERIS STABIT

Halfpenny.

20.   Similar to last, excepting in size and value.

Farthing.

21.   Similar to last, excepting in size and value.

         There are bronzed and copper proofs of the last three pieces. Patterns also occur of No. 19 dated 1841, and 1859; of No. 20 dated 1841, and 1860; and of No. 21, dated 1860, and 1864. These, however, were never issued as coins.

Silver Tokens.

22. *O* : View of Peel Castle and harbour. PEEL
           CASTLE above, ISLE OF MAN below.

     R : PROMISE | TO PAY | THE BEARER | ON
           DEMAND | 5 SHILLINGS | BRITISH |
           1811, in seven lines. THE DOUGLAS
           BANK Co. ❋ AT THEIR BANK, DOUG-
           LAS ❋ in an outer circle.

23. *O* : Similar to the last.

     R : Similar to the last, excepting that the fifth line
           of *R* : is 2*s* 6*d*.

24. *O* : View of Peel Castle and harbour, no legend.

     R : DOUGLAS | BANK TOKEN | ONE SHIL-
           LING | BRITISH | 1811 in five lines.

           I have seen a small copper token as follows.

25. *O* : As last.

     R : S . ASH . in centre of the field of the coin.

Copper Tokens.

26. *O* : View of Peel Castle and harbour, PEEL
           CASTLE above, ISLE OF MAN below.

     R : DOUGLAS | BANK TOKEN | ONE PENNY
           | 1811. in four lines.

27.   Similar to preceding, excepting that the word
           BANK is omitted on the reverse.

28.   Halfpenny similar to No. 26, excepting in size
           and value.

29. *O* : Atlas supporting a globe, PAYABLE AT THE
           OFFICE DOUGLAS.

     R : The triune, MANKS TOKEN ONE PENNY
           1811.

30.   Halfpenny similar, excepting in size and value.

31. *O* : BANK | PENNY in two lines in centre within
           a circle, ISLE OF MAN · 1811 ·

     R : The triune, QVOCVNQVE IECERIS STABIT.

32.   Halfpenny similar, excepting in size and value.

Penny.

33. *O*: Bust to right, GOD : SAVE : THE : KING 1830.
(George III. ?)

R. FOR ⚜—⚜ PUBLICK ACCOMODATION,
displayed in three lines. This is struck in
copper and brass, there is a variety in brass
which has a square top to the figure 3.

Halfpenny.

34. Similar excepting in size and value.

35. *O*: HALF | PENNY | TOKEN in three lines in
the centre, PRO BONO PUBLICO 1831.

R: The triune. QUOCUNQUE . IECERIS . STABIT,
The legend on both sides is incuse on a broad
thick rim. This also occurs in copper and
brass.

To make our list as complete as possible we add a
description of the only 17th Century token known to exist.

36. *O*: HIS | PENNY | I * M in three lines within a
circle. IOHN ✶ MVRRAY ✶ 1668.

R: The triune, QVOCVNQVE . GESSERIS · STA-
BIT *.

GIBRALTAR.

THE ancient Calpe, a town on a rock in South Spain, on which is placed a fortress considered impregnable. It was attacked by the British, and taken on July 24th, 1704. The Spaniards attempted to retake it in 1705, and again in 1727, but were repulsed with great loss on both occasions.

Again in 1779 it was besieged by an immense force of French and Spaniards combined, and kept in a state of siege for upwards of three years, but the English garrison, under General Eliott, were successful in withstanding all their efforts, and the blockade ceased on February 5th, 1783.

The only coins are copper, struck in 1842, and are for two, one, and half quarts respectively.

The tokens are not numerous, and are of copper only.

COINS.

1. *O:*   Bust to left.   VICTORIA D : G : BRITAN-
          NIAR : REGINA F : D : 1842.

   R: A castle with a key under it, GIBRALTAR
          above, TWO QUARTS below.

2.   ONE QUART.   Similar, excepting in size and
          value.

3.   HALF QUART.   Similar.

          There are bronzed and copper proofs of
          each of these, and I have also seen a set dated
          1861.   These latter were never issued, but
          are only patterns.

TOKENS.

4. *O:*   View of Gibraltar, PAYABLE AT R. KEEL-
          INGS above, GIBRALTER below.

   R: Castle and key VALUE TWO QUARTS 1802.

5.   ONE QUART. Similar to last, excepting in size and value.

✓6. *O*: A lion holding a key. PAYABLE AT ROBERT KEELING & SON'S. GIBRALTAR.

  R: A castle. VALUE TWO QUARTS above, 1810 below.

7.   ONE QUARTO. Similar to last, excepting in size and value.

8. *O*: Similar to No. 6, excepting that there is no dot before or after Gibraltar.

  R: Similar to last, excepting that the figures of date are smaller.

9.   ONE QUARTO. Similar to No. 8, excepting in size and value.

10. *O*: Lion and key, PAYABLE AT RICHARD CATTONS GOLDSMITH. GIBRALTAR 1813.

  R: **2. QUARTOS** within a wreath, a crown over. AGENTE PARA LA FABRICA DE DIA-MANTES PATENTES. DE DUDDELL. HOLBORN. LONDRES.

11.   **1 QUART0.** Similar, but without the legend on reverse.

12. *O*: Lion and key. PAYABLE AT JAMES SPITTLE'S above, GIBRALTAR below.

  R: View of fortifications. VALUE TWO QUARTOS 1818.

13. *O*: Same as last.

  R: Similar view, VALE DOS QUARTOS 1820.

14.   UN QUARTO. Similar to last, excepting in
size and value.

There are Spanish Dollars with their various divisions
found, which are countermarked on both sides with the
floriated capitals ⟨GR⟩ in a circular indent. These are
mentioned by Boyne in his work on Silver Tokens, and
supposed by him to have been so marked for use in some
of the Colonies. I have been informed, on pretty good
authority, that they were used early in the present century
for the payment of the troops at Gibraltar. I have, therefore, taken this opportunity of mentioning them, although I
do not positively assign them to this purpose. See also a
note to a somewhat similar piece assigned to the West
Indies.

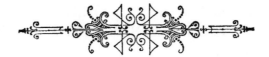

MALTA,

T<small>HE</small> ancient Melita, was given to the Knights Hospitallers in 1530, and taken from them by the French in 1798. It surrendered to the British in 1800, and was confirmed in their possession by the treaty of Paris in 1814.

Ruding, in his "Annals of the Coinage," says that the third of a farthing was ordered to be struck for this island on February 26th, 1827, and again on March 10th, 1835. It has also been struck in both copper and bronze during the reign of Victoria.

C<small>OPPER</small>.

1. *O* :   Laureated bust to left. GEORGIUS IV DEI GRATIA. 1827.

   R :   Britannia seated holding trident; rose, shamrock, and thistle under, BRITANNIAR : REX FID : DEF :

2. *O* :   Bust to right, GULIELMUS IIII DEI GRATIA 1835.

   R :   Same as last.

      There are bronzed and copper proofs of Nos. 1 and 2.

3. *O* :   Bust to left, the hair filleted. VICTORIA DEI GRATIA 1844.

   R :   Britannia as before, BRITANNIAR : REG : FID : DEF :

2

BRONZE.

4. *O*: Laureated bust to left, VICTORIA D.G. BRITT.
          REG. F.D.

    R: ONE THIRD | FARTHING | 1866 in three
          lines within an oak wreath, a crown over.

5.   Similar to last, excepting date, which is 1868.
6.   Similar to last, excepting date, which is 1876.
7.   Similar to last, excepting date, which is 1878.
8.   Similar to last, excepting date, which is 1881.
✓ 9.   Similar to last, excepting date, which is 1884.
10.   Similar to last, excepting date, which is 1885.

IONIAN ISLANDS.

THESE islands were taken under the protection of Great Britain in 1815, and remained so until 1864 when they were handed over to the kingdom of Greece. According to Ruding, a penny, halfpenny, and farthing were ordered to be struck for these islands on February 11th, 1819. And on August 23rd, 1834, a silver piece of 30 oboli, as well as a copper obolus, was ordered; the latter being of the weight of 240 to the pound.

SILVER.

30 *Oboli.*

1. O: **30** within an oak wreath. IONIKON ΚΡΑΤΟΣ above it, 1834 below.

    R: Britannia seated facing right, holding a trident. BRITANNIA.

2. Similar to last, excepting date, which is 1849.
3. Similar to last, excepting date, which is 1851.
4. Similar to last, excepting date, which is 1852.
5. Similar to last, excepting date, which is 1857.
6. Similar to last, excepting date, which is 1862.

Proofs occur of all these coins.

COPPER.

Penny (or 10 *Oboli).*

7. O: The winged lion of St. Mark. IONIKON ΚΡΑΤΟΣ 1819.

    R: Britannia seated facing left, holding olive branch and trident. BRITANNIA.

2 *

Halfpenny (or 5 Oboli).

8.   Similar to last, excepting in size and value.

Farthing (or 2½ Oboli).

✔9. ⁊   Similar to last, excepting in size and value.
✔10.   Similar excepting date, which is 1820.
             There are bronzed and copper proofs of Nos. 7-10.

Obolus.

√11.   O: Winged lion of St. Mark. IONOKON ΚΡΑΤΟΣ.
             1834.

        R: Britannia seated facing right holding trident.
             BRITANNIA.
                     There is a bronze proof of this.

12.   Similar to last, excepting date, which is 1835.
13.   Similar to last, excepting date, which is 1848.
14.   Similar to last, excepting date, which is 1849.
⌐ 15.   Similar to last, excepting date, which is 1851.
16.   Similar to last, excepting date, which is 1853.
17.   Similar to last, excepting date, which is 1857.
18.   Similar to last, excepting date, which is 1862.

             There are copper proofs of Nos. 16, 17, and
             18, and there are also " mules " or varieties
             made by combining the obverses of Nos. 7
             and 8 with the obverses of the Irish penny
             of Geo. IV. and the Ceylon stiver of Geo. III.
             respectively.

CYPRUS.

THIS, the latest acquisition of England in the Mediterranean, was ceded by the Sultan of Turkey for administrative purposes, under the Anglo-Turkish Convention of June 4th, 1878.

The following bronze coins have been struck for use in the island :—

Piastre.

1. *O* : Coroneted bust to left. VICTORIA QUEEN, 1879.

   R : **1** within a circle of dots. CYPRUS ° ONE PIASTRE °.

2. Similar to last, excepting date, which is 1880.
3. Similar to last, excepting date, which is 1881.
4. Similar to last, excepting with initial H. for Heaton.
5. Similar to last, excepting date, which is 1885, but without the H.
6. Similar to last, excepting date, which is 1886.
7. Similar to last, excepting date, which is 1887.

Half Piastre.

8. Similar to No. 1 excepting in size and value, 1879.
9. Similar to last, excepting date, which is 1880.
10. Similar to last, excepting date, which is 1881.
11. Similar to last, excepting with initial H.
12. Similar to last, excepting date, which is 1885, but without the H.
13. Similar to last, excepting date, which is 1886.
14. Similar to last, excepting date, which is 1887.

Quarter
Piastre.

15.   Similar to No. 1 excepting in size and value,
                1879.
16.   Similar to last, excepting date, which is 1880.
17.   Similar to last, excepting date, which is 1881.
18.   Similar to last, excepting with initial H.
19.   Similar to last, excepting date, which is 1885, but
                without the H.
20.   Similar to last, excepting date, which is 1886.
21.   Similar to last, excepting date, which is 1887.
            There are proof sets of 1879.

THE ANGLO-HANOVERIAN COINS.

THE electorate and kingdom of Hanover, together with the dukedoms of Brunswick and Luneberg, became a portion of the British empire by the accession of George Lewis, Elector, in 1714, to the throne of England. From this time, therefore, to the death of William IV. in 1837, the coins of these States come within the scope of this work.

The majority of these coins were struck at the mints at Clausthall or Zellerfeld, the Hanover mint only commencing its operations in 1814.

The coins of the Clausthall mint usually bear the bust or arms of the sovereign on obverse, and the running horse on reverse, but when the metal of which the coins were made was brought from the mines at Andreasberg, then the reverse bears St. Andrew with his cross.

The Zellerfeld coins usually bear a wild man holding a fir-tree, the symbol of Brunswick Luneberg. The wild man holds the tree in his right hand. (The coins of Brunswick Wolfenbuttel bear the same wild man holding the tree in his left hand.) The tree usually has branches on one side only, but the mint at Zellerfeld being closed in 1789, and its business transferred to Clausthal from that time to the opening of the Hanover mint in 1814, the fir-tree has branches on both sides. On the smaller silver and many of the copper coins, the royal cypher appears on obverse, and the value on reverse.

On most of the coins the initials of the mint master appear; it will be as well, therefore, to give a list of their names during the English connection. On some of the coins the initial C. only appears; this denotes commission, and only occurs in those years in which there was a vacancy in the office of mint master.   The initial A. also occurs, and denotes administrator.

Clausthal Mint.

HEINRICH CHRISTIAN BONHORST, 1702-1725.
CHRISTIAN PHILIP SPANGANBERG, 1725-1751.
JOHAN WILHELM SCHLEMN, 1753-1788.
PHILIP LUDWIG MAGIUS, 1792-1800.
GEORG FRIEDRICH MICHAELIS, 1802-1807.
JOHAN WILHELM LUNDE, 1807-1819, Director.
WILHELM AUGUST JULIUS ALBERT, 1821-1838,
    Administrator.

Zellerfeld Mint.

HEINRICH HORST, 1711-1719.
ERNEST PETER HECHT, 1723-1731.
JOHAN ALBRECHT BRAUNS, 1731-1739.
JOHAN BENJAMIN HECHT, 1739-1763.
JOHAN ANTON PFEFFER, 1763-1773.
LUDWIG CHRISTIAN RUPERTT, 1773-1778.
CHRISTOF ENGLEHARD SEIDENSTICKER, 1780-
    1785.

Hanover Mint.

CHRISTIAN HEINRICH HAASE, 1814-1818.
LUDWIG AUGUST BRUEL, 1818-1838.

For the more convenient identification of the coins which follow, a table giving the shape of the various coats of arms, and shields, in outline, is here placed.   For easy reference the arms, and shields, are numbered separately, and will be referred to in the description of the coins, by the numbers which are placed under them.   There are minor variations in the shape of shields, which are impossible to specify, but these given will be found to embrace all the most striking differences.

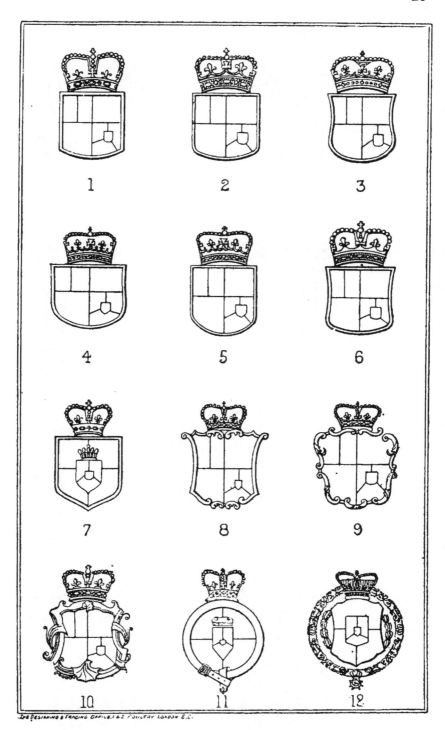

The Designing & Tracing Office, 1 & 2 Poultry London E.C.

1   2

3   4

GOLD COINS.
GEORGE I.   1714-27.

Ducats or Gulden.

1.   *O* :   Bust to right. GEORGIUS . D . G . M . BRIT .
            FR . ET . HIB . REX . F . D.

     R :   Four shields crosswise, sceptres in saltire.
            H . C . B . at the sides of the Irish shield,
            BR . ET . LUN . DUX . S . R . I . A . T . &
            EL.   1715.

2.   Similar to last, but with AUR[B] HERC. under bust.
                 This is made from gold brought from the
             Hartz Mountains.

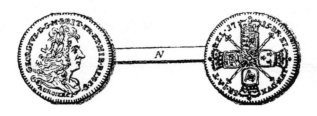

3. *O*: Bust as before, H.C.B. under, GEORG.
D.G.M.BRIT.F.&H.REX.F.D.

R: Four shields crosswise, two sceptres in saltire, a
star in centre, BR.& LUN.D.S.R.I.A.T.
& EL. 1716.

4. *O*: Bust as before, B. under. GEORG.D.G.M.
BRIT.F.&H.REX.F.D.

R: Four shields crosswise, and sceptres in saltire,
a star in centre, BR.&L.D.S.R.I.A.T
& EL. 1717.

5. Similar to last, but with AURI HERC. under
bust.

6. Similar to last, but dated 1719.

7. Similar to No. 4, excepting date, which is 1721.

8. Similar to No. 4, excepting date, which is 1724.

9. *O*: Four shields crosswise, a star in centre. GEORG.
D.G.M.BR.FR.ET.H.REX.F.D.

R: Wild man and tree. E.P.H. under. BRUN.
& LUN.DUX.S.R.I.A.TH.& EL.
1726.

10. Similar to No. 5, excepting date, which is 1727.

Half Ducat.

11. *O*: Bust to right, B. under, GEORG.D.G.M.B.F.
& H.REX.F.D.

R: Running horse. BR.&.L.DVX.
S.R.I.A.TH.& E. 1724.

GEORGE II. 1727-60.

Four Gulden.

12. *O*: Bust to left. GEORG.II.D.G.M.B.F.
& H.REX. Under the bust is F.D.

R: **IIII** GOLD | GULDEN | 8 THALER | N.D.
FUS. | I.A.S. in six lines. BRUNS.ET.
LUN.DUX.S.R.I.A.TH.ET.EL.
1749.

13. Similar to last, excepting date, which is 1750.

14.   *O* :   As No. 12, excepting the latter part of legend, which is F . ET . H . REX . F . D.

     R :   As No. 12, excepting the latter part of legend, which is T . ET . EL . and date 1752.

Five Thalers.

15.   *O* :   Shield No. 8, crowned. GEORG . II . D . G . M . B . F . & H . REX . F . D.

     R :   ❧ **V** ❧ | THALER | ⚬ 1758 ⚬ | ❊ I . A . s ❊ in four lines. BRUNS . ET LUN . DUX . S . R . I . A . TH . ET . EL.

16.   Similar to last, excepting the shield, which is No. 10.

Two Gulden.

17.   *O* :   Similar to No. 12.

     R :   **II** GOLD | GULDEN | 4 THALER | N . D . R . FUS. | s. | in five lines. BRUNS . ET . LUN . DUX . S . R . I . A . TH . ET . EL.   1749.

18.   *O* :   Shield No. 3. GEORG . II . D . G . M. BRIT . FR . ET . HIB . REX . F . D.

     R :   Similar in all respects to last.

19.   Similar to No. 17, excepting date, which is 1751, and initials I . w . s.

20.   Similar to last, but dated 1752.

21.   Similar to last, but dated 1753.

22.   Similar to No. 18, excepting date, which is 1754, and initials I . w . s.

23.   *O* :   Shield No. 8. GEORG . II . D . G . M . B . F . ET . H . REX . F . D.

     R :   Similar to No. 17, excepting date, which is 1754, and initials I . w . s.

Ducats or Gulden.

24.   *O* :   Four shields crosswise, two sceptres in saltire. GEORG . II . D . G . M . BR . F . & H . REX . F . D . B . & L . DUX . S . R . I . A . TH . & EL.

     R :   Running horse, AUR ˢ HERC 1727 under, NEC ASPERA TERRENT.

25. *O* : Shield No. 3, legend as last.

    R : Running horse, 17$\frac{3}{8}$2 under, NEC ASPERA TERRENT.

26. *O*. Bust to left. GEORG . II . D . G . M . B . F . ET . H . REX . F . D.

    R : Shield No. 3. BR . ET . LUN . DUX . S . R . I . A . T . ET EL . 1732.

27. Similar to No. 25, excepting date, which is 1737.

28. Similar to No. 25, excepting date, which is 1744, and EX . AÜR . HERCHIN in a curve under horse.

29. Similar to last, excepting date, which is 1748.

30. *O* : Bust to left, GEORG . II . D . G . M . B . F . ET . H . REX . F . D.

    R : 1 GOLD | GULDEN | 2 THAL : | N . D . R . FUS. | s. in five lines, BR . ET LUN . DUX . S . R . I . A . TH . ET . EL. 1749.

31. Different bust, otherwise as last, but dated 1750.

32. Similar to No. 30, but dated 1751.

33. Similar to last, excepting date, which is 1756, and EX . AURO . HERC | I . B . H. under horse.

34. *O* : As No. 30.

    R : 1 | DUCAT | N . D . R . FUS . | I . A . s. in four lines, BR . ET . LUN . DUX . S . R . I . A . T . ET . EL. 1751.

35. *O* : Running horse, legend as last.

    R : As last.

36. *O* : As No. 23.

    R : As No. 30, excepting date, which is 1752.

37. Similar to No. 30, excepting date, which is 1753.

38. Similar to last, excepting date, which is 1754.

39. Similar to No. 36, excepting date, which is 1754.

40. Similar to No. 36, excepting date, which is 1755.

Half Gulden or Thaler.

41. *O* : Bust to left, s. under. Legend as No. 30.

    R : Shield as centre of Arms No. 1, crown divides date, 1730. BR . ET . L . DUX . S . R . I . A . TH . ET . EL.

42. *O :* As last.

    R : Shield No. 3, crown divides date, 1737. BR .
        ET . L . DUX . S . R . I . A . T . ET . EL.

43. *O :* Bust to left, GEORG . II . D . G . M . B . F .
        ET . H . REX . F . D.

    R : $\frac{1}{2}$ GOLD | GULDEN | I.THAL: | N.D.R.F. |
        s . in five lines. BR . ET . LUN . DUX .
        S . R . I . A . T . ET . EL. 1749.

44. *O :* As last.

    R : $\frac{1}{2}$ GOLD | GULDEN | I THALER | N . D . R .
        F . | I . A . s . in five lines, BRUN . ET . LUN .
        DUX . S . R . I . A . TH. ET . EL. 1750.

45.   Similar to last, but legend on *R :* reads BR .
        ET . LUN . DUX . S . R . I . A . T. ET . EL.
        1750, and s. only, in place of initials I . A . S.

46.   Similar to No. 44, excepting date, which is 1754.

47.   Similar to No. 44, excepting date, which is 1756.

Half Thaler or Quarter Gulden.

48. *O :* $\mathcal{G}$. $\mathcal{R}$. in monogram crowned, s. under.

    R : Running horse, NEC ASPERA TERRENT.
        1730.

49. *O :* Bust to left. GEORG . II . D . G . M . B . F .
        ET . H . REX . F . D.

    R : ✿ $\frac{1}{4}$ ✿ | GOLD G: | $\frac{1}{2}$ THAL: | N.D.R.F. |
        s . in five lines. BR . ET . LUN . DUX .
        S . R . I . A . T. ET. EL. 1754.

50. *O :* Similar to last, but with s. under bust.

    R : As last, excepting date, 1757, and end of legend,
        which is T . & EL.

        These last coins are usually found as proofs.

George III. 1760-1820.

George d'or.

51. *O :* Bust to right, c . under. GEORGIVS III .
        D . G . M . B . F . ET . H . REX . F . D.

    R : Shield of arms, crowned, BRVNS . ET . LVN .
        DVX . S . R . I . A . T . ET . EL . 1768.

52. *O* : Bust to right, different to preceding GEORGIVS . III . DEI . GRATIA.

R : Shield of arms, crown divides date, 17—83. M . B . F . ET . H . REX . F . D . B . ET . L . D . S . R . I . A . T . ET . E.

Ten Thalers.

53. *O* : Running horse, c . H . H . under. GEORGIUS III D . G . BRITANNIARUM REX F . D ✸

R : ❖**X**❖ | THALER | 1814. | in three lines. BRUNS . ET LUNEB . DUX . S . R . I . A . TH . ET ELECT ✸

Five Thalers.

54. *O* : Shield as centre of Arms No. 2, with garter depending from it; legend as last.

R : ❖**V**❖ | THALER | ❧1813❧ | T. W. in four lines. BRUNSVICENSIS ET LUNEBURG DUX . S . R . I . A . T . ET . E.

55. Similar to last, but dated **1814**.

56. *O* :　Running horse, EX AURO | HEROINIÆ in two lines
　　　　　under.　GEORG . III . D . G . BRITAN-
　　　　　NIARUM . REX . F . D. ✽

　　R :　✽ **V** ✽ | THALER | 1814 | c . in four lines,
　　　　　BRUNS . ET . LUNEB . DUX . S . R . I .
　　　　　A . TH . ET . ELECT. ✽

57. 　　　Similar to No. 54, but dated 1815.
　　　　　　　The initials T . w on Nos. 54, 55, and 57,
　　　　　are for Thomas Wyon.　These coins are only
　　　　　met with as proofs and are most probably
　　　　　patterns.

Two-and-a-Half Thalers.

58. *O* :　Running horse, c . H . H . under.　GEORGIUS
　　　　　III . D . G. BRITANNIARUM REX . F . D.

　　R :　✢ **2½** ✢ | THALER | 1814.　in three lines.
　　　　　BRUNS . ET . LUNEB . DUX . S . R . I . A .
　　　　　TH . ET . ELECT ✽ |

59. 　　　Similar to last, excepting date, which is 1815.

Ducats or Gulden.

60. *O* :　Shield No. 3.　GEORG . III. D. G. M. BR .
　　　　　F . ET . H . REX . F . D . B . & L . DUX .
　　　　　S . R . I . A . TH . & EL.

　　R :　Running horse, EX . AURO . HERC . | 1767 |
　　　　　I . A . P . in three lines under; no legend.

61. 　　　Similar to last, excepting date, which is 1768.

62. 　　　Similar to No. 60, excepting date, which is 1774.

63. *O* :　Shield No. 1, otherwise as No. 60.

　　R :　Similar to No. 60, excepting date, 1776, and
　　　　　initials, L . C . R.

64. *O* :　Shield No. 2, otherwise as last.

　　R :　Similar to last, excepting date, 1783, and initials,
　　　　　C . P . S.

65. 　　　Similar to last, excepting date, which is 1789.

66. *O* :　As last.

　　R :　Running horse, EX . AURO . HERC . | 1791, in
　　　　　two lines under, no legend.

67. Similar to No. 65, excepting date, which is 1795 and initials P . L . M.

68. Similar to last, excepting date, which is 1797.

69. *O:* Bust to right. GEORGIUS III . D . G . M . B . F . ET . H . REX . F . D.

    R: Shield No. 10. BRUNS . ET . LUN . DUX . S . R . I . A . T . ET . EL. 1798.

70. Similar to No. 66, excepting date, which is 1799.

71. Similar to No. 66, excepting date, which is 1802, and initials G . F . M.

72. *O:* Running horse, c. under. GEORG . III . D . G . M . BRIT . REX . F . D . B . & L . DUX . S . R . I . A . TH . & EL. ✻

    R: ✻ **1** ✻ | PISTOLE | 1803. In three lines.

73. Similar to No. 66, excepting date, which is 1804.

74. *O:* Running horse. GEORG . III . D . G . BRIT . & HANNOV . REX . BR . & L . DUX.

    R: **1** | DUCAT | 1805 | c. in four lines. EX AURO HERCINIAE

75. Similar to last, excepting date, which is 1815.

76. Similar to last, excepting date, which is 1818.

George IV.   1820—30.

Ten Thalers.

77. *O :*   Bust to left. GEORGIUS IV . D . G . BRIT .
             & HANOV . REX . F . D.

    R :   **X** | THALER | 1821 | B. in   four   lines.
             BRUNSVICENSIS & LUNEBURGENSIS
             DUX

78.   Similar to last, excepting date, which is 1822.
79.   Similar to last, excepting date, which is 1823.
80.   Similar to last, excepting date, which is 1824.
81.   Similar to last, excepting date, which is 1825.
82.   Similar to last, excepting date, which is 1827.
83.   Similar to last, excepting date, which is 1828.
84.   Similar to last, excepting date, which is 1829.
85.   Similar to last, excepting date, which is 1830.

Five Thalers.

86. *O :*   As last.

    R :   **V** | THALER | 1821 | B. in four lines.   Legend
             as before.

87.   Similar to last, excepting date, which is 1822.
88.   Similar to last, excepting date, which is 1823.
89.   Similar to last, excepting date, which is 1824.
90.   Similar to last, excepting date, which is 1825.
91.   Similar to last, excepting date, which is 1827.
92.   Similar to last, excepting date, which is 1828.
93.   Similar to last, excepting date, which is 1829.
94.   Similar to last, excepting date, which is 1830.

Two-and-a-Half Thalers.

95. *O :*   As before.

    R :   **$2\frac{1}{2}$** | THALER | 1821 | B. in four lines, legend
             as before.

96.   Similar to last, excepting date, which is 1827.
97.   Similar to last, excepting date, which is 1830.

Ducat.

98. *O :* Running horse, GEORG . IV . D . G . BRIT .
& HANOV . REX . BR . & L . DUX ✿

R : I | DUCAT | 1821 | c in four lines, EX AURO
HERCINIÆ.

99. Similar to last, excepting date, which is 1824.

100. Similar to last, excepting date, which is 1827.
All these occur as proofs.

WILLIAM IV. 1830-37.

Ten Thalers.

101. *O :* Bust to right. GULIELMUS IV D . G . BRIT .
ET HANOV . REX F . D . &c.

R : Shield of arms in a garter, inscribed NEC
ASPERA TERRENT. The date over, 1832,
ZEHN THALER under.

102. *O :* Bust to right; B. under. WILHELM IV
KOENIG V . GR . BRIT . U . HANNOVER.

R : Shield No. 12, ZEHN THALER under, date
over 1833.

103. *O :* Similar to last, excepting date, which is 1835.

104. Similar to last, but the date 1836 under the
shield, and ZEHN THALER over.

105. Similar to last, excepting date, which is 1837.

Five Thalers.

106. *O :* As No. 102.

R : Shield No. 12. FUNF THALER over, date
under, 1835.

Two-and-a-Half Thalers.

107. *O :* Bust to right. GULIELM . IV . D . G . BRIT .
& HANNOV . REX . F . D.

R : $2\frac{1}{2}$ | THALER | 1832 | B. in four lines.
BRVNSVICENSIS & LUNEBURGENSIS
DUX. ✿

108. Similar to last, excepting date, which is 1833.

109. Similar to last, excepting date, which is 1835.

110. Similar to last, excepting date, which is 1836.

Ducat.

111. *O*: Running horse, WILHELM IV V . G . G .
KONIG D . v . R . GROSSB . U . IRL ✻

    R: As No. 98. 1 | DUCAT | 1831 | c in four lines,
EX AURO HERCINIÆ.

SILVER COINS.
GEORGE I. 1714—27.

Thalers.

112. *O*: Bust to right. GEORGIVS . D . G . M . BRIT .
FR . ET . HIB . REX . F . D.

    Arms No. 2, supporters, &c. H . C . B . under.
BRVNS . ET . LVN . DVX . S . R . I . A .
THES . ET . EL . 1716.

113.   Similar to last, excepting date, which is 1717, and
initials are under bust on *O :*

114. *O*: Bust as before, H . C . B . under it. GEORGIVS .
D . G . MAG. BRIT . FR . ET . HIB . REX .
F . D.

    R: Four shields crosswise, a star in the centre.
BR . ET . LVN . D . S . R . I . A . TH . ET .
EL. 1717.

115. *O*: Four shields crosswise, a star in the centre.
GEORGIVS . D . G . MAG . BR . FR . ET .
HIB . REX . FID . D.

    R: Wild man and tree, H . ⚹ H. under. BRVN .
& LVN . DVX . S . R . I . AR . THES . &
EL. 1717.

116. *O*: Arms No. 2, supporters, &c. GEORGIUS .
D . G . MAG . BRIT . FRANC . ET . HIB .
REX . FID . D .

    R: As last.

117. *O*: Four shields crosswise, a star in centre,
GEORGIUS . D . G . MAG . BRIT . FR .
ET . HIB . REX . F . D. 1717.

    R: Running horse. H . C . B . under, BRUN . ET .
LUN . DUX . S . R . I . ARCHITHES . ET . EL.

118. *O* :   Bust as No. 114.

    R :   Arms No. 2, supporters, &c. BRUN . ET . LUN . DUX . S . R . I . ARCHITH . ET . EL . 1718.

119. *O* :   Bust as No. 114.

    R :   Arms No. 3, supporters, &c. BRUNS . ET . LUN . DUX . S . R . I . A . THES . ET . EL . 1718.

120. *O* :   Arms No. 3, supporters, &c. GEORGIUS . D . G . MAG . BRIT . FR . ET . HIB . REX . F . D. 1718.

    R :   St. Andrew and his cross, H . C . B . under. BRUNS . ET . LUN . DUX . S . R . I . A . THES . ET . EL.

121. *O* :   Arms No. 2, supporters, &c. Legend and date as last.

    R :   Running horse, H . C . B . under it. BRUNS . ET . LUN . DUX . S . R . I . A . THES . ET . ELECT . *

122.   Similar to No. 115, excepting date, which is 1718.

123. *O* :   Bust as No. 114.

    R :   Arms No. 2, supporters, &c. BRVNS . ET . LVN . DVX . S . R . I . A . THES . ET . EL. 1719.

124.   Similar to No. 120, excepting date, which is 1719.

125. *O* :   Arms No. 2, supporters, &c. GEORGIUS . D . G . MAG . BRIT . FR . ET . HIB . REX . F . D. 1719.

    R :   Running horse, H . C . B . under, BRVNS . ET . LVN . DVX . S . R . I . A . THES . ET . ELECT . ✤

126.   Similar to No. 119, excepting date, which is 1720.

127. *O* :   Four shields as No. 115.

    R :   Wild man and tree, C . under. Legend as No. 115, date 1720.

128. *O* :   Arms No. 2, supporters, &c. GEORGIUS . D .
             G . MAG . BRIT . FRANC . ET . HIB . REX .
             FID . D .

    R :   Same as last.

129.   Similar to No. 121, excepting date, which is 1720.

130.   Similar to No. 121, excepting date, which is 1721.

131.   Similar to No. 120, excepting date, which is 1721.

132.   Similar to No. 127, excepting date, which is 1721.

133. *O* :   Bust as No. 114.

    R :   Arms No. 1, supporters, &c. BRVNS . ET . LVN .
             DVX . S . R . I . A . THES . ET . EL . 1722.

134. *O* :   Arms No. 1, supporters, &c. GEORGIUS . D . G .
             M . BRIT . FR . ET . HIB . REX . F . D. 1722.

    R :   St. Andrew, as No. 120.

135.   Similar to No. 128, excepting date, which is 1722.

136. *O* :   Four shields as No. 117.

    R :   As No. 127, date 1722.

137. *O* :   As last.

    R :   As No. 125, date 1722.

138.   Similar to No. 128, excepting date, which is 1723,
             and E . P . H . under Wild man.

139.   Similar to No. 125, but legend is GEORGIVS .
             D . G . M . BRIT . FR . ET . HIB . REX .
             F . D. 1723.

140.   Similar to No. 133, excepting date, which is 1724.

141. *O* :   Arms, &c., similar to No. 134, excepting date,
             which is 1724.

    R :   Runnin horse as No. 121.

142.   Similar to No. 115, but E . P . H . under Wild man, and date, 1724.

143.   Similar to No. 128, but E . P . H . under Wild man, and date 1724.

144.   Similar to No. 115, but E . P . H . under Wild man, and date 1725.

145.   Similar to No. 128, but E . P . H . under Wild man, and date 1725.

146. *O :*   Bust as before, C . P . S . under, legend as No. 139. The date is on *R :*

    R :   Arms No. 1, supporters, &c. BRVNS . ET . LVN . DVX . S . R . I . A . THES . ET . EL. 1726.

147. *O :*   Arms No. 2, supporters, &c. GEORGIVS . D . G . M . BRIT . FR . ET . HIB . REX . F . D. 1726.

    R :   St. Andrew with his cross, C . P . S . under, legend as last.

148. *O :*   As last.

    R :   Running horse, C . P . S . under, legend as before, date 1726.

149.   Similar to No. 115, excepting date, which is 1726, and E . P . H . under Wild man.

150.   Similar to No. 128, but E . P . H . under Wild man, and date 1726.

151.   Similar to No. 133, but C . P . S . under bust, and date 1727.

152.   Similar to No. 148, excepting date, which is 1727.

153.   Similar to No. 149, excepting date, which is 1727.

154.   Similar to No. 150, excepting date, which is 1727.

Two-third Thalers.

155. *O :*   Bust to right, H . C . B . under. GEORGIUS . D . G . MAG . BRIT . FR . ET . HIB . REX . F . D .

    R :   Four shields crosswise, ($\frac{2}{3}$) FE-IN-SI-LB in centre. BR . & LUN . D . S . R . I . A . TH . & EL. 1715.

156.   Similar to last, excepting date, which is 1716.

157.   Similar to last, but V^S in legend instead of U$^{S.}$

158. *O*:   Bust as before, H . C . B . under. GEORGIUS .
     D . G . M . BRIT . FR . ET . HIB . REX . F . D.

   R: Four shields crosswise, ($\frac{2}{3}$) FE-IN-SI-LB in the
     centre. BR . ET . LUN . D . S . R . I . A .
     TH . ET . EL. 1717.

159. *O*:   Four shields crosswise, ($\frac{2}{3}$) FE-IN-SI-LB in centre.
     GEORGIUS . D . G . MAG . BR . FRA . & .
     HIB . REX . FID . D.

   R: Wild man and tree, . H ✖ H . under. BRUN .
     & LUN . D . S . R . I . A . THES . & .
     EL. 1717.

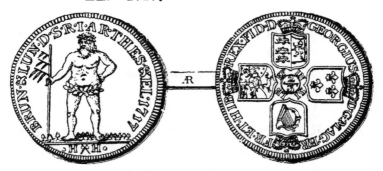

160.   Similar to No. 158, excepting date, which is 1718.

161.   Similar to No. 159, excepting date, which is 1718.

162.   Similar to last, excepting date, which is 1719,
     and C . under Wild man.

163.   Similar to last, excepting date, which is 1720.

164.   Similar to No. 158, excepting date, which is 1720.

165.   Similar to No. 158, excepting date, which is 1721.

166.   Similar to No. 162, excepting date, which is 1721.

167.   Similar to No. 158, excepting date, which is 1722.

168. *O*:   Four shields crosswise, ($\frac{2}{3}$) FE-IN-SI-LB in centre.
     GEORG . D . G . M . BR . FR . ET . HIB .
     REX . F . D

   R: Running horse, H . C . B . under. BRUNS . ET .
     LUN . DUX . S . R . I . A . THES . ET .
     EL. 1722.

169.   Similar to No. 162, excepting date, which is
              1722.

170.   Similar to last, excepting date, which is 1723,
              and E . P . H . under Wild man.

171.   Similar to No. 158, excepting date, which is 1723.

172.   Similar to No. 168, excepting date, which is 1723.

173.   Similar to No. 158, excepting date, which is 1724.

174.   Similar to No. 170, excepting date, which is 1724,
              and 24 at the side of Wild man.

175.   Similar to last, excepting date, which is 1725.

176.   Similar to No. 168, excepting date, which is 1725.

177.   Similar to No. 174, excepting date, which is 1726.

178.   Similar to No. 168, excepting date, which is 1726,
              and C . P . S . under horse.

179.   Similar to No. 158, excepting date, which is 1727.

180.   Similar to No. 174, excepting date, which is 1727.

181.   Similar to No. 178, but C . P . S . under horse,
              and date 1727.

One-third Thalers.

182. *O* :   Bust to right, H . C . B . under. GEORGIUS .
              D . G . M . BRIT . FR . ET . HIB . REX .
              F . D.

      R :   Four shields crosswise ($\frac{1}{3}$) FE-IN-SI-LB in the
              centre. BR . ET . LUN . D . S . R . I .
              A . TH . ET EL.   1716.

183.   Similar to last, but date 1717 and LVN on
              reverse.

184. *O* :   Bust to right, H . C . B . under. GEORG . D .
              G . M . BR . FR . ET . H . REX . F . D.

      R :   Four shields crosswise, ($\frac{1}{3}$) FE-IN-SI-LB in centre.
              BR. ET . L . DUX . S . R . I . A . T . ET .
              E . 1718.

185. *O* :   As reverse of last, GEORGIUS . D . G . MAG .
              BR . ERA . & HIB . REX . F . D .

      R :   Wild man and tree, H ✗ H under. BRUN . &
              LUN . D . S . R . I . A . TH . & . EL.   1718.

186. *O*: As reverse of No. 184. GEORG . D . G .M . B . FR . ET . H . REX . F . D.

    R: St. Andrew and cross, H . C . B . under. BR . ET . LUN . DUX . S . R . I . A . TH . ET . EL. 1719.

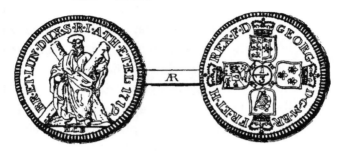

187. *O*: Same as last.

    R: Running horse, H . C . B . under it. BRUNS . ET . LUN . DUX . S . R . I . A . TH . ET . EL. 1720.

188. Similar to No. 185, but C . under wild man, and THES . & EL . 1720 . on reverse.

189 *O*: Bust to right, H . C . B. under. GEORG . D . G . M . BRIT . F . ET . H . REX . F . D.

    R: Four shields as before. BR . ET . L . DUX . S . R . I . A . TH . ET . EL. 1721.

190. Similar to No. 186, excepting date, which is 1721.

191. Similar to No. 186, excepting date, which is 1722.

192. Similar to No. 189, but reverse legend is BR . ET . LUN . D . S . R . I . A . T . ET . E. 1722.

193. ˙ Similar to No. 188, excepting date, which is 1722.

194. *O*: Four shields as before, GEORGIUS . D . G . MAG . BR . FR . & . HIB . REX . FID . D.

    R: Wild man holding tree, E . P . H . under, 12 in the field. BRUN . & LUN . D . S . R . I . AR . TH . & EL. 1723.

195.   Similar to No. 185, excepting date, which is 1723, and E . P . H . under wild man.

196.   Similar to No. 187, excepting date, which is 1723.

197.   Similar to No. 189, excepting date, which is 1724.

198.   Similar to No. 186, excepting date, which is 1724.

199.   Similar to No. 189, excepting date, which is 1725.

200.   Similar to No. 194, excepting date, which is 1725.

201. *O* :   Bust to right, C . P . S . under. GEORG . D . G . M . BRIT . F . ET . H . REX . F . D.

R :   Similar to No. 184. BR . ET . L . DUX . S . R . I . A . T . ET . E. 1726.

202.   Similar to No. 194, excepting date, which is 1726.

203.   Similar to No. 194, excepting date, which is 1727.

Quarter Thaler.

204. *O* :   Four shields crosswise, a star in centre. GEORG . D . G . M . BRIT . FR . ET . HIB . REX . F . D.

R :   Running horse, $\begin{smallmatrix} \text{R} & (\frac{1}{4}) & \text{T} \\ & \text{H . C . B} & \end{smallmatrix}$ under. BRUN . ET . LUN . DUX . S . R . I . A . TH . ET . EL. 1718.

205. *O* :   Bust to right, $\overset{R\ (\frac{1}{4})\ T}{\text{H . C . B}}$ under. GEORG . D . G .
             M . BR . F . ET . H . REX . F . D.

   R :   Four shields crosswise, a star in centre. B .
             ET . L . DVX . S . R . I . A . T . ET . E.
             1726.

One-sixth Thalers.

206. *O* :   Bust to right, $\text{FEIN}\overset{B}{.}\text{SILB}$. under. GEORG .
             D . G . M . BRIT . FR . ET . HIB . REX .
             F . D.

   R :   Four shields crosswise, $(\frac{1}{6})$ in centre. BR . ET .
             L . DUX . S . R . I . A . T . & EL. 1716.

207.   Similar to last, excepting date, which is 1717.
208.   Similar to last, excepting date, which is 1718.
209. *O* :   Four shields crosswise, $(\frac{1}{6})$ FE-IN-SI-LB in centre.
             Legend as before.

   R :   St. Andrew and cross, H . C . B . under. BR .
             ET . LVN . D . S . R . I . A . T . & . E. 1719.

210. *O* :   As last.

   R :   Running horse, H . C . B . under. BRUNS .
             ET . LVN . DVX . S . R . I . A . TH . ET .
             ELECT. 1719 ✠

211.   Similar to last, excepting date, which is 1720.
212. *O* :   Four shields as before, GEORGIUS . D .
             G . MAG . BR . FRA . & HIB . REX .
             FID . D.

   R :   Wild man and tree, $\overset{\text{FEIN}}{}\underset{\text{C.}}{}\text{SILB}$ under. BRUN .
             & . LUN . D . S . R . I . A . TH . & EL.
             1720.

213.   Similar to last, excepting date, which is 1721.
214.   Similar to No. 206, excepting date, which is
             1722.
215   Similar to No. 210, excepting date, which is
             1722.

216.   *O*:   As No. 209.

      R: Wild man and tree, $\frac{\text{FEIN SILB}}{\text{C}}$ under.   BR .
ET . LVN . DVX . S . R . I . A . TH . ET .
EL.   1722.

217.   Bust similar to No. 206, excepting date, which is
1723.

218.   Similar to last, but legend on reverse is BR .
& . L . DUX . S . R . I . A . T. ET . EL .
1723.

219.   Similar to last, excepting date, which is 1724.

220.   ·   Similar to No. 210, but legend on reverse ends
TH . ET . EL.   1724 ✿

221.   Similar to No. 209, excepting date, which is
1724.

222.   Similar to No. 212, but $\frac{\text{C . P . S .}}{\text{FEIN SILB :}}$ under wild
man, and dated 1725.

223.   Similar to No. 206, but $\frac{\text{C . P . S .}}{\text{FEIN SILB :}}$ under bust,
and dated 1726.

224.   Similar to No. 210, but c . p . s . under horse,
and V$^{\underline{S}}$ instead of U$^{\underline{S}}$, dated 1727. ✿

One-eighth Thalers.

225.   *O*:   Four shields crosswise, a star in centre,
GEORG . D . G . M . BR . FR . ET . H .
REX . F . D.

      R: Running horse, $\frac{\text{R } (\frac{1}{8}) \text{ T}}{\text{H . C . B}}$ under, BR . ET . L .
DUX . S . R . I . A . TH . ET . EL.   1718.

226.   *O*:   Bust to right, h . c . b . under. GEORGIUS
D . G . M . BRIT . F . ET . H . REX . F . D.

      R: Four shields crosswise, a star in centre. BR .
ET . L . DVX . S . R . I . A . T . ET . EL.
1720.

227.   *O*:   Bust to right, $\frac{\text{C . P . S .}}{\text{R } (\frac{1}{8} \text{ T}}$ under GEORG . D .
G . M . BRIT . FR . ET . HIB . REX . F . D.

      R: As last, but LVN and date 1726.

Four Groschen.

228. *O* :   Four shields crosswise, $\frac{1}{9}$ in the centre. K .
            GR . BRIT . UND C . F . LAND . M.

      R :   ✳ **IIII** ✳ | MARIEN | GROS : | 1717 | H
            C . B.   In five lines.

229.   Similar to last, excepting date, which is 1726.

230. *O* :   *G . R* . in monogram, crowned.

      R :   ✽ **IIII** ✽ | MARIEN | GROSCH . | 1717 |
            H ✿ H in five lines.   VON FEINEM
            SILBER.

231. *O* :   Shield as centre of arms No. 3, crowned.
            GEORG . D . G . M . BRIT . FR . HIB .
            REX . F . D.

      R :   **IIII** | MARIEN | GROS: | 1718 | H . C . B .
            in five lines.   BR . ET . LVN . DVX .
            S . R . I . A . TH . ET . EL.

232.   Similar to last, excepting date, which is 1720,
            and BR . ET LUN . DUX . S . R . I . A.
            THES . ET . EL ✳.

233.   Similar to last, excepting date, which is 1721.
            Legend on reverse as 228.

234.   Similar to last, excepting date, which is 1722.
            BR . ET . LUNEB . DUX . S . R . I . A .
            THES . ET . EL . ✳.

235. *O* :   *G . R* . in monogram crowned.

      R :   ° **IIII** ° | MARIEN | GROSCH : | 1723 . in
            four lines within a beaded circle.   VON
            FEINEM SILBER ✢ ✢ ✢ .

236. *O*: Shield as centre of arms No. 1.   Legend as
            No. 231.

      R: Similar to No. 231, excepting date, which is 1724.

237.   Similar to last, excepting date, which is 1727,
            and initials c . p . s .

Three Groschen.

238. *O*: **12** | EINEN | THALER | 1716, in four lines.
            K . GR . BRIT . und C . F . BR . LVN
            LAND MVNTZ .

      R: Running horse, h . c . b . under.

239.   Similar to last, excepting date, which is 1717.

240. *O*: *G . R* . in monogram crowned. h . c . b . under.

      R: ✚ **III** ✚ | MARIEN | GROS : | 1717 | in four
            lines. K . GR . BRIT . und C . F . BR .
            LUN . LAND . MUNTZ *⸰

Two Groschen.

241. *O*: *G . R* . in monogram crowned.

      R: * **II** * | MARIEN | GROSCH : | 1717 | h ✗
            h in five lines, VON FEINEM SILBER.

242.   Similar to last, but GROS : | 1718 | h . c . b .
            on reverse.

243. *O*: As last, excepting with h . c . b . under mono-
            gram.

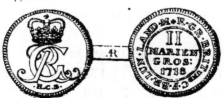

      R: **II** | MARIEN | GROS : | 1718 in four lines.
            K . GR . BRIT . und C . F . BR . LVN .
            LAND MVNTZ.*

244.   Similar to No. 242, but GROSCH : | 1719 | c .
            on reverse.
245.   Similar to No. 243, excepting date, which is
            1719, and initials under monogram, H . C . B.
246.   Similar to last, excepting date, which is 1720.
247.   Similar to last, excepting date, which is 1727,
            and initials under monogram C . P . S.

One Twenty-fourth Thaler.
248.   O :   *G . R* . in monogram crowned, H . C . B . under.
       R :   **24** | EINEN | THAL : | 1718, in four lines.
249.   Similar to last, excepting date, which is 1724.

One Gute Groschen.
250   O :   As last.
      R :   **I** | GUTER | GROS | 1717, in four lines.

One Marien Groschen.
251   O :   As last.
      R :   ✣ **I** ✣ | MARIEN | GROS : | 1717, in four lines,
            K . GR . BRIT . UND C . F . BR . L .
            LAND . M . ✳ .
252.   Similar to last, excepting date, which is 1718.
253.   Similar to last, excepting date, which is 1719.
254.   Similar to last, excepting date, which is 1727,
            c . P . S . under monogram.

Six Pfennige.
255.   O :   *G . R* . in monogram crowned. H . C . B . under.
       R :   ° **VI** ° | PFENN : | 1717 | ✳ in four lines.
256.   O :   *G . R* . in monogram crowned.
       R :   Orb and cross, inscribed VI. dividing date 17-18.
257.   Similar to last, but date 17-21.

Four Pfennige.
258.   O :   *G . R* . in monogram crowned. H ✗ H under.
       R :   ° **IIII** ° | PFEN . | 1717 in three lines, K . GR .
            BR . UND C . F . BR . LUN . LAND . M . ✳
259.   O :   As last. H . C . B . under.
       R :   **IIII** | PFENN : | 1718, in three lines. Legend
            as last.

260. Similar to last, excepting date, which is 1719.

261. Similar to last, excepting date, which is 1720.

Three Pfennige.

262.   *O :*   *𝒢 . ℛ .* in monogram crowned.   H 𝕏 H under.

      R :   Orb and cross, inscribed 5, dividing date 17-17.

263. Similar to last, excepting date, which is 1718, H . C . B . under monogram.

264. Similar to last, excepting date, which is 1719.

265. Similar to last, excepting date, which is 1720.

266. Similar to last, excepting date, which is 1723.

The following synopsis of the principal silver coins of George I. will be found useful by the collector.

WITH KING's BUST.				WITH THE WILD MAN.			
THALER.	$\frac{2}{3}$	$\frac{1}{3}$	$\frac{1}{6}$	THALER.	$\frac{2}{3}$	$\frac{1}{3}$	$\frac{1}{6}$
1716.	1715.	1716.	1716.	1717.	1717.	1718.	1720.
1717.	1716.	1717.	1717.	1718.	1718.	1720.	1721.
1718.	1717.	1718.	1718.	1720.	1719.	1722.	1722.
1719.	1718.	1721.	1722.	1721.	1720.	1723.	1725.
1720.	1720.	1722.	1723.	1722.	1721.	1725.	
1722.	1721.	1724.	1724.	1723.	1722.	1726.	
1724.	1722.	1725.	1726.	1724.	1723.	1727.	
1726.	1723.	1726.		1725.	1724.		
1727.	1724.			1726.	1725.		
	1727.			1727.	1726.		
					1727.		

WITH ST. ANDREW.			WITH THE RUNNING HORSE.			
THALER.	$\frac{1}{3}$	$\frac{1}{6}$	THALER.	$\frac{2}{3}$	$\frac{1}{3}$	$\frac{1}{6}$
1718.	1719.	1719.	1717.	1722.	1720.	1719.
1719.	1721.	1721.	1718.	1723.	1723.	1720.
1721.	1722.	1724.	1719.	1725.		1722.
1722.	1724.		1720.	1726.		1724.
1726.			1721.	1727.		1727.
			1722.			
			1723.			
			1724.			
			1726.			
			1727.			

George II. 1727-60.

Thalers.

267. *O:* Four shields crosswise, a star in centre. GEORG . II . D . G . MAG . BR . FR . ET . HIB . REX . FID . D.

    R: Wild man and tree, E . P . H . under. BRUN . & LUN . DUX . S . R . I . AR . THES . & EL. 1727.

268. *O:* Arms No. 1, supporters, &c. GEORGIVS . II . D . G . M . BRIT . FR . ET . HIB . REX . F . D. 1727.

    R: St. Andrew and cross, C . P . S . under. BRVNS . ET . LVN . DVX . S . R . I . A . THES . ET . EL.

269. *O:* Arms No. 2, supporters, &c. GEORG . II . D . G . MAG . BRIT . FRANC . ET . HIB . REX . FID . D.

    R: Wild man and tree, E . P . H . under. BRUN . & . LUN . DUX . S . R . I . AR . THES . & EL. 1728.

270. *O:* Bust to left, C . P . S . under. GEORGIUS . II . D . G . M . BRIT . FR . ET . HIB . REX . F . D.

    R: Arms No. 1, supporters, &c. BRUN . ET . LUN . DUX . S . R . I . A . THES . ET . EL. 1729.

271. *O:* Bust to left, C . only, under bust. Legend as last.

    R: Four shields crosswise, a star in centre. BRUN . ET . LUN . DUX . S . R . I . A . THES . ET . ELECT. 1729.

272. *O:* Four shields crosswise, a star in centre. GEORG . II . D . G . MAG . BR . FR . ET . HIB . REX . FID . D.

    R: Similar to 269, excepting date, which is 1729.

273. *O*: Arms No. 2, supporters, &c. GEORG . II .
D . G . M . BRIT . F . & H . REX . F .
D . B . & L . DVX . S . R . I . A . TH . &
EL.

R: Running horse, 1729 and c . p . s . under.
NEC ASPERA TERRENT.

274. Similar to No. 270, excepting date, which is
1730.

275. *O*: Shield No. 3, crown divides date 17—30.
GEORG . II . D . G . MAG . BR . FR . ET .
HIB . REX . F . D.

R: Wild man, as No. 267.

276. *O*: Shield No. 2, crown divides date, 17—30.
GEORG . II . D . G . M . BRIT . FR . ET .
HIB . REX . F . D.

R: St. Andrew, as No. 268.

277. *O*: Shield No. 3, crowned. GEORG . II . D . G .
M . BRIT . F . & H . REX . F . D . BR . &
. L . DVX . S . R . I . A . TH . & E.

R: Horse as No. 273, date 1730.

278. Similar to last, but legend on obverse reads,
GEORG . II . D . G . M . BR . F . & . H .
and S . R . I . A . T . & E.

279. *O*: Shield No. 3, crowned. GEORG . II . D . G .
M . BRIT . FR . & H . REX . F . D . BR .
& L . DVX . S . R . I . A . TH . & EL ✢ .

R: Running horse, with MDCCXXX and e . p . h .
under. NEC ASPERA TERRENT.

280. Running horse as before, with MDCCXXXI
and initial c . under.

281. Similar to No. 273, excepting date, which is
1731.

282. Similar to No. 273, excepting date, which is
✳ 1732 ✳.

283. Similar to No. 275, excepting date, which is
1732, and initials ι . A . B . under wild man.

4 ✳

284. *O* :   Shield No. 3, crowned. GEORG . II . D . G .
             M . BRIT . FR . & H . REX . F . D . BR .
             & L . DVX . S . R . I . A . TH . & EL. ✿

     R :   Running horse, MDCCXXXII and I . A. B .
             under. NEC ASPERA TERRENT.

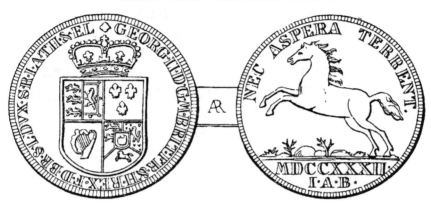

285.   Wild man as No. 283, but dated 1733.

286.   Running horse as No. 284, but dated
             MDCCXXXIV.

287.   St. Andrew as No. 276, but dated 1735.

288.   Wild man as No. 283, but dated 1736.

289.   Running horse as No. 284, but dated
             MDCCXXXVI.

290.   Wild man as No. 283, but dated 1738.

291. *O* :   Shield No. 3, crowned, date over, 1738.
             GEORG . II . D . G. M . BRIT . FR . ET .
             HIB . REX . F . D.

     R :   St. Andrew and cross, C . P . S . under. BRVNS .
             ET . LVN . DVX . S . R . I . A . TH . ET EL.

292.   Similar to last, but reverse legend is, BR . ET .
             LVN . DVX . S . R . I . A . TH . ET . EL.

293. *O* :   Shield No. 3, crowned. GEORG . II . D . G .
             BRIT . FR . & H . REX . F . D . B . & L .
             D . S . R . I . A . TH . & EL.

     R :   Running horse as No. 273, date under, 1739.

294.   As last, but legend ends, S . R . I . A . T . & E.

295.   As last, but date 1740.

296.   As No. 293, but date 1741.

297.   As No. 293, but date 1743.

298.   As No. 293, but date 1744, and legend on obverse ends S . R . I . A . T . & E.

299.   *O* :   Shield No. 3, crown divides date 17—44. GEORGIUS II . D . G . M . BRIT . F . & . H . REX . F . D.

    R :   St. Andrew and cross, c . p . s . under. BR . ET . LUN . DUX . S . R . I . A . TH . ET . EL.

300.   *O* :   Shield No. 6 crowned. GEORG . II . D . G . M . B . F . & . H . REX . F . D . B . & . L . DUX . S . R . I . A . T . & EL.

    R :   Running horse, 1745, and c . p . s . under. NEC ASPERA TERRENT.

301.   Similar to No. 299, excepting date, which is 17—45.

302.   Similar to No. 299, excepting date, which is 17—46.

303.   Similar to No. 300, excepting date, which is 1746, and legend on obverse ends T . & EL.

304.   Similar to No. 300, excepting date, which is 1747, and legend on obverse BR . & L . DVX.

305.   Similar to No. 299, excepting date, which is 17—47.

306.   Similar to No. 299, excepting date, which is 17—49.

307.   Running horse as No. 300, but dated ❊ 1749. ❊

308.   Wild man as No. 275; but dated 1750, and initials i . b . h .

309.   *O* :   Bust to left, c . under. GEORGIVS II . D . G . M . BRIT . F . & H . REX . F . D.

    R :   Shield No. 3, crown divides date, 17—51. BRVNS . ET . LVN . DVX . S . R . I . A . TH . ET . EL.

310. *O* :   Shield No. 3, crowned, date over, 1751.
              GEORG . II . D . G . M . BRIT . FR . ET .
              HIB . REX . F . D.
      R :   St. Andrew and cross, c . under. BRVNS . ET .
              LVN . DVX . S . R . I . A . TH . ET . EL.

311.   Similar to last, but crown divides date, which
              is 17—52.

312.   Similar to last, excepting date, which is 1753,
              and initials ɪ . w . s.

313. *O* :   Shield No. 9, crowned. Legend as No. 285.
      R :   Running horse, MDCCLIII and ɪ . ʙ . ʜ .
              under. NEC ASPERA TERRENT.

314.   ⸳   Similar to No. 310, excepting date, which is
              1754, and initials ɪ . w . s.

315.   Similar to No. 310, excepting date, which is
              1756, and initials ɪ . w . s . under St. Andrew.

316.   Similar to No. 300, excepting date, which is
              1756, and initials ɪ . w . s. under the horse.

317.   Similar to No. 300, excepting date, which is
              1757, and initials ɪ . w . s.

318.   Similar to No. 300, excepting date, which is
              1758, and initials ɪ . w . s.

319.   Similar to No. 310, excepting date, which is
              1758, and initials ɪ . w . s.

320.   Similar to No. 300, excepting date, which is
              1759, and initials ɪ. w . s.

321.   Similar to No. 300, excepting date, which is
              1760, and initials ɪ . w . s.

322.   Similar to No. 310, excepting date, which is
              1760, and initials ɪ . w . s.

Two-third Thalers.

323. *O* :   Bust to left, c . ᴘ . s . under. GEORG . II . D .
              G . M . BRIT . FR . ET . HIB . REX . F . D.
      R :   Shield No. 3, crown divides date 17-27. ꜰᴇɪɴ
              ($\frac{2}{3}$) sɪʟʙ. under shield in a curve. BR . ET.
              LVN DVX . S . R . I . A . TH . ET . EL.

324. *O* : Shield No. 3, crowned. GEORG . II . D . G .
M . B . F . & . H . REX . F . D . B . & . L .
DUX . S . R . I . A . T . & . EL.

R : Running horse, $\dfrac{\text{FEIN} \ (\frac{2}{3}) \ \text{SILB}}{17 \qquad 27}$—E . P . H .
under. NEC ASPERA TERRENT.

325. *O* : Four shields crosswise, ($\frac{2}{3}$) FE-IN-SI-LB in centre.
GEORG . II . D . G . M . BRIT . FR . ET .
HIB . REX . F . D.

R : Wild man and tree, E . P . H . under. 24 in the
field. BR . ET . LVN . DVX . S . R . I . A .
TH . ET . EL. 1727.

326. *O* : As No. 323.

R : Four shields crosswise, ($\frac{2}{3}$) FE-IN-SI-LB in centre.
BR . ET . LVN . DVX . S . R . I . A . TH .
ET . EL. 1728.

327. Similar to last, excepting date, which is 1729.

328. *O* : Shield No. 4, crowned. GEORG . II .
D . G . M . BR . F . & . H . REX . F . D . B .
& L . DVX . S . R . I . A . TH . & EL✿

R : Running horse, FEIN ($\frac{2}{3}$) SILB | 1730 |
E . P . H . in three lines under, NEC ASPERA
TERRENT.

329. *O* : Shield No. 3, crowned, FEIN ($\frac{2}{3}$) SILB. under.
GEORG . II . D . G . M . BR . F . & H .
REX . F . D . B . & L . DVX . S . R . I . A . T .
& EL.

R : Running horse, C . P . S . under. NEC ASPERA
TERRENT. 1730.

330. Similar to No. 325, excepting date, which is
1731.

331. Similar to No. 329, excepting date, which is
1731.

332. As last, but dated 1732, and legend reads F . & .
H . REX . F . D . BR . & L . DVX .
S . R . I . A . T . & E.

333. *O:* Shield No. 3, crown divides date 17—32. FEIN
            ($\frac{2}{3}$) SILB under GEORG . II . D . G . M . BR .
            FR . ET . HIB . REX . F . D.

      R: Wild man and tree, I . A . B . under, 24 in the
            field. BR . ET . LVN . DVX . S . R . I . A
            TH . ET . EL.

334.   Similar to last, excepting date, which is 17—33.

335.   Similar to No. 328, excepting date, which is
            17—33, and I . A . B . under horse.

336.   Similar to No. 329, excepting date, which is
            1733.

337.   Similar to No. 329, excepting date, which is
            1734.

338.   Similar to No. 333, excepting date, which is
            17—34.

339.   Similar to No. 333, excepting date, which is
            17—35.

340.   Similar to No. 333, excepting date, which is
            17—36.

341.   Similar to No. 333, excepting date, which is
            17—37.

342.   Similar to No. 328, excepting date, which is
            1737.

343.   As last, but with N . D . LEIPZ . F . ($\frac{2}{3}$) FEIN SILB
            in a curve under shield, dated 1738.

344.   Similar to No. 333, excepting date, which is 1738.

345. *O:* As No. 323.

      R: Shield No. 2, crown divides date, 17-39. N . D .
            LEIPZ . F . ($\frac{2}{3}$) FEIN . SILB . under in a curve.
            BR . ET . LVN . DVX . S . R . I . A . TH .
            ET . EL.

346.   Similar to No. 333, excepting date, which is
            17—39, and c . under wild man.

347.   Similar to No. 329, excepting date, which is
            1739, and legend B . & . L . D . S . R . I . A .
            T . & EL.

348. *O* : Shield No. 3, crown divides date, 17—40.
FEIN ($\frac{2}{3}$) SILB. in a curve under. GEORG . II .
D . G . M . BR . FR . ET . HIB . REX . F . D .

R : Wild man and tree, I . B . H . under. 24 in the
field. BR . ET. LVN . DVX . S . R . I . A .
TH . ET . EL.

349. Similar to No. 328, excepting date, which is
1740, and I . B . H . under horse.

350. Running horse as 329, but N . D . REICHS F . ($\frac{2}{3}$)
FEIN SILB under shield, and date 1740.

351. Similar to No. 348, excepting date, which is
17—42.

352. Similar to last, excepting date, which is 17—43.

353. *O* : Shield No. 3, crowned GEORG . II . D . G .
M . BR . F . & H . REX . F . D . B . & L .
DVX . S . R . I . A . T . & EL. Under the
shield in a curve is N . D . REICHS F . ($\frac{2}{3}$) FEIN SILB.

R : Running horse, c . P . s . under. NEC
ASPERA TERRENT. 1743.

354. *O* : Bust to left, c . P . s . under. GEORGIVS II .
D . G . M . BR . FR . ET . HIB . REX . F . D.

R : Shield No. 4, crowned. N . D . REICHES . F . ($\frac{2}{3}$)
FEIN . SILB . in a curve under. BR . ET . LVN .
DVX . S . R . I . A . TH . ET . EL . 1744.

355. Similar to No. 348, excepting date, which is
17—44.

356. *O* : Shield No. 9, crown divides date, 1745. FEIN .
($\frac{2}{3}$) SILB . under. GEORG . II . D . G . M . BR .
FR . ET . HIB . REX . F . D.

R : As No. 348.

357. *O* : Shield No. 9, crowned. GEORG . II . D . G . M .
BR . F . & . H . REX . F . D . B . & L .
DVX . S . R . I . A . TH . & . EL.

R : Running horse. $\frac{\text{FEIN}}{17}$ ($\frac{2}{3}$) $\frac{\text{SILB}}{45}$: I . B . H .

arranged under. NEC ASPERA TERRENT.

358.   Similar to No. 354, excepting date, which is
            1746.

359.   Similar to No. 348, excepting date, which is
            17—46.

360.   Similar to No. 353, excepting date, which is
            1746.

361.   Similar to No. 348, excepting date, which is
            17—47.

362. *O :* Shield No. 4, crowned. N . D . REICHES ⋮ F .
            (⅔) FEIN . SILB . in a curve under. GEORG .
            II . D . G . M . B . F . & H . REX . F .
            D . B . & L . DVX . S . R . I . A . T . &
            EL.

     R : Running horse, 1747. C . P . S . in two lines
            under. NEC ASPERA TERRENT.

363.   Similar to No. 328, excepting date, which is
            1748, and I . B . H . under horse.

364.   Similar to No. 356, excepting date, which is
            17—49.

365.   Similar to No. 362, excepting date, which is
            ✶ 1750 ✶

366. *O :* **XXIV** | GUTE GROSCH : | N . D . REICHES .
            FUS . | I . W . S . in four lines in centre.
            GEORG . II . D . G . M . BRIT . FR . ET .
            HIB . REX . F . D . 1750.

     R : Running horse, R . (⅔) T . under. NEC
            ASPERA TERRENT.

367.   Similar to No. 362, excepting date, which is
            ✿ 1751 ✿ and initial . C.

368.   Similar to No. 348, excepting date, which is
            1752.

369. *O :* Bust to left, I . W . S . under. GEORG . II .
            D . G . M . B . F . ET . H . REX . F . D.

     R : Shield No. 8, crowned, N . D . REICHES . F . (⅔)
            FEIN . SILBER : in a curve under. BRVNS . ET .
            LVN . DVX . S . R . I . A . T . ET . EL . 1754.

370.   Similar to No. 362, excepting date, which is 1754, and initials I . W . S.

371.   Similar to No. 348, excepting date, which is 17—54.

372.   Similar to No. 328, excepting date, which is 1755, and I . B . H . under horse.

373.   Similar to No. 362, excepting date, which is *1755*, and I . W . S . under horse.

374. *O*: Shield No. 9, crown divides date, 17—57. GEORG . II . D . G . M . BRIT . FR . ET . HIB . REX . F . D.

    R: Wild man and tree, I . B . H . under. BR . ET . LVN . DVX . S . R . I . A . TH . ET . EL.

375. *O*: Shield No. 9, crowned. GEORG . II . D . G . M . B . F . & H . REX . F . D . B . & . L . DVX . S . R . I . A . T . & . E.

    R: Running horse, $\frac{\text{FEIN}}{17}$ ($\frac{2}{3}$) $\frac{\text{SILB}}{57}$ and I . B . H . under. NEC ASPERA TERRENT.

376.   Similar to No. 362, excepting date, which is 1757, and initials I . W . S.

377.   Similar to No. 374, excepting date, which is 1758.

378.   Similar to No. 374, excepting date, which is 1759.

379. *O*: Shield No. 3, crowned, legend as No. 375.

    R: Running horse, 1759 under. NEC ASPERA TERRENT.

380.   Similar to No. 362, excepting date, which is 1760, and initials I. W. S.

381.   Similar to No. 374, excepting date, which is 1760.

382.   Similar to No. 375, excepting date, which is 1760.

Half Thalers.

383. *O* :   Bust to left, R ($\frac{1}{2}$) T under. GEORG . II .
            c . P . s
            D . G . M . BR . F . ET . H . REX . F . D.

R :   Shield No. 3, crown divides date . 1732 . BR .
        ET . LVN . DVX . S . R . I . A . T . ET .
        EL.

384. *O* :   **XVI** | GVTE | GROSCH : | N . D . REICHES . |
            FVS . | C . P . S . in six lines within an inner
            circle. GEORG . II . D . G . M . B . F . & .
            H . REX . F . D . B . & . L . DVX . S . R . I .
            A . T . & . E.

R :   Running horse, R ($\frac{1}{2}$) T under. NEC ASPERA
        TERRENT 1739.

385.   Similar to last, excepting date, which is 1740.

386. *O* :   Bust to left, R ($\frac{1}{2}$ T under. GEORG . II .
            c . P . s
            D . G . M . BRIT . F . & . H . REX . F . D.

R :   **XVI** | GVTE GROSCH : | N . D . REICHES . FVS .
        in three lines. BRVNS . ET . LVN . DVX .
        S . R . I . A . THES . ET . EL .   1741.

387.   Similar to No. 384, excepting date, which is
            1741, and initials C . P . s . on *R* : instead
            of on *O* :

388. *O* :   As last.

R :   As last, but in five lines within a circle, and
        date 1742.

389.   Similar to No. 384, excepting date, which is
            1752, and C . instead of C . P . s.

390. *O*: Bust to left, R ($\frac{1}{2}$) T under. GEORG . II .
D . G . M . BRIT . FR . ET . HIB . REX . F . D.

R: **XVI** | GVTE | GROSCH : | N . D . REICHES . |
FVS . | I . W . S . in six lines, legend as last,
date 1756.

One-third Thalers.

391. *O*: Bust to left, C . P . S . under. GEORG . II .
D . G . M . BRIT . F . & . H . REX . E . D.

R: Four shields crosswise, ($\frac{1}{3}$) FE-IN-SI-LB in the
centre. BR . ET . L . DVX . S . R . I . A .
T . ET . E. 1729.

392. *O*: As last.

R: Shield No. 3, crowned, FEIN . ($\frac{1}{3}$) SILB . under.
BR . ET . LVN . DVX . S . R . I . A . TH .
ET . EL. 1730.

393. *O*: Shield No. 2, crown divides date 17—31. FEIN
($\frac{1}{3}$) SILB under. GEORG . II . D . G . M .
BR . FR . ET . HIB . REX . F . D.

R: Wild man and tree, C . under. BR . ET .
LVN . DVX . S . R . I . A . TH . ET . EL.

394. *O*: Shield No. 3, crowned. FEIN ($\frac{1}{3}$) SILB under.
GEORG . II . D . G . M . BR . FR . & HIB .
REX . F . D.

R: St. Andrew, with his cross, C . P . S . under.
BR . ET . LVN . DVX . S . R . I . A . TH .
ET . E. 1731.

395. Similar to last, but date 1732, and legend on *O* :
reads M . BRIT . FR . ET . HIB . REX . F . D.

396. Similar to No. 392, but with $\frac{R\ (\frac{1}{3})\ T}{C . P . S .}$ under bust,
and date 1732.

397. *O*: Shield No. 2, crowned. PEIN ($\frac{1}{3}$) SILB under.
GEORG . II . D . G . M . BR . F . & H .
REX . F . D . BR . & L . DVX . S . R . I . A .
TH . & EL.

R: Running horse, ✱ 1734 ✱, and C . P . S . under.
NEC ASPERA TERRENT.

398.   Similar to No. 393, excepting date, which is 1734.

399.   Similar to No. 393, excepting date, which is 1735.

400.   Similar to No. 393, excepting date, which is 1736.

401.   Similar to No. 392, excepting date, which is 1736.

402. *O* : Shield No. 2, crown divides date 17—37. FEIN . ($\frac{1}{3}$) SILB . under. GEORG . II . D . G. M . BR . FR . ET . HIB . REX . F . D .

R : Wild man and tree, I . A . B . under, 12 in the field. BR . ET . LVN . DVX . S . R . I . A . TH . ET . EL.

403.   Similar to last, excepting date, which is 1740.

404. *O* : Shield No. 3, crowned. N . D . REICHES . F . ($\frac{1}{3}$) FEIN . SILB . under, in a curve. GEORG . II . D . G . M . BR . FR . ET . H . REX . F . D . 1740.

R : St. Andrew with his cross, C . P . S . under. BR . ET . LVN . DVX . S . R . I . A . TH . ET . EL.

405.   Similar to No. 402, excepting date, which is 1741, and initials I . B . H.

406.   Similar to last, excepting date, which is 1742.

407.   Similar to No. 404, excepting date, which is 1742.

408.   Similar to No. 404, excepting date, which is 1743.

409.   Similar to No. 405, excepting date, which is 1744.

410.   Similar to No. 405, excepting date, which is 1746.

411.   Similar to No. 405, excepting date, which is 1747.

412.   Similar to No. 404, excepting date, which is 1749.

413.   Similar to No. 405, excepting date, which is 1750.

414.   Similar to No. 405, excepting date, which is 1751.

415.   Similar to No. 405, excepting date, which is 1752.

416.   Similar to No. 405, excepting date, which is 1754.

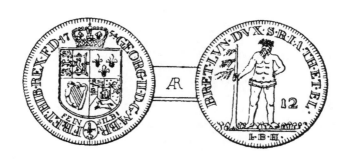

417.   Similar to No. 397, excepting date, which is ✱1754✱, and initials ɪ . w . s.

418.   Similar to No. 404, excepting date, which is 1757, and initials ɪ . w . s.

419.   Similar to No. 405, excepting date, which is 1757.

420.   Similar to No. 404, excepting date, which is 1758.

421.   Similar to No. 405, excepting date, which is 1760.

Quarter Thalers.

422. *O* : Bust to left $\frac{R \; (\frac{1}{4}) \; T}{\text{c.p.s.}}$ under. GEORG . II . D . G . M . BRIT . F . & . H . REX . F . D.

 R : Four shields crosswise, a star in centre. BR . ET . LVN . DVX . S . R . I . A . TH . ET . EL. 1728.

423. *O* : As last.

 R : Shield No. 3, crowned, date above, 1732. Legend as before.

424. *O* : Bust to left, $\underset{\text{c . p . s}}{\text{R } (\frac{1}{4}) \text{ T}}$ under. GEORG . II .
D . G . M . BRIT . F . ET . H . REX . F . D .

R : **VIII** | GVTE | GROSCH. | N . D . REICHES |
FVS | in five lines. BRVNS . ET . LVN .
DVX . S . R . I . A . T . & E . 1742.

425. *O* : **VIII** | GVTE | GROSCH. | N.D.REICHS |
FVS in five lines in centre. GEORG . II .
D . G . M . B . F . & H . REX . F . D . B .
& L . DVX . S . R . I . A . T . & E . 1742.

R : Running horse $\underset{\text{c . p .s .}}{\text{R } (\frac{1}{4}) \text{ T}}$ under. NEC ASPERA
TERRENT.

One-sixth Thalers.

426. *O* : Bust to left, c . p . s . under. GEORG . II .
D . G . M . BR . F . & H . REX . F . D .

R : Four shields crosswise ($\frac{1}{6}$) FE - IN - SI - LB in centre.
BR . & L . DVX . S . R . I . A . T . & EL . 1727.

427. *O* : Four shields crosswise ($\frac{1}{6}$) in the centre.
GEORG . II . D . G . M . BR . F & H . REX .
F . D . B & L . D . S . R . I . A . T . & E ✳ .

R : Running horse, 1727 | c . p . s . | FEIN   SILB
under. NEC ASPERA TERRENT.

428. *O* : Four shields crosswise, ($\frac{1}{6}$) FE - IN - SI - LB in
centre. GEORG . II . D . G . M . BR . F .
& HIB . REX . F . D .

R : Running horse, c . p . s . and FEIN . SILB . under.
NEC ASPERA TERRENT. 1729.

429. *O* : As last.

R : St. Andrew with his cross, c . p . s . under.
BR . ET . LVN . DVX . S . R . I . A . TH .
ET . E . 1729.

430. *O* : Bust to left, c . p . s . under. GEORG . II .
D . G . M . BR . F . & H . REX . F . D .

R : Shield No. 3, crown divides date 17—30, FEIN
($\frac{1}{6}$) SILB under. BR . ET . L . DVX .
S . R . I . A . T . ET . E .

431. *O*: Shield No. 3, crowned FEIN ($\frac{1}{6}$) SILB under.
GEORG . II . D . G . M . B . F . & H . REX .
F . D . B . & L . D . S . R . I . A . T . & .
EL.

R: Running horse, 1730, and c . p . s . under. NEC
ASPERA TERRENT.

432. *O*: Shield No. 2, crown divides date 17—30.
GEORG . II . D . G . M . BR . ER . ET .
HIB . REX . F . D.

R: Wild man and tree, E . P . H . under, 6 in the
field. BR . ET . LVN . DVX . S . R . I . A .
TH . ET . EL.

433. Similar to No. 429, excepting date, which is
1730.

434. Similar to No. 429, excepting date, which is
1731, and legend BR . & LVN . and A . T .
& E.

435. Similar to last, excepting date, which is 1732.

436. Similar to No. 432, excepting date, which is
1732, and initials I . A . B.

437. Similar to No. 431, excepting date, which is
1732.

438. Similar to No. 432, excepting date, which is
1733, and initials I . A . B.

439. Similar to last, excepting date, which is 1734.

440. Similar to last, excepting date, which is 1735.

441. Similar to last, excepting date, which is 1736.

442. *O*: Similar to No. 430, excepting date, which
is 1736, and the bust is different.

443. *O* : Shield No. 3, crown divides date **17-37**, ꜰᴇɪɴ ($\frac{1}{6}$)
             ꜱɪʟʙ under.   GEORG . II . D . G . M . BR .
             FR . ET . HIB . REX . F . D.

       R : Wild man and tree, ɪ . ᴀ . ʙ . under, 6 in field.
             BR . ET . LVN . DVX . S . R . I . A . TH .
             ET . EL.

444.   Similar to last, but date **17-38**.

445. *O* : As No. 430.

       R : Shield No. 5, crowned, ɴ . ᴅ . ʀᴇɪᴄʜᴇꜱ . ꜰ . ($\frac{1}{6}$)
             ꜰᴇɪɴ . ꜱɪʟʙ . in a curve under. BR . ET .
             LVN . DVX . S . R . I . A . TH . ET . EL.
             1739.

446.   Similar to No. 443, excepting date, which is
             17-39, and initials ɪ . ʙ . ʜ.

447.   Similar to No. 443, excepting date, which is
             17-40, and initials ɪ . ʙ . ʜ.

448.   Similar to No. 443, excepting date, which is
             17-41, and initials ɪ . ʙ . ʜ.

449.   Similar to No. 443, excepting date, which is
             17-42, and initials ɪ . ʙ . ʜ.

450.   Similar to No. 443, excepting date, which is
             17-43, and initials ɪ . ʙ . ʜ.

451.   Similar to No. 443, excepting date, which is
             17-44, and initials ɪ . ʙ . ʜ.

452.   Similar to No. 443, excepting date, which is
             17-45, and initials ɪ . ʙ . ʜ.

453.   Similar to No. 430, excepting date, which is **1746**.

454. *O* : Shield No. 5, crown divides date **17-46**. ɴ . ᴅ :
             ʀᴇɪᴄʜᴇꜱ . ꜰ . ($\frac{1}{6}$) ꜰᴇɪɴ . ꜱɪʟʙ . in a curve under.
             GEORG . II . D . G . M . BR . F . ET . HIB .
             REX . F . D.

       R : St. Andrew with his cross, ᴄ . ᴘ . ꜱ . under.
             BR . ET . LVN . DVX . S . R . I . A . TH .
             ET . EL.

455.   Similar to No. 443, excepting date, which is
             17-46, and initials ɪ . ʙ . ʜ.

456. Similar to No. 443, excepting date, which is 17-48, and initials I . B . H.

457. Similar to No. 443, excepting date, which is 17-49, and initials I . H . B.

458. Similar to No. 443, excepting date, which is 17-50, and initials I . B . H.

459. Similar to No. 443, excepting date, which is 17-51, and initials I . B . H.

460. Similar to No. 443, excepting date, which is 17-53, and initials I . B . H.

461. Similar to No. 454, excepting date, which is 17-53, and initials I . W . S.

462. Similar to No. 443, excepting date, which is 17-54, and initials I . B . H.

463. Similar to No. 443, excepting date, which is 17-56, and initials I . B . H.

464. Similar to No. 454, excepting date, which is 17-56, and initials I . W . S . and legend on O: reads M . B . F . ET . H and on R: BR . & LVN . and TH . & EL.

465. Similar to No. 454, but dated 17-57, and R: legend as last.

466. Similar to No. 454, but dated 17-59, legend as No. 463, but ends T . & EL.

467. Similar to No. 443, excepting date, which is 17-60, and initials I . B . H.

Four Marien Groschen.

468. O: Shield as centre of arms No. 1. GEORG . II . D . G . M . BR . FR . & H . REX . F . D.

R: **IIII** | MARIEN | GROS : | 1727 | C . P . S in five lines. BR . ET LVN . DVX S . R . I . A . TH . ET . EL✼

469. Similar to last, excepting date, which is 1728.

470. Similar to last, excepting date, which is 1730.

5 *

471. *O:* *IIII* | MARIEN | GROSCH: | FEIN SILB: |
           E . P . H . in five lines.   GEORG . II . D . G .
           M . BR . FR . ET . HIB . REX . F . D. 1730. *

    R: Wild man and tree, 4 on field. BR . ET . LUN .
           DUX . S . R . I . A . TH . ET . EL.

472.   Similar to No. 468, excepting date, which is
           1731, and legend HIB . REX . F . D and
           U<u>s.</u> instead of V<u>s.</u>

473.   Similar to No. 471, excepting date, which is
           1732, and initials I . A . B.

474.   Similar to No. 468, excepting date, which is
           1734, and legend on *R*: BRVNS . & LVN .
           DVX . S . R . I . A . TH . & EL❋

475.   Similar to last, excepting date, which is 1735.

476.   Similar to last, excepting legend on *O*: F . &
           H . REX.

477.   Similar to No. 471, excepting date, which is
           1735, and initials I . A . B.

478.   Similar to No. 471, excepting date, which is
           1736, and initials I . A . B.

479.   Similar to No. 471, excepting date, which is
           1737, and initials I . A . B.

480.   Similar to No. 471, excepting date, which is
           1738, and initials I . A . B.

481. *O:* As No. 468, but legend, BRIT . F . ET . H.

    R: IIII | MARIEN | GROS: | N . D . LEIPZ. |
           FVS | C . P . S.   1738.

482.   Similar to No. 471, excepting date, which is
           1739, and initial c.

483.   As last, but with initials I . B . H.

484.   Similar to last, excepting date, which is 1740.

485.   Similar to last, excepting date, which is 1741.

486.   Similar to last, excepting date, which is 1742.

487.   Similar to last, excepting date, which is 1743.

488.   Similar to last, excepting date, which is 1744.

489.	Similar to last, excepting date, which is 1745.

490.	*O*:	Shield as centre of arms No. 1. GEORG . II .
D . G . M . BRIT . F . & . H . REX .
F . D . B . & L . DUX . S . R . I . A .
TH . ET . EL. *

R:	**IIII** | MARIEN | GROS: | C . P . S . in four
lines. NACH DEM LEIPZIGER FVS.
1745. *

491.	Similar to last, excepting date, which is 1746.

492.	Similar to No. 471, excepting date, which is
1747, and initials I . A . B.

493.	Similar to No. 471, excepting date, which is
1749, and initials I . A . B.

494.	Similar to No. 471, excepting date, which is
1751, and initials I . A . B.

495.	Similar to No. 490, excepting date, which is
1752.

496.	Similar to No. 471, excepting date, which is
1756, and initials I . A . B.

497.	As last, but date 1760.

One-twelfth Thaler.

498.	*O*:	Running horse, C . P . S . under.

R:	**12** | EINEN | THAL : 1732 in four lines.
K . GR . BRIT . UND C . F . B . L .
LAND . MVNTZ. *

499.	Similar to last, excepting date, which is 1735.

500.	*O*:	Horse as before, 1738, and C . P . S . under.

R:	**12** | EINEN | THAL: | N . D . LEIPZ. |
FVS . in five lines, legend as before except
C . F . BR . L.

501. Similar to last, excepting date, which is 1740.

502. *O*: Horse as before, 1741, and C . P . S . under.
R: **12** | EINEN | THAL: | in three lines. NACH . DEM . LEIPZIGER . F. ❋

503. *O*: Running horse, 1742, and C . P . S . under.
R: **12** | EINEN | THAL: in three lines. NACH DEM LEIPZIGER FUS.

504. Similar to last, excepting date, which is 1743.

505. Similar to last, excepting date, which is 1744, and legend ends FVS ❋

506. Similar to last, excepting date, which is 1747.

507. Similar to last, excepting date, which is 1748.

508. Similar to last, excepting date, which is 1749.

509. Similar to last, excepting date, which is ✤ 1751 ✤ and initial C.

510. Similar to last, excepting date, which is 1752, and initial C.

511. *O*: Running horse, 1760 under.
R: **12** | EINEN | THAL: | I . A . S . in four lines. NACH DEM REICHES FUS. *

Two Marien Groschen.

512. *O*: ***II*** | MARIEN | GROSCH: | FEIN SILB. | E . P . H . in five lines. GEORG . II . D . G . M . BR. FR . ET H . REX . F . D. 1730 ❋
R: Wild man holding tree, 2 in the field. BR . ET . LVN . DVX . S . R . I . A . TH . ET . EL.

513. *O:*   *G. R.* in monogram crowned c . p . s.

    R: **II** | MARIEN | GROS: | 1730. in four lines.
        G . R . BRIT . und . C . F . BR . & LVN
        LAND MUNTZ.

514. *O:*   As last.

    R: **II** | MARIEN | GROS : 1730. in four lines
        NACH DEM LEIPZIGER FUS.

515.   Similar to last, excepting date, which is 1732,
        and initials i . a . b.

516.   Similar to last, excepting date, which is 1733.

517.   Similar to last, excepting date, which is 1734.

518.   Similar to last, excepting date, which is 1736.

519.   Similar to last, excepting date, which is 1737.

520.   Similar to No. 513, excepting date, which is
        1737.

521.   Similar to No. 512, excepting date, which is
        1738, and initial i . a . b.

522. *O:*   **II** | MARIEN | GROSCH | fein silb .
        i . b . h. in five lines. GEORG . II . D . G . M .
        BR . FR . ET . H . REX . F . D . 1739.

    R: Wild man and tree, 2 in field. BR . ET .
        LVN . DVX . S . R . I . A . TH . ET . EL.

523.   Similar to last, excepting date, which is 1740.

524.   Similar to last, excepting date, which is 1741.

525.   Similar to No. 514, excepting date, which is
        1741.

526.   Similar to No. 514, excepting date, which is
        1744.

527.   Similar to No. 514, excepting date, which is
        1745.

528.   Similar to No. 522, excepting date, which is
        1745.

529.   Similar to No. 514, excepting date, which is
        1748.

530.   Similar to No. 522, excepting date, which is
        1748.

531.   Similar to No. 514, excepting date, which is
            1749.

532.   Similar to No. 522, excepting date, which is
            1750.

533.   Similar to No. 514, excepting date, which is
            1751, and initial c.

534.   Similar to No. 514, excepting date, which is
            1752, and initial c.

535. *O* : 𝒢 . ℛ . in monogram, crowned.

   R : **II** | MARIEN | GROS: c . p . s . in four
            lines.
            NACH DEM LEIPZIGER FVS.   1752.

536.   Similar to No. 522, excepting date, which is
            1753.

537.   Similar to No. 514, excepting date, which is
            1754, and initials ɪ . w . s.

538.   Similar to No. 522, excepting date, which is
            1756

539.   Similar to No. 522, excepting date, which is
            1758.

540.   Similar to No. 522, excepting date, which is
            1759.

541.   Similar to No. 514, excepting date, which is
            1759, and initials ɪ . w . s.

542.   Similar to No. 522, excepting date, which is
            1760.

One Twenty-fourth Thaler.

543. *O* : Running horse, 1732, and c . under.

   R : **24** | EINEN | THAL : in three lines. NACH
            DEM LEIPZIGER FVS.

544. *O* : Running horse, c . p . s . under.

   R : **24** | EINEN | THAL : | 1733 in four lines.
            K . GR . BRIT . und C . F . B . L .
            LANDMVNTZ *

545. *O :* $\mathcal{G} . \mathcal{R}$. in monogram, crowned, c . p . s . under.

     R : **24** | EINEN | THAL : | 1735 in four lines. NACH DEM LEIPZIGER FVS.

546. Similar to last, excepting date, which is 1745.

547. Similar to last, excepting date, which is 1746, and legend ends FVS &

One Groschen.

548. *O :* $\mathcal{G} . \mathcal{R}$. in monogram, crowned, c . p . s . under.

     R : **I** | MARIEN GROS : 1730. in four lines, GR . BRIT . und . C. F . BR . & LVN . LAND MVNTZ.

549. *O :* As last.

     R : **I** | MARIEN | GROS : | 1733 . | in four lines. NACH DEM LEIPZIGER FVS.

550. Similar to No. 549, excepting date, which is 1739.

551. Similar to No. 548, excepting date, which is 1741, and initials i . b . h.

552. Similar to No. 549, but date follows legend on *R :* 1742.

553. Similar to last, but date follows legend 1744.

554. Similar to No. 549, but date follows legend 1745.

555. Similar to No. 247, excepting date, which is 1746.

556. Similar to No. 247, excepting date, which is 1753.

557. Similar to No. 542, excepting date, which is 1755, and initials i . w . s.

558. Similar to No. 548, excepting date, which is 1760.

Six Pfennige.

559. *O :* $\mathcal{G} . \mathcal{R}$. in monogram, crowned, c . p . s . under.

     R : Orb and cross inscribed VI. NACH DEM LEIPZ. FVS. 1733.

560. Similar to last, excepting date, which is 1743.

561. Similar to last, excepting date, which is 1751.
562. Similar to last, excepting date, which is 1753.
563. Similar to No. 559, but without legend on reverse and date 1754.

Four Pfennige.

564. *O :* *G. R.* in monogram, crowned, c . p . s . under.
    R : **IIII** | PFENN | 1732 in three lines. K . GR . BRIT . und C . F . B . L . LANDM *

565. Similar to last, excepting date, which is 1733.

566. *O :* As before.
    R : **IIII** | PFENN | 1739 in three lines. NACH . DEM . LEIPZ . FVS *

567. *O :* *G . R .* in monogram, as before.
    R : **IIII** | PFENN : | 1741 . in three lines, NACH . DEM. LEIPZ. FVS.

568. Similar to last, excepting date, which is 1743.
569. Similar to last, excepting date, which is 1744.
570. Similar to last, excepting date, which is 1756.

Three Pfennige.

571. *O :* *G . R .* in monogram, crowned, c . p . s . under.
    R : Orb and cross inscribed 3, divides date 17—32.

572. Similar to last, excepting date, which is 17—33.
573. Similar to last, excepting date, which is 1743.
574. Similar to No. 571, excepting date, which is 1743, and legend NACH. DEM. LEIPZ. FUS.

575. Similar to No. 574, excepting date, which is 1748.

576.   Similar to No. 574, excepting date, which is
        1751.

A synoptical table of the principal series of the silver coins of George II. will be placed here, similar to that of the preceding reign.

WITH KING'S BUST.				WITH THE WILD MAN.			
THALER.	$\frac{2}{3}$	$\frac{1}{3}$	$\frac{1}{6}$	THALER.	$\frac{2}{3}$	$\frac{1}{3}$	$\frac{1}{6}$
				1727.	1727.	1731.	1730.
1729.	1727.	1729.	1727.	1728.	1731.	1734.	1732.
1730.	1728.	1730.	1730.	1729.	1732.	1735.	1733.
1751.	1729.	1732.	1736.	1730.	1733.	1736.	1734.
	1739.	1736.	1739.	1732.	1734.	1737.	1735.
	1744.		1746.	1736.	1735.	1740.	1736.
	1746.			1738.	1736.	1741.	1737.
	1754.			1750.	1737.	1742.	1738.
					1738.	1744.	1739.
					1739.	1746.	1740.
					1740.	1747.	1741.
					1742.	1750.	1742.
					1743.	1751.	1743.
					1744.	1752.	1744.
					1745.	1754.	1745.
					1746.	1757.	1746.
					1747.	1760.	1748.
					1749.		1749.
					1752.		1750.
					1754.		1751.
					1757.		1753.
					1758.		1754.
					1759.		1756.
					1760.		1757.
							1759.
							1760.

WITH ST. ANDREW.

THALER.	$\frac{1}{3}$	$\frac{1}{6}$
1727.	1731.	1729.
1730.	1732.	1730.
1735.	1740.	1731.
1738.	1742.	1732.
1744.	1743.	1746.
1745.	1749.	1753.
1746.	1757.	1756.
1747.	1758.	1757.
1749.		1759.
1751.		
1752.		
1753.		
1754.		
1756.		
1758.		
1760.		

WITH THE RUNNING HORSE.

THALER.	$\frac{2}{3}$ WITH FEIN SILB on O:	on R:	$\frac{1}{3}$	$\frac{1}{6}$
1729.	1728.	1727.	1734.	1727.
1730.	1730.	1730.	1754.	1729.
MDCCXXX	1731.	1733.		1730.
1731.	1732.	1736.		1732.
MDCCXXXI	1733.	1737.		
1732.	1734.	1740.		
MDCCXXXII	1738.	1744.		
MDCCXXXIV	1739.	1745.		
MDCCXXXVI	1740.	1748.		
1739.	1743.	1755.		
1740.	1744.	1757.		
1741.	1746.	1759.		
1743.	1747.	1760.		
1744.	1750.			
1745.	1751.			
1746.	1754.			
1747.	1755.			
1749.	1757.			
MDLIII	1759.			
1756.	1760.			
1757.				
1758.				
1759.				
1760.				

A few dates will be found in this table which came to hand too late for insertion in the body of the work.

GEORGE III. 1760-1820.

Thalers.

577. O :   Shield No. 3, crown divides date, 17—61. GEORG . III . D . G . M . BRIT . FR . & . HIB . REX . F . D.

     R :   St. Andrew with his cross, ɪ . w . s . under. BR . & LUN . DUX . S . R . I . A . T . & ELECT.

578. *O*: Shield No. 2, crown divides date 17—62. GEORG . III . D . G . M . BRIT . FR . & . HIB . REX . F . D.

  R: St. Andrew with his cross . ı . w . s . under, BR . & . LUN . DUX . S . R . I . A . TH . & EL.

579. Similar to last, excepting date, which is 1763.

580. Similar to last, excepting date, which is 1764.

581. *O*: Shield No. 9, crown divides date 17—64. Legend as before.

  R: Wild man holding tree. ı . A . P . under, BRUN . & . LUN . DUX . S . R . I . A . THES . & . EL.

582. Similar to No. 578, excepting date, which is 17—65.

583. Similar to No. 578, excepting date, which is 17—66.

584. Similar to No. 578, excepting date, which is 17—67.

585. Similar to No. 578, excepting date, which is 17—68.

586. Similar to No. 578, excepting date, which is 17—69.

587. Similar to No. 578, excepting date, which is 17—70.

588. Similar to No. 578, excepting date, which is 17—71.

589. Similar to No. 578, excepting date, which is 17—72.

590. *O*: Bust to right. GEORG . III . D . G . M . BR . FR . & . HIB . REX . F . D.

  R: Shield No. 10 crowned, date over, 1773. ı . w . s . under. BRUNS . & . LUN . DUX S . R . I . A . TH . & ELECT.

591. Similar to No. 578, excepting date, which is 17—73.

592. Similar to No. 590, excepting date, which is 1774.

593. *O*: Shield No. 9, crown divides date, 17—75. GEORG . III . D . G . MAG . BRIT . FR . ET . HIB . REX . F . D.

R: Wild man holding tree, L . C . R . under. BRVN . & LVN . DVX . S . R . I . A . TH . ET . EL.

594. Similar to last, excepting date, which is 17—76.

595. *O*: As No. 590.

R: Arms No. 4, supporters, &c. I . W . S . under. Legend as before, date 17—77.

596. Similar to No. 590, excepting date, which is 1779.

597. Similar to No. 590, excepting date, which is 1791, and initial C.

598. Similar to No. 590, excepting date, which is 1792, and initials P . L . M.

599. Similar to No. 590, excepting date, which is 1794, and initials P . L M.

600. Similar to No. 590, excepting date, which is 1797, and initials P . L . M .

601. *O*: Bust to right. GEORG . III . V . G . G . KÖNIG . UND CHÜRFÜRST ❋.

R: ✣ **I** ✣ | THALER | HANNOVERISCH | CASSEN = GELD | ❋1801❋ | ❋C❋ in six lines.

Two-third Thalers.

602 *O*: Shield No. 3, crowned, N . D . REICHES . F . (⅔) FEIN . SILBER in a curve under. GEORG . III . D . G . M . BRIT . FR . & HIB . REX . F . D.

R: **24** | MARIEN | GROSCH | 1761 | I . W . S . in five lines. BRUNS . & LUN . DUX . S . S . R . I . A . TH . & ELECT ❋.

603. Similar to last, excepting date, which is 1762, and legend on R : ends TH . & . EL.

604. O : Shield No. 10, crown divides date, 17—62. FEIN ($\frac{2}{3}$) SILB under. GEORG . III . D . G . M . BR . FR . ET . HIB . REX . F . D.

  R : Wild man holding tree . I . B . H . under, 24 in field. BR . ET . LVN . DVX . S . R . I . A . TH . ET . EL.

605. Similar to No. 602, excepting date, which is 1763.

606. Similar to No. 604, excepting date, which is 17—63, and initials I . A . P.

607. Similar to No. 602, excepting date, which is 1764.

608. Similar to No. 606, excepting date, which is 17—64.

609. Similar to No. 602, excepting date, which is 1765.

610. O : Shield No. 9, crown divides date 17—65. FEIN ($\frac{2}{3}$) SILB under . GEORG . III . D . G . M . BR . FR . ET HIB . REX . F . D.

  R : Wild man holding tree I . A . P . under, 24 in field. BR . ET . LVN . DVX . S . R . I . A . TH . & ELECT.

611. Similar to last, but dated 17—67.

612. Similar to No. 602, excepting date, which is 17—67.

613. Similar to No. 602, excepting date, which is 1768.

614. Similar to No. 610, excepting date, which is 17—68.

615. Similar to No. 602, excepting date, which is 1769.

616. Similar to No. 610, excepting date, which is 17—69.

617. Similar to No. 602, excepting date, which is 1770.

618.   Similar to No. 610, excepting date, which is
                17—70.

619.   Similar to No. 610, excepting date, which is
                17—71.

620.   Similar to No. 610, excepting date, which is
                17—72.

621. *O:*   Bust to right, I . W . S . under . GEORG . III .
                D . G . M . BR . FR . & HIB . REX . F . D.

      R: Shield No. 10, crown divides date 17—72. N . D .
                REICHES. F ($\frac{2}{3}$) FEIN. SILBER in a curve under.
                . BRUNS . & . LUN . DUX . S . R . I˙. A ˙.
                TH . & ELECT.

622. *O:*   Shield No. 2 crowned, N . D . REICHES . F ($\frac{2}{3}$) FEIN.
                SILBER in a curve under GEORG . III .
                D . G . M . BR . FR . & . HIB . REX .
                F . D.

      R: **24** | MARIEN | GROSCH | 1772 | I . W . S :
                in five lines. BRUNS . & . LUN . DUX .
                S . R . I . A . TH . & . ELECT ✻ .

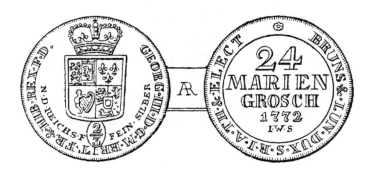

623.   Similar to No. 621, excepting date, which is
                17—73.

624.   Similar to No. 622, excepting date, which is
                1773.

625.   Similar to No. 621, excepting date, which is
                1774, and not divided by the crown but
                over it.

626.   Similar to No. 622, excepting date, which is 1774.

627.   Similar to No. 610, excepting date, which is 17—74, and initials under wild man L . C . R .

628.   Similar to No. 621, excepting date, which is 17—75.

629.   Similar to No. 622, excepting date, which is 1775.

630.   Similar to No. 627, excepting date, which is 17—75.

631.   Similar to No. 621 excepting date, which is 17—76.

632.   *O* :   Bust as No. 621.

    R :   Arms No. 4 supporters, &c.   N . D . R . F ($\frac{2}{3}$) F . SILB . under.   BRUNS . & . LUN . DUX . S . R . I . A . TH . & ELECT .   1776.

633.   Similar to No. 610, excepting date, which is 17—76, and initials L . C . R . under Wild man.

634.   Similar to No. 622, excepting date, which is 1776.

635.   Similar to No. 622, excepting date, which is 1777.

636.   Similar to No. 627, excepting date, which is 17—77.

637.   Similar to No. 621, excepting date, which is 17—78.

638.   Similar to No. 633, excepting date, which is 17—78.

639.   *O* :   Shield No. 1, otherwise as No. 622.

    R :   Similar to No. 622, excepting date, which is 1778.

640.   Similar to No. 622, excepting date, which is 17—79.

641.   Similar to No. 633, excepting date, which is 17—79, and initial c. under Wild man.

642.   Similar to No. 639, excepting date, which is 1780.

643.   Similar to No. 641, excepting date, which is 1780, and initials under wild man, c . e . s .

644.   Similar to No. 621, excepting date, which is 1781, and n . d . r . f . ($\frac{2}{3}$) f . silb under shield.

645.   Similar to No. 632, excepting date, which is 1781.

646.   Similar to No. 639, excepting date, which is 1781.

647.   Similar to No. 643, excepting date, which is 17—81.

648.   Similar to No. 621, excepting date, which is 17—82.

649.   Similar to No. 622, excepting date, which is 1782.

650.   Similar to No. 643, excepting date, which is 1782.

651.   Similar to No. 639, excepting date, which is 1783.

652.   Similar to No. 643, excepting date, which is 1783.

653.   Similar to No. 639, excepting date, which is 1784.

654.   Similar to No. 643, excepting date, which is 1784.

655.   Similar to No. 639, excepting date, which is 1785.

656.   *O* :   Shield No. 1, crowned, date at sides of shield 17—85. fein ($\frac{2}{3}$) silb . under, legend as before.

    R :   Wild man and tree, c . under, BR . ET . LUN . DUX . S . R . I . A . TH . ET . EL.

657.   Similar to No. 621, excepting date, which is 17—86.

658.   Similar to No. 656, excepting date, which is 17—86.

659.   Similar to No. 621, excepting date, which is 17—87, and legend on *O* : reads D . G . M . BRIT.

660.   Similar to No. 639, excepting date, which is 1787.

661.   Similar to No. 643, excepting date, which is 1787.

662.   Similar to No. 621, excepting date, which is 17—88.

663.   *O* :   Shield No. 1, crowned, N . D . REICHES . F . ($\frac{2}{3}$) FEIN . SILBER . in a curve under. GEORG . III . D . G . M . BRIT . FR . & . HIB . REX . F . D .

     R :   **24** | MARIEN | GROSCH : | 1788 | P . L . M . in five lines . BRUNS . & . LUN . DUX . S . R . I . A . TH . & ELECT. ✳

664.   Similar to No. 643, excepting date, which is 1788.

665.   Similar to No. 663, excepting date, which is 1789.

666.   Similar to No. 621, excepting date, which is 17—89.

667.   Similar to No. 656, excepting date, which is 17—89.

668.   Similar to No. 663, excepting date, which is 1790, and initial c.

669.   Similar to No. 621, excepting date, which is 17—90.

670.   Similar to No. 621, excepting date, which is 17—91.

671.   Similar to No. 663, excepting date, which is 1791, and initial c.

672.   Similar to No. 663, excepting date, which is 1792, and initial c.

673.   Similar to No. 663, excepting date, which is 1793, and initials P . L . M.

674.   Similar to last, excepting date, which is 1794.

675.   Similar to last, excepting date, which is 1795.

676.   Similar to No. 621, excepting date, which is 17—95, and initials P . L . M . under bust.

677.   Similar to No. 621, excepting date, which is
          17—96, and initials P . L . M . under bust.

678.   Similar to No. 673, excepting date, which is
          1796.

679.   Similar to No. 621, excepting date, which is
          17—97, and initials P . L . M .

680.   Similar to No. 673, excepting date; which is 1797.

681.   Similar to No. 673, excepting date, which is
          1798.

682.   Similar to No. 621, excepting date, which is
          17—99, and initials P . L . M .

683.   Similar to No. 673, excepting date, which is
          1799.

684.   Similar to No. 663, excepting date, which is
          1800, and initials, E. C.

685.   Similar to No. 621, excepting date, which is
          1800, and initials P . L . M.

686.   As last, but with initial C.

687.   Similar to No. 663, excepting date, which is
          1800, and initials P . L . M.

688. O: Bust to right, GEORG . III . D . G . BRIT .
          REX . F . D . B . & L . DUX . S . R . I .
          A . TH . & EL . ✿

     R: $\frac{2}{3}$ in the centre, ✿ C ✿ under, 18 STUCK
          EINE MARK FEIN ✿ 1801.

689. O: Shield No. 7, crowned, C under, GEORGIUS .
          III . D . G . BRITANNIARUM . REX .
          F . D.

     R: $\frac{2}{3}$ in the centre, N . D . REICHES . FUS . FEIN .
          SILBER . under in a curve, BRUNS . & LUN .
          DUX . S . R . I . A . TH . & ELECTOR .
          1801. ✿

690.   Similar to last, but dated 1802, and initials
          G . F . M.

691.   Similar to last, but dated 1803, and initials
          G . F . M.

692. *O*: Shield No. 7 (not so pointed as last), G . F . M .
under, legend as last.

R: Similar to last, excepting date, which is 1804,
and legend under numerals reads FUSS.

693. Similar to last, excepting date, which is 1805.

694. *O*: Shield No. 11, G . M . under, GEORGIUS . III .
D . G . BRITANNIARUM . REX . F . D.

R: Similar to No. 689, excepting date, which is
1805.

695. Similar to last, excepting date, which is 1806.

696. Similar to last, excepting date, which is 1807.

697. *O*: Shield No. 7, with garter depending from it,
GEORGIUS III . D . G . BRITANNIARUM
REX . F . D.

R: $\frac{2}{3}$ in centre, BRUNSVICIENSIS ET LUNE-
BERG DUX . S . R . I . A . T . ET E .
1813. 20 EINE MARK FEIN.

I have only met with this coin in proof
condition and I suspect it was a pattern.

698. *O*: Bust to right, C. under, legend as last.

R: Centre as No. 689. BRUNS . & LUNEB .
DUX S . R . I . A . TH . & . ELECT . 1813. ✿

699. Similar to last, excepting date, which is 1814. ✿

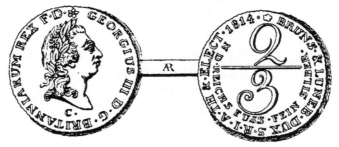

Half Thalers.

700. *O*: Bust to right. GEORG . III . V . G . G . KÖNIG
UND CHURFÜRST.

R: ✛ $\frac{1}{2}$ ✛ | THALER | HANNOVERISCH |
CASSEN=GELD | ✿1801✿ | ✿C✿ in six
lines.

701. *O*: Running horse, xx EINE F . MARK under,
          GEORGIUS III D. G. BRITANNIARUM
          & ❊

R: ❊ **16** ❊ | GUTE | GROSCHEN | CONVEN-
          TION | MUNZE | FEIN SILBER in six lines
          in the centre. HANNOV . REX BRUNS .
          & LUNEBURG . DUX . 1820.

One Third Thalers.

702. *O*: Shield No. 6, crown divides date, 17—64.
          N . D . R . F . ($\frac{1}{3}$) F . SILB . in a curve under.
          GEORG . III . D . G . M . B . F . & . H .
          REX . F . D.

R: St. Andrew with his cross, I . W . S . under, BR .
          & . LUN . DUX . S . R . I . A . TH . & . EL.

703. *O*: Shield No. 3, crown divides date 17—64 . FEIN .
          ($\frac{1}{3}$) SILB . in a curve under, legend as before.

R: Wild man holding tree, I . A . P . under, legend
          as last.

704.   Similar to last, excepting date, which is 17—65.

705.   Similar to No. 702, excepting date, which is
          17—66.

706.   Similar to No. 703, excepting date, which is
          17—67.

707. *O*: Shield No. 10, N . D . REICHES . F . ($\frac{1}{3}$) FEIN . SILBER
          in a curve under, legend as before.

R: Running horse ⚘ C ⚘ under, legend as before,
          date follows legend 1767.

708.   Similar to No. 703, excepting date, which is
          17—68.

709.   Similar to No. 703, excepting date, which is
          17—70.

710.   Similar to No. 703, excepting date, which is
          17—72.

711. *O*: Bust to right, I . W . S . under. GEORG . III .
          D . G . M . BRIT . FR . & HIB . REX .
          F . D.

R: Shield No. 10, crown divides date, 17—74, N . D . R . r ($\frac{1}{3}$) F . SILB in a curve under, BR . & LUN . DUX . S . R . I . A . TH . ET . EL.

712.   Similar to No. 703, excepting date, which is 17—74, and initials L . C . R. under Wild man.

713.   Similar to last, excepting date, which is 17—75.

714.   Similar to last, excepting date, which is 17—76.

715.   Similar to last, excepting date, which is 17—77.

716. O: Bust to right, I . W . S . under. GEORG . III . D . G . M . BRIT . FR . & . HIB . REX . F . D.

    R: Arms No. 4, supporters, &c.; crown divides date 17—78. N . D . R . F . ($\frac{1}{3}$) F . SILB. under in a curve, BRUNS . & LUN . DUX . S . R . I . A . TH . & ELECT.

717.   Similar to last, excepting date, which is 17—79.

718. O: Shield No. 10, date over 1781. N . D . R . F . ($\frac{1}{3}$) F . SILB . in a curve under GEORG . III · D . G . M . BR . FR . & HIB . REX . F . D.

    R: St. Andrew as No. 702.

719. O: As No. 716.

    R.   Shield No. 10, crown divides date 17—82, N . D . R . F . ($\frac{1}{3}$) F . SILB . in a curve under, legend as last.

720.   Similar to No. 703, excepting date, which is 17—82, and initials C . E . S. under Wild man.

721.   Similar to last, excepting date, which is 17—83.

722.   Similar to No. 718, excepting date, which is 1783.

723. O: Shield No. 2, crown divides date 17—84, legend as before.

    R: Wild man holding tree, C . E . S . under, 12 in field, BR . ET . LUN . DUX. S . R . I . A . TH . ET . EL.

724.　　　　　Similar to No. 718, excepting date, which is 1784.

725. *O* :　Shield No. 1, date at sides of shield 17—85, FEIN . ($\frac{1}{3}$) SILB . under. GEORG . III . D . G . M . BR . FR . ET . HIB . REX . F . D.

　　R :　Similar to No. 723.

726.　　　　　Similar to No. 711, excepting date, which is 17—85.

727.　　　　　Similar to No. 725, excepting date, which is 17—86, and initial c. under Wild man.

728.　　　　　Similar to No. 711, excepting date, which is 17—86.

729.　　　　　Similar to No. 725, excepting date, which is 17—87, and initial c.

730.　　　　　Similar to No. 725, excepting date, which is 17—88, and initial c.

731.　　　　　Similar to No. 725, excepting date, which is 17—89, and initial c.

732. *O* :　Bust to right, c . under, GEORG . III . D . G . M . BRIT . FR . & HIB . REX . F . D.

　　R :　Shield No. 1, crown divides date 17—89, N . D . R . F . ($\frac{1}{3}$) F . SILB . in a curve under. BRUNS . & . LUN . DUX . S . R . I . A . TH . & ELECT.

733.　　　　　Similar to last, excepting date, which is 17—90.

734.　　　　　Similar to last, excepting legend on *R* : which reads BR . & LUN . DUX . S . R . I . A . TH . & E.

735.　　　　　Similar to No. 732, excepting date, which is 17—91.

736.   Similar to No. 732, excepting date, which is 17—93.

737.   Similar to No. 702, excepting date, which is 17—93, and N . D . REICHES . F . ($\frac{1}{3}$) FEIN . SILBER . in a curve under shield.

738.   Similar to No. 732, excepting N . D . REICHES . F . ($\frac{1}{3}$) FEIN . SILBER is under shield, and date is 17—94.

739. *O* : Bust to right, P . L . M . under, legend as 732.

     R : Similar to last, excepting date, which is 17—95.

740.   Similar to last, excepting date, which is 17—96.

741.   Similar to last, excepting date, which is 17—97.

742.   Similar to last, excepting date, which is 17—98.

743.   Similar to last, excepting date, which is 18—00, and C. under bust.

744. *O* : Bust to right, G . F . M . under, GEORGIUS . III . D . G . BRITANNIARUM . REX . F . D.

     R : Shield No. 7, crown divides date 18—03, N . D . REICHES . F . ($\frac{1}{3}$) FEIN . SILBER in a curve under, BRUNS . & LUN . DUX . S . R . I . A . TH . & . ELECT.

745.   Similar to last, but with much smaller bust, the date, which is 1804, follows the legend, and is not divided by the crown.

746. *O* : Shield No. 7, N . D . REICHES . F . ($\frac{1}{3}$) FEIN . SILBER . in a curve under, GEORGIUS . III. D . G . BR . REX . F . D . 1804.

     R : St. Andrew with his cross, G . F . M . under, BR . & . LUN . DUX . S . R . I . A . TH . & . ELECT.

One-sixth Thalers.

747. *O* : Shield No. 3, crown divides date 17—61, N . D . R . F . ($\frac{1}{6}$) F . SILB under GEORG . III. D . G . M . B . F . & H . REX . F . D.

     R : St. Andrew and cross, I . W . S . under, BR . & LUN . DUX . S . R . I . A . TH . & . EL.

748.   ¦   Similar to last, excepting date, which is 17—62.

749.   O:¦   Shield No. 2, crown divides date 17—62, FEIN.
        ($\frac{1}{6}$) SILB . under in a curve, legend as last.

    R: Wild man holding tree, I . B . H . under, 6 in the
        field, legend as last.

750.   ¦   Similar to last, excepting date, which is 17—63.

751.   ¦   Similar to last, excepting date, which is 17—64.

752.   Similar to No. 747, excepting date, which is
        17—64.

753.   Similar to No. 749, excepting date, which is
        17—67.

754.   Similar to No. 749, excepting date, which is
        17—68, and initials I . A . P.

755.   Similar to No. 747, excepting date, which is
        17—69.

756.   Similar to No. 749, excepting date, which is
        17—70, and initials I . A . P.

757.   Similar to No. 747, excepting date, which is
        17—71.

758.   Similar to No. 749, excepting date, which is
        17—72, and initials I . A . P.

759.   Similar to No. 749, excepting date, which is
        17—73, and initials L . C . R . under Wild
        man.

760.   O: Bust to right, I . W . S . under, GEORG . III .
        D . G . M . B . F . ET . H . REX . F . D.

    R: Shield No. 10, crown divides date 17—73,
        N . D . R . F . ($\frac{1}{6}$) F . SILB . in a curve under,
        BR . & . LUN . DUX . S . R . I . A . TH . & .
        EL.

761.   Similar to No. 759, excepting date, which is
        17—74.

762.   Similar to No. 760, excepting date, which is
        17—76.

763.   Similar to No. 759, excepting date, which is
        17—76.

764.   Similar to No. 759, excepting date, which is 17—78.

765. *O*: Bust to right, ɪ . w . s . under, GEORG . III . D . G . M . BRIT . FR . & . HIB . REX . F . D.

     R: Shield No. 10, crown divides date 17—78, N . D . R . F . ($\frac{1}{6}$) F . SILB . in a curve under, BRUNS . & LUN . DUX . S . R . I . A . TH . & . ELECT.

766.   Similar to last, excepting date, which is 17—79.

767.   Similar to last, excepting date, which is 17—80.

768. *O*: Shield No. 1, crown divides date, 17—80, legend as No. 765.

     R: St. Andrew and cross . ɪ . w . s . under, BR . & LUN . DUX . S . R . I . A . TH . & ELECT.

769.   Similar to No. 749, excepting date, which is 17—80, and initials c . ᴇ . s . under Wild man.

770.   Similar to last, excepting date, which is 17—81.

771.   Similar to last, excepting date, which is 17—82.

772.   Similar to No. 765, excepting date, which is 17—82.

773.   Similar to No. 769, excepting date, which is 1783.

774.   Similar to No. 769, excepting date, which is 17—84.

775. *O*: Bust as No. 765.

     R: Shield No. 1, crown divides date, 17—84, N . D . R . F . ($\frac{1}{6}$) F . SILB . under, and legend as *R*: of No. 765.

776. *O*: Shield No. 1, crown divides date, 17—85, N . D . R . F . ($\frac{1}{6}$) F . SILB . in a curve, legend as *O*: of No. 765.

     R: St. Andrew with his cross, ɪ . w . s . under, BR . & LUN . DUX . S . R . I . A . TH . & . ELECT.

777.   Similar to No. 769, excepting date, which is 17—85.

778.   Similar to No. 749, excepting date, which is
                     17—86, and initial c . under Wild man.

779.   O :   Bust to right, I . W . S . under, GEORG . III .
                     D . G . M . BRIT . FR . ET HIB . REX .
                     F . D.

         R :   Shield No. 1 within a garter, crown over divides
                     date 17—86, N . D . R . F . ($\frac{1}{6}$) F . SILB . in a
                     curve under, BRUNS . ET . LUN . DUX .
                     S . R . I . A . TH . ET . ELECT.

780.   Similar to last, excepting date, which is 17—87.

781.   Similar to No. 778, excepting date, which is
                     17—88.

782.   Similar to No. 779, excepting date, which is
                     17—89.

783.   Similar to No. 778, excepting date, which is
                     17—89.

784.   Similar to No. 776, excepting date, which is
                     17—89.

785.   Similar to No. 776, excepting date, which is
                     17—90, and initial c . only, under St. Andrew.

786.   O :   Shield No. 1, crowned, date at sides 17—91,
                     N . D . R . F . ($\frac{1}{6}$) F . SILB . under, in a curve
                     legend as No. 765.

         R :   Wild man holding tree, c. under, 6 in field,
                     BRUNS . & . LUN . DUX . S . R . I . A . TH .
                     & . ELECT.

787.   Similar to last, excepting date, which is 17—92.

788.   Similar to No. 779, excepting date, which is
                     17—92, and initial c.

789.   Similar to No. 786, except date, which is
                     17—93, and initials P . L . M.

790.   Similar to No. 779, excepting date, which is
                     17—94, and initials P . L . M.

791.   Similar to No. 786, excepting date, which is
                     17—94, and initials P . L . M.

792.   Similar to last, but dated 17—95.

793.   Similar to No. 779, excepting date, which is 17—95, and initials P . L . M.

794.   Similar to No. 779, excepting date, which is 17—96, and N. D. R. F ($\frac{1}{6}$) F. SILBER under shield.

795.   Similar to last, but dated 17—97.

796.   Similar to No. 786, excepting date, which is 17—97, and initials P . L . M.

797.   Similar to No. 779, excepting date, which is 17—98, and initials P . L . M . under bust, and N . D . REICHES . F . FEIN . SILBER, in a curve under shield.

798.   Similar to No. 749, excepting date, which is 17—98, and initials P . L . M . and as last under shield.

799.   Similar to last, but dated 17—99.

800.   Similar to No. 797, excepting date, which is 17—99.

801.   Similar to No. 797, excepting date, which is 18—00, and initial c. under bust.

802. *O*:   Shield No. 1, crown divides date 1800. N . D . R . F . ($\frac{1}{6}$) F . SILB . in a curve under, GEORG . III . D . G . M . BRIT . FR . & HIB . . REX . F . D.

   R: Wild man holding tree, P . L . M . under, 6 in the field. BRUNS . & LUN . DUX . S . R . I . A . TH . & ELECT.

803. *O*:   Bust to right, c. under, GEORGIUS . III . D . G . BRITANNIARUM . REX . F . D.

   R: Shield No. 3, crown divides date, 18—02, N . D . R . F . ($\frac{1}{6}$) F . SILBER under, BRUNS . & LUN . DUX . S . R . I . A . TH . & ELECT.

804.   Similar to last, excepting date, which is 18—03.

805.   Similar to last, excepting date, which is 18—04.

806.   Similar to No. 802, excepting date, which is 18—04.

807. *O* : Shield No. 7, crowned, N . D . R . F . $(\frac{1}{6})$ F .
SILB. in a curve under, GEORGIUS . III .
D . G . BR . REX . F . D . 1804.

R : St. Andrew with his cross, G . F . M . under,
BR . & LUN . DUX . S . R . I . A . TH . &
ELECT.

808. *O* : Bust to right, G . $(\frac{1}{6})$ M . under, GEORGIUS . III .
D . G . BRITANNIARUM . REX . F . D .

R : Arms in garter, crowned, N . D . R . F—F . SILB .
in a curve under, BRUNS . & LUN . DUX .
S . R . I . A . TH & ELECT . 1807.

Four Marien Groschen.

809. *O* : ✳ **IIII** ✳ | MARIEN | GROSCH : | FEIN
SILB : | I . B . H in five lines, GEORG . III .
D . G . M . BR . FR . ET . HIB . REX .
F . D . 1762. ✳

R : Wild man holding tree, 4 in the field, BR . ET .
LUN . DUX . S . R . I . A . TH . ET . EL.

810. Similar to last, excepting date, which is 1764,
and initials I . A . P.

811. Similar to last, excepting date, which is 1766.

812. Similar to last, excepting date, which is 1767.

813. Similar to last, excepting date, which is 1769.

814. Similar to last, excepting date, which is 1770.

815. Similar to last, excepting date, which is 1771.

816. Similar to last, excepting date, which is 1774,
and initials L . C . R.

817.   Similar to last, excepting date, which is 1775.
818.   Similar to last, excepting date, which is 1776.
819.   Similar to last, excepting date, which is 1777.
820.   Similar to last, excepting date, which is 1778.
821.   Similar to last, excepting date, which is 1779, and initial c.
822.   Similar to last, excepting date, which is 1780, and initials c . e . s.
823.   Similar to last, excepting date, which is 1781.
824.   Similar to last, excepting date, which is 1783.
825.   Similar to last, excepting date, which is 1784.
826.   Similar to last, excepting date, which is 1786, and f . silber . | c . in centre of O :
827.   O :   ❃ IIII ❃ | MARIEN | GROSCH : | f . silber . | 1787 | c. in six lines, legend as before.
    R :   As before.

One-twelfth Thaler or 3 Groschen.

828.   O :   **12** | EINEN | THAL : | i . w . s . in four lines in centre, NACH DEM REICHES FUS ❃
    R :   Running horse, with date under 1760.
829.   As last, but with initials i . a . s . and legend NACH DEM LEIPZIGER FUS *
830.   Similar to No. 828, excepting date, which is 1761.
831.   Similar to last, excepting date, which is 1762.
832.   Similar to last, excepting date, which is 1763.
833.   As last, but initial ❃ c ❃
834.   Similar to last, excepting date, which is 1764.
835.   Similar to last, excepting date, which is 1765.
836.   Similar to last, excepting date, which is 1767.
837.   Similar to last, excepting date, which is 1768.
838.   Similar to last, excepting date, which is 1769, and initials i . w . s.
839.   Similar to last, excepting date, which is 1770.

840.		Similar to last, excepting date, which is 1771.
841.		Similar to last, excepting date, which is 1772.
842.		Similar to last, excepting date, which is 1773.
843.		Similar to last, excepting date, which is 1774.
844.		Similar to last, excepting date, which is 1776.
845.		Similar to last, excepting date, which is 1778.
846.		Similar to last, excepting date, which is 1780.
847.		Similar to last, excepting date, which is 1781.
848.		Similar to last, excepting date, which is 1783.
849.		Similar to last, excepting date, which is 1784.
850.		Similar to last, excepting date, which is 1786.
851.		Similar to last, excepting date, which is 1788.
852.		Similar to last, excepting date, which is 1789.
853.		Similar to last, excepting date, which is 1791, and initial c.
854.		Similar to last, excepting date, which is 1792.
855.		Similar to last, excepting date, which is 1793, and initials P . L . M .
856.		Similar to last, excepting date, which is 1795.
857.		Similar to last, excepting date, which is 1796.
858.		Similar to last, excepting date, which is 1798.
859.		Similar to last, excepting date, which is 1799.
860.		Similar to last, excepting date, which is 1800.
861.		Similar to last, excepting date, which is 1801, and initials E . C .
862.		Similar to last, excepting date, which is 1802, and initial c.
863.		Similar to last, excepting date, which is 1803.
864.		Similar to last, excepting date, which is 1804.
865.		Similar to last, excepting date, which is 1805.
866.		Similar to last, excepting date, which is 1806.
867.		Similar to last, excepting date, which is 1807.
868.	O :	**12**	EINEN	THALER	c . in four lines, NACH DEM REICHES FUSS ✽
	R :	Running horse, with date under, 1814.

869.   Similar to last, excepting date, which is 1815.

870.   Similar to last, excepting date, which is 1816.

871.   *O* :   3 | MARIEN | GROSCHEN | 1816 in four
            lines, KÖN . HANNOVERSCHE CON-
            VENTIONS-MUNZE.

       R :   Running horse, c . h . h . under, 160 EINE
            FEINE MARK.

872.   Similar to last, excepting date, which is 1817.

873.   Similar to last, excepting date, which is 1818.

874.   Similar to last, excepting date, which is 1819,
            and initials L . B . under horse.

875.   As last, but initials under horse L . A . B .

Two Marien Groschen.

876.   *O* : $\mathcal{G}.\mathcal{R}$. in monogram, crowned, I . W . S . under.

       R :   II | MARIEN | GROSCH | 1760 in four lines,
            NACH DEM LEIPZIGER FUS ✻

877.   *O* :   ✻II✻ | MARIEN | GROSCH : | FEIN SILB : |
            I . A . P . in five lines, GEORG . III . D . G .
            M . BR . FR . ET . HIB . REX . F . D .
            1763 ✢

       R :   Wild man holding tree, 2 in field, BR . ET .
            LVN . DVX . S . R . I . A . TH . ET . EL .

878.   Similar to last, excepting date, which is 1766.

879.   Similar to last, excepting date, which is 1768.

880.   Similar to last, excepting date, which is 1770.

881.   Similar to last, excepting date, which is 1773.

882.   Similar to last, excepting date, which is 1774,
            and initials L . C . R .

883.   Similar to last, excepting date, which is 1778.

884.   Similar to last, excepting date, which is 1779.
885.   Similar to last, excepting date, which is 1780,
             and initials c . ᴇ . s .
886.   Similar to last, excepting date, which is 1781.
887.   Similar to last, excepting date, which is 1782.
888.   Similar to last, excepting date, which is 1783.
889.   Similar to last, excepting date, which is 1785.

One Twenty-fourth Thaler.

890. *O :*   Running horse, with the date under, 1760.

      R :   **24** | EINEN | THAL : | ɪ . ᴀ . s . in four
              lines, NACH DEM REICHES FUS ❉

891.   As last, but initials ɪ . w . s .
892.   Similar to No. 890, excepting date, which is
             1761.
893.   Similar to last, excepting date, which is 1764.
894. *O :*   Running horse, with date under, 1814.

      R :   **24** | EINEN | THALER | c in four lines,
              NACH DEM REICHES FUSS ❉

895. *O :*   *G. R* . in monogram   crowned, CONVEN.
              TIONS—MÜNZE.

      R :   **24** | EINEN | THALER | 1817 | ʜ . in five .
              lines.

896.   Similar to last, but dated 1818.

Marien Groschen.

897. *O :*   *G. R* . in monogram crowned, ɪ . w . s . under.

      R :   **1** | MARIEN | GROS | 1762 in four lines,
              NACH DEM REICHS FUS ❉

898.   Similar to last, but date 1763 and legend ends
             FVS.

899   O :   *G . R* . in monogram crowned, I . A . P . under.

      R :   ✳ **1** ✳ | MARIEN | GROS : | 1764 in four lines, K . GR . BRIT . UND . C . F . BR . LVN . LAND . M ✳

900.   Similar to last, excepting date, which is 1765.

901.   Similar to No. 898, excepting date, which is 1766.

902.   Similar to No. 898, excepting date, which is 1768.

903.   Similar to No. 897, excepting date, which is 1769.

904.   Similar to No. 897, excepting date, which is 1770.

905.   Similar to No. 899, excepting date, which is 1770.

906.   Similar to No. 899, excepting date, which is 1771.

907.   Similar to No. 897, excepting date, which is 1775.

908.   Similar to No. 899, excepting date, which is 1777.

909.   Similar to No. 898, excepting date, which is 1778.

910.   Similar to No. 897, excepting date, which is 1781.

911.   Similar to No. 897, excepting date, which is 1784.

912.   Similar to No. 897, excepting date, which is 1785.

913.   Similar to No. 897, excepting date, which is 1790, and initial c.

914.   Similar to last, excepting date, which is 1791.

915.   Similar to No. 897, excepting date, which is 1793, and initials P . L . M.

916.   Similar to last, excepting date, which is 1797.

917.   Similar to last, excepting date, which is 1799.

918.   Similar to last, excepting date, which is 1802, and legends ends FUSS.

919.   Similar to last, excepting date, which is 1803, and initials G . F . M.

920.   Similar to last, excepting date, which is 1804.

921.   Similar to last, excepting date, which is 1814.

922. *O:* *G . R* . in monogram crowned, CONVEN-TIÖNS-MUNZE.

     R: **1** | MARIEN | GROS . | 1816 . | H . in five lines.

923.   Similar to last, excepting date, which is 1817.

924.   Similar to last, excepting date, which is 1818.

Six Pfennige.

925. *O:* *G . R* . in monogram crowned, I . W . S . under.

     R: Orb and cross inscribed (VI), NACH DEM REICHS FUS 1763.

926.   Similar to last, excepting date, which is 1764.

Four Pfennige.

927. *O:* *G . R* . in monogram crowned, I . W . S . under.

     R: **IIII** | PFENN | 1761 in three lines, NACH DEM LEIPZIGER FUS ✿

928. *O:* As last.

     R: **IIII** | PFENN | 1762 in three lines, NACH DEM REICHS FUS ✿

929. *O:* As before, I . A . P . under monogram.

     R: **IIII** | PFEN . | 1763, in three lines, K . GR . BR . UND C . F . BR . LVN . LANDM . ✿

930.   Similar to No. 928, excepting date, which is 1763.

931.   Similar to last, excepting date, which is 1764.

932.	Similar to last, excepting date, which is 1765.
933.	Similar to No. 929, excepting date, which is 1765.
934.	Similar to No. 929, excepting date, which is 1766.
935.	Similar to last, excepting date, which is 1770.
936.	Similar to last, excepting date, which is 1772.
937.	Similar to last, excepting date, which is 1775, and initials L . C . R.
938.	Similar to No. 928, excepting date, which is 1776.
939.	Similar to No. 929, excepting date, which is 1779, and initial C.
940.	Similar to No. 928, excepting date, which is 1780.
941.	Similar to last, excepting date, which is 1784.
942.	Similar to last, excepting date, which is 1785.
943.	Similar to last, excepting date, which is 1787.
944.	Similar to last, excepting date, which is 1791, and initial C.
945.	Similar to last, excepting date, which is 1792.
946.	Similar to last, excepting date, which is 1793, and initial P . L . M.
947.	Similar to last, excepting date, which is 1797.
948.	Similar to last, excepting date, which is 1799.
949.	Similar to last, excepting date, which is 1802, initial C and legend ends FUSS.

950. *O* : *G . R* . in monogram crowned, G . F . M . under.

    R : **IIII** | PFEN : | 1804 in three lines, NACH DEM REICHS FUSS ✽

951.	Similar to No. 948, but dated 1814.
952.	Similar to last, but dated 1815, and initial H.

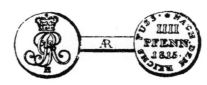

953. *O* : 𝒢 . ℛ . in monogram crowned, CONVENT-
MÜNZE.

   R :   **IIII** | PFENN . | 1816 | H . in four lines.

954.   Similar to last, but dated 1817.

955.   Similar to last, but dated 1818.

A synopsis of the principal silver coins of George III.

WITH THE KING'S BUST.				WITH THE WILD MAN.			
THALER.	$\frac{2}{3}$	$\frac{1}{3}$	$\frac{1}{6}$	THALER.	$\frac{2}{3}$	$\frac{1}{3}$	$\frac{1}{6}$
1773.	1772.	1774.	1773.	1764.	1762.	1764.	1762.
1774.	1773.	1778.	1776.	1765.	1763.	1765.	1763.
1776.	1774.	1779.	1778.	1775.	1764.	1767.	1764.
1777.	1775.	1782.	1779.	1776.	1765.	1768.	1767.
1778.	1776.	1785.	1780.		1767.	1770.	1768.
1779.	1778.	1786.	1782.		1768.	1772.	1769.
1780.	1781.	1789.	1784.		1769.	1774.	1770.
1786.	1782.	1790.	1786.		1770.	1775.	1772.
1791.	1786.	1791.	1787.		1771.	1776.	1773.
1792.	1787.	1793.	1789.		1772.	1777.	1774.
1797.	1788.	1794.	1792.		1774.	1782.	1775.
1801.	1789.	1795.	1794.		1775.	1783.	1776.
	1790.	1796.	1795.		1776.	1784.	1778.
	1791.	1797.	1796.		1777.	1785.	1780.
	1795.	1798.	1797.		1778.	1786.	1781.
	1796.	1800.	1798.		1779.	1787.	1782.
	1797.	1803.	1799.		1780.	1788.	1783.
	1799.	1804.	1800.		1781.	1789.	1784.
	1800.		1802.		1782.		1785.
	1801.		1803.		1783.		1786.
	1802.		1804.		1784.		1788.
	1813.		1807.		1785.		1789.
	1814.				1786.		1790.
					1787.		1791.
					1788.		1792.
					1789.		1793.
							1794.
							1795.
							1797.
							1798.
							1799.
							1800.
							1804.

With St. Andrew.			There are no large pieces of George III. with the Running Horse.		
Thaler.	$\frac{1}{3}$	$\frac{1}{6}$			With large fraction.
1761.	1764.	1761.			$\frac{2}{3}$
1762.	1766.	1762.	XXIV Groschen.		
1763.	1779.	1764.			
1764.	1781.	1768.	1761.	1782.	1801.
1765.	1783.	1769.	1762.	1783.	1802.
1766.	1784.	1771.	1763.	1784.	1803.
1767.	1790.	1780.	1764.	1785.	1804.
1768.	1793.	1782.	1765.	1787.	1805.
1769.	1804.	1785.	1767.	1788.	1806.
1770.		1786.	1768.	1789.	1807.
1771.		1789.	1769.	1790.	1813.
1772.		1790.	1770.	1791.	(Pattern.)
1773.		1804.	1772.	1792.	
			1773.	1793.	
			1774.	1794.	
			1775.	1795.	
			1776.	1796.	
			1777.	1797.	
			1778.	1798.	
			1779.	1799.	
			1780.	1800.	
			1781.		

A few dates will be found here which came to hand too late to be included in the body of the work.

George IV. 1820-30.

Two-third Thalers.

956. *O :* Bust to left, c. under, GEORGIUS IV . D . G . BRITANN & HANNOV . REX . F . D .

R : $\frac{2}{3}$ in centre N . D . LEIPZIGER FUSSE FEINES SILBER . in a curve under. BRUNSVICENCIS & LUNEBERGENSIS DUX . 1822.

957. Similar to last, excepting date, which is 1823.

958. Similar to last, excepting date, which is 1824.

959. Similar to last, excepting date, which is 1825.

960. Similar to last, excepting date, which is 1826.

961. *O* :   Bust to left, smaller than before. GEORG IV .
              D . G . BRIT . & HANNOV . REX F . D .
              BR . & LUN . DUX.

      R : $\frac{2}{3}$ in the centre with B . under.   18 STUCK
              EINE MARK FEINE . 1826.

962.   Similar to last, excepting date, which is 1827.

963.   Similar to No. 955, excepting date, which is
              1827, and with c under bust.

964.   Similar to last, excepting date, which is 1828.

965.   Similar to No. 961, excepting date, which is
              1828.

966.   Similar to last, excepting date, which is 1829.

967.   Similar to No. 956 excepting date, which is
              1829.

Half-Thaler.

968. *O* :   Running horse XX . EINE . F . | MARK . in two
              straight lines under, GEORGIUS IV. D . G .
              BRITAN . & . HANNOV . REX ✽

      R :   ✽ **16** ✽ | GUTE | GROSCHEN | CON-
              VENTIONS | MÜNZE in five lines, and
              in a curve under FEIN SILBER. BRUNS-
              VICENSIS . & . LUNEBURGENSIS .
              DUX . 1820 ✽

969. *O* :   Similar to last.

      R :   ✽ **16** ✽ | GUTE | GROSCHEN | CONV.
              MÜNZE | FEIN . SILBER . in five lines,
              BRUNSVICENSIS . & . LUNEBURGEN-
              SIS . DUX . 1820 ✽

970. *O* :   Running horse XX . E . F . MARK . in a curve
              under, GEORGIUS . IV . D . G . BRITAN .
              ET . HANNOV . REX.

      R :   **16** | GUTE | GROSCHEN in three lines,
              CONV . MÜNZE . FEIN SILB . in a curve under,
              BRUNSVICENSIS ET LUNEBURGEN-
              SIS DUX . 1821.

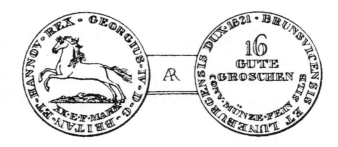

971. As last, but legend BRITANN . ET HANNOV REX.

972. *O* : As last.

    R : **16** | GUTE | GROSCHEN | 1822. in four lines, FEINES SILBER in a curve under, BRUNS-VICENSIS ET LUNEBURGENSIS DUX.

973. Similar to last, excepting date, which is 1823.

974. Similar to last, excepting date, which is 1824.

975. Similar to last, excepting date, which is 1825.

976. Similar to last, excepting date, which is 1826.

977. Similar to last, excepting date, which is 1827.

978.   Similar to last, excepting date, which is 1828.

979. Similar to last, excepting date, which is 1829.

980. Similar to last, excepting date, which is 1830.

One-sixth Thaler.

981. *O* : **6** | EINEN | THALER | 1821. in four lines. KON . HANNOV . CONVENT-MUNZE.

    R : Running horse, B . under, 80 EINE FEINE MARK.

Three Groschen.

982. *O* : **3** | MARIEN | GROSCHEN | 1820. in four lines. KON . HANNOVERSCHE . CONVENTIONS-MUNZE.

    R : Running horse L . B . under. 160 EINE FEINE MARK.

983. Similar to last, excepting date, which is 1821.

984. *O* : **12** | EINEN | THALER | 1822. in four lines.
    KON . HANNOV . CONVENT-MUNZE.

   R : As 982.

985.   Similar to last, excepting date, which is 1823.

986.   Similar to last, excepting date, which is 1824.

One Twenty-fourth Thalers.

987. *O* : *G . R* . in monogram, crowned IV. under,
    CONVENTIONS-MUNZE.

   R : **24** | EINEN | THALER | 1826 | B . in five
    lines.

988.   Similar to last, excepting date, which is 1827.

989.   Similar to last, excepting date, which is 1828.

Four Pfennige.

990. *O* : *G . R* . in monogram, crowned IV. under,
    CONVENT MUNZE.

   R : **IIII** | PFENN . | 1822 | B . in four lines.

991.   Similar to last, excepting date, which is 1824.

992.   Similar to last, excepting date, which is 1826.

993.   Similar to last, excepting date, which is 1828.

994.   Similar to last, excepting date, which is 1830.

WILLIAM IV. 1830-37.

Thalers.

995. *O* : Bust to right, B. under, WILHELM IV
    KOENIG V . GR . BRIT . U. HANNOVER.

   R : Shield No. 12, date under 18—34. EIN
    THALER XIV EINE F . M.

996. *O* : Bust to right, A . under, WILHELM IV
    KOENIG V . GR . BRIT . U . HANNOVER .

   R : **1** | THALER | 1834, in three lines XIV EINE
    FEINE MARK FEINES SILBER.

997. Similar to last, excepting date, which is 1835.

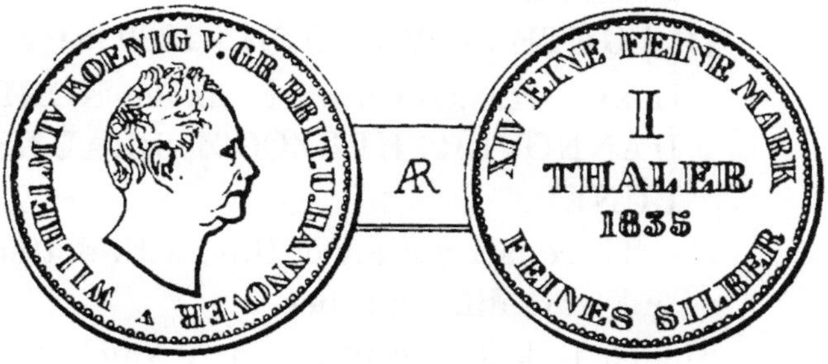

998. *O*: As No. 996.

R: Shield No. 12, EIN THALER XIV EINE F . M. FEINES 1835 SILBER.

999. Similar to last, excepting date, which is 1836.

1000. Similar to No. 996, excepting date, which is 1836.

1001. Similar to 998, excepting date, which is 1837.

Two-third Thaler.

1002. *O*: Arms within a garter, crowned. WILHELM IV . v . G . G . KÖNIG v . GROSS BRIT . IRL . u . HANNOVER .

R: $\frac{2}{3}$ in the centre. NACH DEM LEIPZIGER FUSSE above, FEINES 1832 SILBER below.

1003. Similar to last, excepting date, which is 1833.

1004. *O*: Bust to right. A small w on the neck, WILHELM IV . v . G . G . KOENIG . v . GR . BRIT . IRL . u . HANNOV.

R: As No. 1002, but with a small A under the fraction in the centre.

Half Thalers.

1005. *O*: Running horse, WILHELM IV . v . G . G . KÖNIG . D . v . R . GROSS BR . u . IRL . ❊

R: **16** | GUTE | GROSCHEN | 1830 | FEINES SILBER in five lines, KÖNIG V . HANNOV . HERZOG . Z . BRAUN . U . LUNE.

1006. *O*: Similar to last, but with xx . ᴇ . ꜰ . ᴍᴀʀᴋ in
a curve under horse.

  R: **16** | GUTE | GROSCHEN | 1830 in four lines,
ꜰᴇɪɴᴇꜱ ꜱɪʟʙᴇʀ in a curve under KÖNIG V.
HANNOVER . HERZOG Z . BRAUNS . U .
LÜNEB.

   There is a variety of this, with dotted rim,
and from different dies.

1007. Similar to last, excepting date, which is 1831.

1008. Similar to last, excepting date, which is 1832,
and initial ᴀ. under date.

1009. Similar to No. 1006, excepting date, which is
1833, and legend on *R* : ends LUNE-
BURG .

1010. Similar to last, excepting date, which is 1834.

One-sixth Thaler.

1011. *O* : Bust to right, WILHELM IV . KÖENIG V .
GR . BRIT . U . HANNOVER ✽

  R : Shield No. 12, VI . EINEN THALER
LXXXIV . EINE F . M . 1834.

1012. Similar to last, excepting date, which is 1835.

1013. Similar to last, excepting date, which is 1836.

One-twelfth Thaler.

✓1014. *O* : Similar to last, but with a small ʙ. under bust.

  R : **12** | EINEN | THALER | 1834 in four lines,
CLXVIII EINE FEINE MARK ᴊᴜꜱᴛɪʀᴛ.

1015. Similar to last, excepting date, which is 1835.

1016. Similar to last, excepting date, which is 1836.

1017. Similar to last, excepting date, which is 1837.

One-twenty-fourth Thaler.

1018. *O* : Horse on a shield crowned, KÖN . HANNOV .
SCHEIDE-MUNZE.

  R : **24** | EINEN | THALER | 1834 | ʙ . in five
lines.

1019.   Similar to last, excepting date, which is 1835.
1020.   Similar to last, excepting date, which is 1836.
1021.   Similar to last, excepting date, which is 1837.
         Nos. 1019 and 1020 have as initials both A .
         and B.

Four Pfennige.

1022. *O* : Horse on a shield crowned, KÖN . HANNOV .
         SCHEIDE-M.
       R : **4** | PFENN. | 1834 | B . in four lines.
1023.   Similar to last, excepting date, which is 1835.
1024.   Similar to last, excepting date, which is 1836.
1025.   Similar to last, excepting date, which is 1837.

COPPER COINS.

GEORGE I. 1714-27.

1026. *O* : *G . L . R* . in monogram crowned. (For George
         Lewis Rex.)
       R : ❀1½❀ | PFENNING | SCHEIDE | MUNTZ
         | 1718 in five lines. ❀ under date.
1027.   Similar to last, but stars instead of quatrefoils
         by the 1½, and nothing under date.
1028.   Similar to last, but with a star under date.
1029.   Similar to No. 1026, excepting date, which is
         1721.
1030.   Similar to No. 1026, excepting date, which is
         1722.
1031. *O* : *G . R* . crowned.
       R : ❀1❀ | PFENNING | SCHEIDE | MUNTZ
         1717 in five lines. ✽ under date.
1032.   Similar to last, excepting date, which is 1719.
1033.   Stars instead of quatrefoils, date 1722.
1034.   Similar to No. 1033, but with a rosette under
         date.

1035.   *G . R* . crowned. H . C . B . under.

    R :   ❖1❖ | PFENNING | SCHEIDE | MÜNTZ

        | 1723.   In 5 lines.   A rosette under date.

1036.   *O* :   Wild man and tree.   E . P . H . under.

    R :   ❖1❖ | PFENNING | SCHEIDE | MÜNTZ

        | 1724.   In 5 lines.

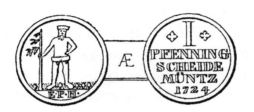

1037.   Similar to No. 1036, excepting date, which is
        1725.

1038.   *O* :   St. Andrew and cross.

    R :   ✳1✳ | PFENNING | SCHEIDE | MÜNTZ |
        1725.

1039.   Similar to last, excepting date, which is 1726.

1040.   Similar to last, excepting roses in place of stars.

1041.   Similar to No. 1036, excepting date, which is
        1726.

GEORGE II. 1727-60.

1042.   *O* :   *G . R* . crowned, c . under.

    R :   1½ | PFENNING | SCHEIDE | MÜNTZ |
        1750.   In five lines.

1043.   Similar to No. 1042, but V instead of Ü in
    MÜNTZ.

In describing the Pfenninges, as there are a large number
of varieties, I shall divide them into three parts or types,
giving the royal cypher first, then those bearing St. Andrew,
and afterwards those with wild man.

1044.   *O* : *G . R* . crowned, c . p . s . under.

      R : ⚜ **1** ⚜ | PFENNING | SCHEIDE | MUNTZ

      | 1729.   In 5 lines.

1045.   Similar to last, but no initials on obverse under the monogram, rosettes instead of quatrefoils on reverse. 1732.

1046.   Similar to last, no initials, on obverse, stars of six rays, quatrefoils on reverse.   1733.

1047.   Similar to No. 1044, quatrefoils by side of numeral.   1734.

1048.   Similar to last, stars of six rays by side of numeral.   1734.

1049.   Similar to last, stars of six rays, 1736.

1050.   Similar to last, but no initials on obverse, stars of six rays.   1739.

1051.   Similar to last, but no initials on obverse, a rose under date.   1740.

1052.   Similar to last, initial s . only, stars of six rays. 1741.

1053.   Similar to last, initial s . only, stars of six rays. 1742.

1054.   Similar to last, initial s . only, roses.   1743.

1055.   Similar to last, c . p . s . on obverse, stars on six rays.   1744.

1056.   Similar to last, quatrefoils.   1745.

1057.   Similar to last, c . p . s . on obverse, quatrefoils.   1745.

1058.   Similar to last, stars of six rays.   1745.

1059.   Similar to last, quatrefoils.   1746.

1060.   Similar to last, stars.   1747.

1061.   Similar to last, quatrefoils, a rosette under date. 1748.

1062.   Similar to last, quatrefoils. 1749.

1063.   Similar to last, quatrefoils. 1750.

1064.   Similar to last, s . on obverse, stars. 1752.

1065.   Similar to last, i . w . s . on obverse, rosettes. 1753.

1066.   Similar to last, quatrefoils. 1753.

1067.   Similar to last, s . on obverse. 1754.

1068.   Similar to last, but with quatrefoils on each side i . w . s . as well as at the sides of numeral on reverse. 1754.

1069.   Similar to No. 1067, quatrefoils. 1755.

1070.   Similar to last, numeral on reverse, quatrefoils. 1756.

1071.   Similar to last, i . w . s . on reverse, rosettes. 1757.

1072.   Similar to last, i . w . s . on reverse. 1758.

1073.   Similar to last, i . w . s . on reverse. 1759.

1074.   *O* : St. Andrew bearing his cross.

      R : ✤ 1 ✤ | PFENNING | SCHEIDE | MÜNTZ | 1729. In 5 lines.

1075.   Similar to last, but rosettes in place of quatrefoils. 1732.

1076.   Similar to last, but rosettes in place of stars. 1734.

1077.   Similar to last, but rosettes in place of stars. 1739.

1078.   *O* : Wild man and tree, with branches on both sides, E . P . H . under.

      R : ∗ 1 ∗ | PFENNING | SCHEIDE | MUNTZ | 1730 in 5 lines.

1079.   Similar to last, but initials i . a . b . and quatrefoils on sides of numeral. 1732.

1080.   Similar to last, but initials i . a . b . and quatrefoils on sides of numeral. 1737.

1081.   Similar to last, but initials ɪ . ʙ. ʜ . and quatre-
           foils on sides of numeral.   1741.
1082.   Similar to last, but initials ɪ . ʙ . ʜ . and quatre-
           foils on sides of numeral.   1742.
1083.   Similar to last, but initials ɪ . ʙ . ʜ . and quatre-
           foils on sides of numeral.   1743.
1084.   Similar to last, but initials ɪ . ʙ . ʜ . and quatre-
           foils on sides of numeral.   1745.
1085.   Similar to last, but initials ɪ . ʙ . ʜ . and quatre-
           foils on sides of numeral.   1747.
1086.   Similar to last, but initials ɪ . ʙ . ʜ . and quatre-
           foils on sides of numeral.   1749.
1087.   Similar to last, but initials ɪ . ʙ . ʜ . and quatre-
           foils on sides of numeral.   1752.
1088.   Similar to last, but initials ɪ . ʙ . ʜ . and quatre-
           foils on sides of numeral.   1754.
1089.   Similar to last, but initials ɪ . ʙ . ʜ . and quatre-
           foils on sides of numeral.   1755.
1090.   Similar to No. 1081, excepting date, which is
           1756.
1091.   Similar to No. 1081, excepting date, which is
           1758.
1092.   Similar to No. 1081, excepting date, and a
           rose under date.   1759.
1093.   Similar to No. 1081, excepting date, and a
           rose under date.   1760.

GEORGE III.   1760-1820.

Four Pfenninges.

1094.   *O* :   St. Andrew with his cross.   c . under.

    R :   **4** | PFENNING | SCHEIDE | MUNTZ |
           1792, in five lines.
1095.   Similar to last, excepting date, which is 1794,
           and initials ᴘ . ʟ . ᴍ.

8

1096.   *O :*   *G . R* . crowned, P . L . M under.

     R :   **4** | PFENNING | SCHEIDE | MÜNTZ |
        1794, in five lines.

1097.   Similar to last, excepting date, which is 1795.

1098.   Similar to last, excepting date, which is 1796.

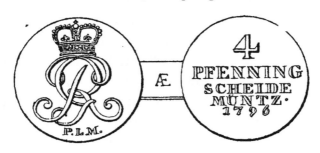

Two Pfenninges.

1099.   Similar to No. 1096, excepting in size and value.
        Date 1794.

1100.   Similar to No. 1096, excepting in size and value.
        Date 1796.

1101.   Similar to No. 1096, excepting in size and value.
        Date 1797.

1102.   Similar to No. 1096, excepting in size and value.
        Date 1798.

1103.   Similar to No. 1096, excepting in size and value.
        Date 1799.

1104.   Similar to No. 1096, excepting in size and value.
        Date 1800.

1105.   Similar to No. 1096, excepting in size and value.
        Initial c. only.   Date 1801.

1106.   Similar to No. 1096, excepting in size and value.
        Initials G . F . M.   Date 1802.

1107.   Similar to No. 1096, excepting in size and value.
        Date 1803.

1108.   Similar to No. 1096, excepting in size and value.
        Date 1804.

1109.   Similar to No. 1096, excepting in size and value.
        Date 1807.

1110. *O:* 𝒢 . ℛ . crowned. The date under. 1817.

 R: A five-leaved rose on each side, numeral on Rev.

1111. Similar to last, excepting date, which is 1818.

One and a half Pfenninges.

1112. *O:* 𝒢 . ℛ . crowned. c . under.

 R: 1½ | PFENNING | SCHEIDE | MUNTZ | 1792.

1113. Similar to last, but P . L . M . under cypher.

In the arrangements of the Pfenninges a similar division will be made to those in the previous reign.

1114. *O:* 𝒢 . ℛ . crowned. I . W . S . under.

 R: 1 | PFENNING | SCHEIDE | MUNTZ.1761.

1115. Similar to last, but 1 PFENN : and date 1762.
1116. Similar to No. 1115. Date 1763.
1117. Similar to No. 1115. Date 1764.
1118. Similar to No. 1115. Date 1765.
1119. Similar to No. 1115. Date 1767.
1120. Similar to No. 1115. Date 1768.
1121. Similar to No. 1115. Date 1769.
1122. Similar to No. 1115. Date 1770.
1123. Similar to No. 1115. Date 1771.
1124. Similar to No. 1115. Date 1772.
1125. Similar to No. 1115. Date 1773.
1126. Similar to No. 1115. Date 1774.
1127. I . W . S . over the crown, not under. 1775.
1128. I . W . S . over the crown, not under. 1776.
1129. I . W . S . over the crown, not under. 1777.
1130. I . W . S . over the crown, not under. 1778.
1131. I . W . S . over the crown, not under. 1779.
1132. With I . W . S . over crown, not under cypher. Date 1780.
1133. With I . W . S . over crown, not under cypher. Date 1781.

8 *

1134.   With I . W . S . over crown, not under cypher.
        Date 1782.

1135.   With I . W . S over crown, not under cypher.
        Date 1783.

1136.   With I . W . S . over crown, not under cypher.
        Date 1784.

1137.   With I . W . S . over crown, not under cypher.
        Date 1785.

1138.   With I . W . S . over crown, not under cypher.
        Date 1786.

1139.   With I . W . S . over crown, not under cypher.
        Date 1787.

1140.   With I . W . S . over crown, not under cypher.
        Date 1788.

1141.   With I . W . S . over crown, not under cypher.
        Date 1789.

1142.   With I . W . S . over crown, not under cypher.
        Date 1790.

1143.   With C . under cypher, nothing above.   Date
        1790.

1144.   With C . under cypher, nothing above.   Date
        1791.

1145.   With C . under cypher, nothing above.   Date
        1792.

1146.   With P . L . M . under cypher, nothing above.
        Date 1793.

1147.   With P . L . M . under cypher, nothing above.
        Date 1794.

1148.   With P . L . M . under cypher, nothing above.
        Date 1795.

1149.   With P . L . M . under cypher, nothing above.
        Date 1796.

1150.   With P . L . M . under cypher, nothing above.
        Date 1797.

1151.   With P . L . M . under cypher, nothing above.
        Date 1798.

1152.   With P . L . M . under cypher, nothing above.
         Date 1799.

1153. ·   With P . L . M . under cypher, nothing above.
         Date 1800.

1154.   With C . only under cypher, nothing above.
         Date 1801.

1155.   With C . only under cypher, nothing above.
         Date 1802.

1156.   With C . only under cypher, nothing above.
         Date 1803.

1157.   With C . only under cypher.   Date 1804.
1158.   With C . only under cypher.   Date 1806.
1159.   With C . only under cypher.   Date 1814.

1160.   Initial C . on rev.   Date on ob. under cypher.
         1817.

1161.   Initial C . on rev.   Date on ob. under cypher.
         1818.

1162.   Initial C . on rev.   Date on ob. under cypher.
         1819.

1163.   Initial C . on rev.   Date on ob. under cypher.
         1820.

1164. O : St. Andrew bearing his cross, I . W . S . under.
       R : 1 | PFENN: | SCHEIDE | MÜNTZ | 1780.

1165.   Similar to last, excepting date, which is 1781.
1166.   Similar to last, excepting date, which is 1782.
1167.   Similar to last, excepting date, which is 1783.
1168.   Similar to last, excepting date, which is 1784.
1169.   Similar to last. excepting date, which is 1785.
1170.   Similar to last, excepting date, which is 1786.
1171.   Similar to last, excepting date, which is 1787.

1172.   Similar to last, excepting date, which is 1788.

1173.   Similar to last, initials P . L . M . 1793.

1174.   Similar to last, but dated 1794.

1175. O :   Wild man and tree, I . B . H . under.

      R :   ❋ **1** ❋ | PFENNING | SCHEIDE | MUNTZ
           | 1762, in five lines.

1176.   Similar to last, but I . A . P . on obv. and date
          1763.

1177.   Similar to last, but I . A . P . on obv. and date
          1764.

1178.   Similar to last, but I . A . P . on obv. and date
          1765.

1179.   Similar to last, but I . A . P . on obv. and date
          1766.

1180.   With I . A . P . under wild man, and date,
          1768.

1181.   With I . A . P . under wild man, and date,
          1769.

1182.   With I . A . P . under wild man, and date,
          1770.

1183.   With L . C . R . under wild man, and date,
          1774.

1184.   With L . C . R . under wild man, and date,
          1775.

1185.   With L . C . R . under wild man, and date,
          1776.

1186.   With L . C . R . under wild man, and date, 1777.

1187.   With L . R . C . under wild man, and date, 1778.

1188.   With C . E . S . under wild man, and date, 1780.

1189.   With C . E . S . under wild man, and date, 1781.

1190.   With C . E . S . under wild man, and date, 1783.

1191.   With C . E . S . under wild man, and date, 1784.

1192.   With C . E . S . under wild man, and date, 1785.

1193.   With C . under wild man, and date, 1788.

1194.   With P . L . M . under wild man, and date, 1792.

1195.   With P . L . M . under wild man, and date, 1794.

1196.	With P . L . M . under wild man, and date, 1795.
1197.	With P . L . M . under wild man, and date, 1796.
1198.	With G . F . M . under wild man, and date, 1804.

GEORGE IV. 1820-30.

Four Pfenninges.

1199.   *O* :   *G . R* . crowned, 1827 under.

   R :   **4** | PFENNING | SCHEIDE | MUNTZ | c.
   in five lines.

Two Pfenninges.

1200.   Similar to last, excepting in size and value.
   Roses on rev., 1821.

1201.	Similar to last.	No roses, 1822.
1202.	Similar to last.	No roses, 1823.
1203.	Similar to last.	No roses, 1824.
1204.	Similar to last.	No roses, 1826.
1205.	Similar to last.	No roses, 1827.
1206.	Similar to last.	No roses, 1828.
1207.	Similar to last.	No roses, 1829.
1208.	Similar to last.	No roses, 1830.
1209.	Similar to last.	No roses, 1830.

Pfenninges.

1210.   *O* :   *G . R* . crowned c. under.

   R :   ✳ **1** ✳ PFENNING | SCHEIDE | MÜNTZ |
   1821.

1211.	Similar, but date 1822.
1212.	Similar, but date 1823.
1213.	Similar, but date 1824.
1214.	Similar, but date 1825.
1215.	Similar, but date 1826.
1216.	Similar, but date 1827.
1217.	Similar, but date 1828.
1218.	Similar, but date 1829.
1219.	Similar, but date 1830.

1220.   With в on R: and date on O: under cypher, 1826.

1221.   Similar to last excepting date, which is **1828**.

1222.   Similar to last, excepting date, which is **1829**.

1223.   Similar to last, excepting date, which is **1830**.

WILLIAM IV.   1830-37.

Four Pfenninges.

1224. O: W . R . in double cypher crowned, 1831 . under.

    R: **4** | PFENNING | SCHEIDE | MÜNTZ | c.
    In 5 lines.

Two Pfenninges.

1225.   Similar to last, excepting in size and value, 1831.

1226.   Similar to last, excepting date, which is 1833.

1227.   Similar to last, excepting date, which is 1834.

1228.   Similar, but having IV. under cypher and date on rev. 1834.

1229. O: Shield with running horse on it, crowned.
    KON : HANNOV. SCHEIDE . MÜNZE.

    R: **2** | PFENNING | 1835 | A.   In four lines.

1230.   Similar, but date 1836.

1231.   Similar, but date 1837.

Pfenninges.

1232.   Similar to No. 1224, excepting in size and value, 1831.

1233.   Similar to last, excepting date, which is 1832.

1234.   Similar to last, excepting date, which is 1833.

1235.   Similar to last, but with initial B., 1833.

1236.   Similar to last, but with initial A., 1833.

1237.   Similar to last, but with initial A., 1834.

1238.   Similar to No. 1228, excepting in size and value, with IV . under cypher, 1834.

1239.   Similar to No. 1229, excepting in size and value. Initial A . on rev., 1835.

1240.   Similar to last. Initial A . on rev., 1836.

1241.   Similar to last. Initial A . on rev., 1837.

1242.   Similar to last. Initial B . on rev., 1835.

1243.   Similar to last. Initial B . on rev., 1836.

1244.   Similar to last, excepting date, which is 1837.

1245. *O* : Running horse not on a shield. WILHELM . HERZOG ZU . BR . U . LUEN .

    R : ✤**1**✤ | PFENNING | SCHEIDE | MÜNZE | 1830. In five lines.

1246.   Similar to last, excepting date, which is 1832.

1247.   Similar to last, excepting date, which is 1834.

I am indebted to an article in the Num. Ch. vol. i. N. S., by the Rev. Henry Christmas, for several dates and varieties of these copper coins.

EAST FRIESLAND.

THE ancient Frisia, formerly governed by its own Counts. On the death of Prince Charles Edward in 1744, it became subject to the King of Prussia. It was annexed to Holland in 1806, and to the French Empire in 1810.. In 1815 it was annexed to Hanover, and so its coins for a short time come within the scope of this work.

Two Stivers.

1. O: *G* . *R* . crowned, IV under.

   R: **2** | STÜBER | OST | FRIESISCH | 1823 | B . in six lines.

Stiver.

2. O: *G* . *R* . crowned, IV . under.

   R: **1** | STÜBER | OST | FRIESISCH | 1823 | B . in six lines.

Half-Stiver.

3. O: *G* . *R* . crowned, IV . under.

   R: $\frac{1}{2}$ | STÜBER | OST | FRIESISCH | 1823 | in five lines.

Quarter Stiver.

4. O: *G* . *R* . IV . crowned.

   R: $\frac{1}{4}$ | STÜBER | OST | FRIESISCH | 1823 | 4 under.

5. Similar to last, excepting with a 5 under date.

6. O: As last.

   R: $\frac{1}{4}$ | STÜBER | OST | FRIESISCH | 1824 in five lines.

7. As last, but dated 1825.

BRUNSWICK-WOLFENBUTTEL.

THE Duchy of Brunswick was in 1409 divided into two branches ; that of Brunswick-Luneburg (from which came George I. of England) and Brunswick-Wolfenbuttel. This latter had for its Duke William Frederick, who, commanding the *avant-garde* at Waterloo under Wellington, was there killed on June 16th, 1815, and who was succeeded by his eldest son, Charles Frederick William. He, being a minor, was placed under the guardianship of George, as Prince Regent, and also as George IV. until 1823, when the young Duke assumed the government.

Under these circumstances it has been thought advisable to include the coins of this State between 1815 and 1823. Although they can scarcely be classed as belonging to the series of English dependencies, still, being found with the name and title of the sovereign upon them they might otherwise somewhat puzzle the inexperienced collector.

GOLD COINS.

Ten Thalers
1. *O :*   Crowned shield of arms. GEORGIVS D . G . PRINC . REGENS

    R :   ✳ X ✳ | THALER | ✢1817✢ | F . R . | ✢ in five lines. TVTOR . NOM . CAROLI DVCIS BRVNS ET LYN ✳

2.   Similar to last, excepting date, which is 1818.
3.   Similar to last, excepting date, which is 1819.

Five Thalers.
4. *O :*   As before.

    R :   ✳ V ✳ | THALER | ✢1816✢ | F . R . | ✢ | in five lines. TVTOR . NOM . CAROLI DVCIS BR . ET LVN ✳

5.   Similar to last, excepting date, which is 1817.

6.   Similar to last, excepting date, which is 1818.

7.   Similar to last, excepting date, which is 1819.

8.   *O :*   Crowned shield as before. GEORG . IV . D . G . REX . BRITANN.

    R :   ✿ **V** ✿ | THALER | ✤1822✤ | C . v . C . | ✤ in five lines, legend as No. 4.

9.   Similar to last, excepting date, which is 1823.

Two-and-a-Half Thalers.

10.   *O :*   As before.

    R :   ✿ **$2\frac{1}{2}$** ✿ | THALER | ✤ 1816 ✤ | F . R . | ✤ in five lines, legend as No. 4, but ending ET LV ✿

11.   Similar to last, excepting date, which is 1818, and legend ends LVN ✿

12.   Similar to last, excepting date, which is 1819.

13.   Similar to last, excepting date, which is 1822, and initials C . v . C.

SILVER COINS.

Twenty-four Groschen.

14.   *O :*   Crowned Shield of Arms. GEORGIVS D . G . PRINC . REGENS.

    R :   ✿ **24** ✿ | MARIEN | GROSCH. | ✿1816✿ | F . R . | FEINES SILBER | In six lines, the lower one curved. TUTOR . NOM . CAROLI DVCIS BRUNS . ET LVN ✿

15.   Similar to last, excepting date, which is 1817.

16.   Similar to last, excepting date, which is 1818.

17.   *O :*   Crowned shield as before. GEORGIVS IV . D . G . REX BRITANNIAR.

    R :   Similar to No. 14, excepting date, which is 1820, and initials under M . C .

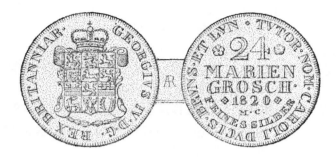

18.   Similar to last, excepting date, which is 1821.
19.   Similar to last, excepting date, which is 1822.
20.   Similar to last, excepting date, which is 1823.

One-Twelfth Thaler.

21.   *O* :   Running horse.   GEORG . D . G . P . R .
              TVT . N . CAROLI . D . BR . ET L . ✳

      R :   ✳ **12** ✳ | EINEN | THALER | ✢ 1816 ✢ |
              F . R . in five lines.   CLX EINE FEINE
              MARK CONVENT M . ✳

22.   Similar to last, excepting date, which is 1817.
23.   *O* :   Horse as before.   GEORG . IV . D . G . R .
              TVT . N . CAROLI . D . BR . ET . L ✳

      R :   As before, but initials in fifth line of legend
              M . C . and date 1820.

24.   Similar to last, but initials C . v. C . and date
              1821.
25.   Similar to last, date 1822.
26.   Similar to last, date 1823.

One Twenty-fourth Thalers.

27.   *O* :   Running horse.   GEORG . IV . D . G . R . T .
              N . CAROLI . D . BR . ET . L.

      R :   ✳ **24** ✳ | EINEN | THALER | ✢ 1820 ✢
              | M . C . in five lines.   BRAUNSCH .
              LÜNEB . LAND MÜNZE ✳

28.   Similar to last, excepting date, which is 1821,
          ,   and initials C . v . C.

29.   Similar to last, excepting date, which is 1823,
               and initials C . v . C.

Marien Groschen.
30.   O :   Running horse, F . R. under. GEORG . T .
               N . CAROLI D . BR . *
       R :   ❀ I ❀ | MARIEN | GROSCH . | ✚ 1819 ✚ |
               ✚ in five lines. DIV EINE FEINE MARK
               CONVENT . M . *

Six Pfenniges.
31.   O :   Running horse, F . R . under. GEORG . T .
               N . CAROLI D . BR . ET . L . *
       R :   ✚ VI ✚ | PFENN : | * 1816 * | ✚ in four lines.
               DCLXXII EINE FEINE MARK CONV .
               M . *
32.   Similar to last, but dated 1819, and legend on
               O : ends D . BR . *
33.   O :   Running horse. GEORG . IV . D . G . T .
               IV . CAR . D . BR . ET . L . *
       R :   As before, but * 1823 * | C . v . C.

Four Pfenniges.
34.   O :   As No. 31.
       R :   ✚ IIII ✚ | PFENN | * 1820 * | ✚ in four lines.
               MVIII E . F . MARK CONV . M . *
35.   O :   As No. 33.
       R :   As last, but dated 1823.

                    COPPER COINS.

Two Pfenniges.
36.   O :   Running horse. GEORG IV . D . G . R .
               TUT . N . CAROLI D . BR . ET L . *
       R :   ✚ II ✚ | PFENNING | SCHEIDE | MÜNZE |
               ✚ 1820 ✚ | M . C . in six lines.
37.   Similar to last, excepting date, which is 1823,
               and initials C . v . C.

Pfennige.

38.   *O* :   Running horse, F . R . under.   GEORG . T . IV. CAROLI D . BR . ET L . *

     R :   ✢ I ✢ | PFENNING | SCHEIDE | MÜNZE | 1816.

39.   Similar to last, but legend on *O* : reads GEORG . P . R . T . N . CAROLI D . BR . ET . L . *

40.   Similar to No. 38, excepting date, which is 1817.

41.   Similar to No. 38, excepting date, which is 1818.

42.   As last, but legend on *O* : ends D . BR . *

43.   Similar to No. 38, excepting date, which is 1819.

44.   As No. 42, dated 1819.

45.   Similar to No. 38, excepting date, which is 1820.

46.   Running horse.   GEORG . IV . D . G . R . T . IV . CAROLI D . BR . ET L . *

     R :   ✢ I ✢ | PFENNING | SCHEIDE | MÜNZE | 1820 | M . C . in six lines.

47.   Similar to last, excepting date, which is 1822, and initials C . v. C.

48.   Similar to last, excepting date, which is 1823.

COINS AND TOKENS

OF THE BRITISH POSSESSIONS

IN

ASIA,

INCLUDING

BOMBAY,	PENANG,
BENGAL,	STRAITS SETTLEMENTS,
MADRAS,	JAVA,
THE INDIAN EMPIRE,	HONG KONG,
CEYLON,	LABUAN,
SUMATRA,	BORNEO,
MALACCA,	SARAWAK,

AND MAURITIUS

INDIA.

THE first commercial intercourse of the English with India was a private adventure of three ships, which were fitted out in 1591.

The information brought home gave rise to another voyage, and ultimately to the establishment of a company, whose first charter was granted by Queen Elizabeth in 1600. Other companies were chartered in 1698 and in 1702, until in 1708 the New East India Company was established. This continued to increase in power and size till 1858, when the Government of India was transferred to the Crown, under a Council of State, when the Company's political power ceased, and the Queen was proclaimed on November 1st, 1858, as Queen of Great Britain and the Colonies. This title was altered in 1877 to Empress of India.

Of the coins of the native princes of India it is not in our province to speak, although they are intimately connected with those of the company. In fact, in some instances such as the "*Surat*" rupee for Bombay, the "*Sicca*" (current) for Bengal, and the "*Arcot*" for Madras, the coins of the latter were exact copies of the former.

It will be necessary to mention, however, for the better understanding of what has to follow, that there were until a very recent period (even if not at present) two distinct monetary systems prevailing in India, the Hindu and the Mussulman, and although the former has become extinct throughout the greater part of Hindustan, by the pre-dominance of the Mussulman power, it is still found in the coins in use in several petty states of Southern India.

The unit of the Hindu system is of gold, and is called "*Hun*" or "*Hoon*," which word in the old Carnatic tongue signifies gold. The name of this coin amongst

Europeans is " *Pagoda,*" a Portuguese appellation derived
from a pyramidical temple, which forms the device on one
side of it.   The Hindu name for it is " *Varaha.*"   The Hun
or Pagoda was subdivided into Fanams, or, more properly,
Panam प नां Faluce or *Faloos*, and Cash or *Kas* ﺱﮐ thus—

20 Cash = 1 Faluce.

80 Cash = 4 Faluce = 1 Fanam

3360 Cash = 168 Faluce = 42 Fanams = 1 Pagoda.

The unit of the Mussulman system is the silver Rupee,
there being nominally 16 Rupees to the gold Mohur ; but as
the weight and quality of the latter varied from time to
time, we find practically that from 14 to 16 Rupees was the
value of a Mohur.   The Rupee is subdivided into Annas
(which is a money of account only) and Pysas, or Pice, and
Pie, thus—

3 Pie =   1 Pysa (or Quarter Anna)

12 Pie =   4 Pysa =   1 Anna

192 Pie = 64 Pysa = 16 Annas = 1 Rupee

The coins of the Hindu system—viz. Pagodas and
Fanams—seem to have been confined to the Madras presi-
dency, whilst on the other hand the coins of Bombay and
Bengal were Rupees, Annas, and Pice.

The earliest coins for the East Indies were either struck
at our own mint by our monarchs, or coined by their
authority.   Of the former kind were the " *Portcullis*"
pieces of Elizabeth struck in 1600-1.   During the reign of
Charles II. the company began by authority from the
Crown to strike coins for their factory at Bombay, all of which
bore either the name, or some reference to, the sovereign.

The first money coined in the East Indies was at Bombay
in the year 1671, when the Court of Directors gave instruc-
tions to their servants to establish a mint, and a few years
later this measure was sanctioned by the Crown.   A clause
in the charter granted 26 Charles II., dated October 5th, 1677,
empowered the company " to stamp money at Bombay,
which money should be current wherever the company's

privilege of trading in the East extended, to be called
Rupees, Pice, and Budgrooks, to bear any seal or impression
as the company shall think proper, so that such money
shall not be called, or bear any impression of, any money
such as was usually current in the Realm of England."
The first record of a regular mint at Bombay is about the
year 1738, and the coins struck then were of like character
to those of the native Surat mint; but about 1790 machinery
like that in use at the royal mint in London was introduced,
and the Rupees thenceforward were carefully stamped, and
bore the entire legend.   Other improvements were made in
1800, in 1823, and again in 1832.

The copper coins for Bombay were from an early period
fabricated in England, many being struck at the Soho
works by Messrs. Boulton and Watt.   Since the construc-
tion of the new mint at Bombay in the year 1832 they have
been struck there, bearing the company's arms on one
side, and a pair of scales with the word *Adel* عدل (Justice)
between, on the other.

The establishment of an independent coinage in Bengal
was of much later date.   Until the year 1757 the only
indulgence granted to the company was the privilege of
having bullion converted into coin at the mints of the
Nawab of Bengal, which were at Dacca, Moorshedabad, and
Patna.   After the taking of Calcutta in 1757 a mint was
established there, although they still continued to imitate
the native currency.

But at last there were so many kinds of Rupees in
existence, all differing in weight and fineness, and causing
so much trouble and loss, that the company resolved in
1773 to remedy this evil by declaring that all Rupees
coined for the future should be of the standard weight of
180 grs., should bear the same date (the 19th of Shah Aulum,
the then king of Delhi), and the same inscription; and
this continued the practice until 1835, although Shah Aulum
died in 1786, and the inscription still stated they were

struck at Moorshedabad, where no mint had existed for very many years.

The mints at Dacca and Moorshedabad were abolished in the year 1793, and mints were established at Benares and Furrukabad subordinate to that at Calcutta. The Furruka-bad mint was abolished in 1825, when one was established at Sagur in its place, and that of Benares was abolished in 1830.

For the Madras Presidency Pagodas, Fanams, &c., were coined about the year 1671 at Fort St. George, and in the charter of 2 James II., dated April 12th, 1686, full power was given to the company to coin any money such as was usually coined by the native princes of that country. (Which, taking into consideration that King James had no shadow of authority there, was a very pretty bit of assumption on his part.)

The first notice of a mint being established is in the year 1743, at Arcot, the capital of the Nawab of the Carnatic. The *Arcot* Rupee was exceedingly rude, and the legend rarely entire; but in 1807 the mint was removed to Madras, and a great improvement was made in the machinery, and in that and the following year a large number of copper coins were struck having the Christian Era in Persian numerals; these were double, single, and half Faloos or Faluce. Meanwhile a great improvement had taken place in the silver coinage, and we now find the Rupee with its divisions as well struck as those of Calcutta or Bombay, and with a neatly milled edge. In the year 1811 a coinage of double Rupees, together with their divisions, took place from Spanish Dollars, and specimens may be found of the double Rupee in which the old impression of the Dollar may still be traced, not being entirely obliterated in the re-striking. Also in the same year pieces of half and quarter Pagodas were struck together with five, two and one Fanams. These continued to be coined until 1818, when still further improvements were introduced, and the Rupee with its half and quarter, was struck with an indented cord milling; and this, with the exception of a coinage of Arcot Rupees with their divisions at the Calcutta mint which took place in 1823-5, remained the case until, in 1835, they all gave way to the company's Rupee which now commenced being issued for the whole of India. This bears the bust of William IV. on the obverse, and on the reverse its value in English and Persian. On the accession of the Queen the type was only altered so far as regards the obverse, of which there are two kinds (with continuous, and with divided legends), and the introduction of a silver piece of two Annas.

When in 1862 the Government of India became vested in a Council of State, the legend of "East India Company" upon the reverse gave way, and an elegant scroll border took its place; and, lastly, in 1877, when the title of Empress of India was assumed, this title was placed upon the obverse of the coins of each denomination.

A copper coinage also of half, quarter, and one-twelfth Annas was commenced in 1862, which in 1877 had the same alteration.

THE ARMS, SUPPORTERS, &C. OF THE EAST INDIA COMPANY

BOMBAY PRESIDENCY.

The gold and silver coins of this Presidency are close imitations of the "*Surat*" Rupee which was copied by the company from 1733 to 1780. It has as a distinguishing mark the year ۴۶ (46) and as a mint-mark, a kind of star (*see illustration to No.* 20). Very few, however, are to be found on which the whole, or any considerable portion of the legend, can be found, as the piece of silver from which the coin was struck was almost invariably smaller than the die. By an agreement with the Nawab of Surat the coins struck by him were to circulate at par with those issued by the company, and they were mutually pledged to preserve their standard. The Nawab's Rupees, however, were soon found to contain 12, and even 15 per cent. of alloy, and as a result the coinage of silver in the Bombay mint was suspended for twenty years. In 1800 there was an issue of silver coins struck at Calcutta for Bombay, as well as at the latter place, which are better formed than the preceding, and bear the whole, or nearly the whole of the legend, but are otherwise similar. From 1818 to 1825 the same were coined with an upright milled edge, and from 1825 to 1835 they have a plain edge and dotted rim. The following is the complete legend in Persian and its translation :—

O: ۱۲۱۵ سکه مبارک شاه عالم بادشاه غازي

1215. The lucky coin of the great Emperor Shah Aulum.

R: ضرب سورت سنه ۴۶ جلوس ميمنت مانوس

Struck at Surat in the forty-sixth year of his propitious reign.

GOLD COINS.

Mohurs.

1. O : A shield within an inner circle, ENGLISH EAST INDIA COMPANY.

   R : BOMBAY | 1765 in two lines, with an ornament above and below.

2. O : BOMBAY | 1770 | 15 Rup̣s in three lines, with an ornament above and also on each side.

   R : Persian inscription.

Half Mohur.

3.   Similar to No. 1, excepting in size and value.

Quarter Mohur.

4.   Similar to No. 1, excepting in size and value. There is a variety in die of this latter piece.

Mohur.

5. O : Persian inscription, "The lucky coin of the great Emperor Shah Aulum 1215."

   R : Ditto. Struck at Surat in the forty-sixth year of his propitious reign.

Half Mohur.

6.   Similar.

Quarter Mohur.

7. ·   Similar.
          These are struck with an upright milled edge.

Mohur.

8.   Similar to No. 5, excepting that it has a plain edge and dotted rim.

Half Mohur.

9.   Similar.

Quarter Mohur.

10.   Similar.
          The weight of these mohurs is 180 grains, and their legal value 15 rupees. The half and quarter in due proportion.

SILVER COINS.

Rupees.

11.   *O* :   Shield of arms between two wreaths.

      R :   PAX DEO in two lines within a beaded circle,
           MONETA BOMBAIENSIS.

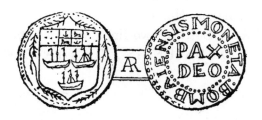

         There are several varieties in the position
and form of letters of the legend on the
reverse of this piece.

Half Rupee.

12.   Similar, excepting in size and value.

Rupee.

13.   *O* :   Shield of arms as No. 11, but without the
           wreaths.

      R :   1673. C . R . in two lines.

         This curious piece, which is in the British
Museum, is struck on a thin piece of silver,
and is evidently a pattern for a rupee.

14.   *O* :   A shield within a beaded circle, HON : SOC :
           ANG : IND : ORI :

      R :   MON | BOMBAY | ANGLIç | REGIMş | Aᵉ
           7ᵉ in five lines within a beaded circle.   A :
           DEO : PAX : & INCREMENTVM.

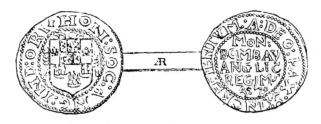

         There are several slight variations in the
form and position of letters on reverse of this.

15. *O*: THE | RVPEE OF | BOMBAIM | in three
lines with two roses under, 1678. BY. AVTHO-
RITY . OF . CHARLES . THE . SECOND ✳

   R: Royal shield crowned. KING . OF . GREAT .
BRITAIN . FRANCE . & IRELAND.

16. *O*: Similar to No. 11.

   R: PAX : DEO in two lines within a beaded circle,
BOMBAIENSIS . MONETA : 1687 :

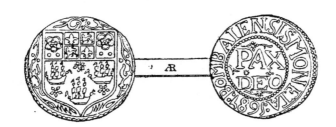

17.　　　　The old *" Surat "* Rupee, a very rudely struck
and ill-formed coin, only showing a small
part of the legend. Struck, in all probability,
from 1773 to 1780. These can only be
distinguished by the date, which is ۴٦ (46) and
a mark thus ⁘

Half Rupee.

18.　　　　Similar, excepting in size and value.

Quarter Rupee.

19.　　　　Similar, excepting in size and value.

　　　　　　There are similar pieces without the star
and which simply have four dots, thus ∻ (*See
illustration to No.* 17.) These were probably
those struck by the Nawab of Surat.

20.   The improved "*Surat*" Rupee, showing more of legend and better struck, coined both at Calcutta and Bombay, 1800 to 1818. Those struck at Bombay bear as mint-mark a small crown.

Half Rupee.

21.   Similar to last, excepting in size and value.

Quarter Rupee.

22.   Similar to last, excepting in size and value.

23.   The "*Surat*" Rupee with upright milling as coined from 1818 to 1825.

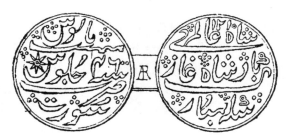

Half Rupee.

24.   Similar to last, excepting in size and value.

Quarter Rupee.

25.   Similar to last, excepting in size and value.

      These have as a mint-mark an arrangement of dots which assumes nearly the form of a fleur de lis, thus

26.   In the year 1825 the old "*Surat*" rupees were coined with a small crown on the obverse in the place of one of the dots, and a label on the reverse with the date incuse (1825)

Half Rupee.

27.   Similar, excepting in size and value.

Quarter Rupee.

28.   Similar, excepting in size and value.

Rupee.

29.   Similar to No. 23, but with a smooth edge and
                   dotted rim; this was coined at the Bombay
                   mint from 1825 to 1835. The figures of the
                   year of reign are better formed than on
                   No. 23.

Half Rupee.

30.   Similar, excepting in size and value.

Quarter Rupee,

31.   Similar, excepting in size and value. In these three
                   latter pieces the mint-mark is a fleur de lis.

COPPER COINS.

Pice.

32.   Similar to No. 14 Æ, and most probably from the
                   same dies.

33.   *O* :   MOET | BOMBAY | ANGLIC | REGIM |
              A ° D ° 9. in five lines within a beaded circle.
              HON : SOC : ANG : IND : ORI :

      R :   Shield of arms within a beaded circle, A :
              DEO : PAX : & INCREMENTVM : (1669 ?)

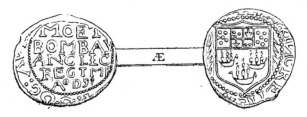

Cash.

34.   *O* :   An orb and cross inscribed 78 (1678 ?)

      R :   Rudely formed Native characters.

Pice.

35.   *O* :   The company's bale-mark, a heart-shaped shield
              with a 4 over it, having in its four compartments
              V. E. I. C. for United East India Company.

      R :   A lion rampaut (1714 ?)

36. *O*: The company's bale-mark as before.

    R: A balance with عدل (*Adel* = justice) between the scales.

37. The company's bale-mark, but with a crown instead of 4 above the heart-shaped shield.

    R: A balance with ᵛ‍‍عدل‍‍ᵛ between the scales.

38. A crown, with two stars on either side of the cross at top.

    R: . . SPIC . | REGIS E . | SENAT . . AN | NGLIC in four lines.

39. *O*: A crown, with G . R . at sides of cross at top, and BOMB under.

    R: AUSPICIO | REGIS ET | SENATUS | AN- GLIÆ in four lines.

Half Pice.

40. Similar, but showing less of the legend. Although a smaller coin, the dies from which it was struck appear, in some instances, to have been larger than the preceding.

    There are varieties of *pice* and *half pice* differing both in shape and size of crown, and also in form and position of letters of legend.

Double Pice.

41. *O*: A crown with G-R and BOMB as before.

    R: AUSPICIO | REGIS ET | SENATUS | AN- GLIÆ | 1728, in five lines.

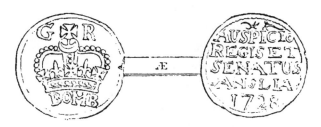

42. Similar to last, excepting date, which is 1730.
43. Similar to last, excepting date, which is 1733.
44. Similar to last, excepting date, which is 1737.

Pice.

45. *O:* A crown with G-R and BOMB as before.

    R: The company's bale-mark.

Half Pice.

46. Similar.

Pice.

47. *O:* A crown with G-R and BOMB as before, with
        the date under 1773.

    R: The company's bale-mark.

48. Similar to last, excepting date, which is 1783.

49. *O:* The company's bale-mark.

    R: The date only 1729.

50. Similar to preceding, dated 1731.

51. Similar to preceding, dated 1734.

52. Similar to preceding, dated 1739.

53. Similar to preceding, dated 1742.

54. Similar to preceding, dated 1743.

55. Similar to preceding, dated 1752.

56. Similar to preceding, dated 1802.

Half Pice.

57. Similar, date 1741.

58. Similar, date 1759.

59. Similar, date 1802.

60. Similar, date 1803.

Quarter Pice.

61. Similar. At present I have been unable to
    discover any dates.

      There are possibly other dates of the *pice*
    and *half pice* than those given.

Pice.

62. *O:* The bale-mark as before.

    R: I | PICE | BOMB | 1773 in four lines.

      There are several varieties, differing in size
    and form of letters.

63. Similar to preceding, but dated 1777.

Half Pice.

64.   *O* :   The bale-mark as before.

      R : $\frac{1}{2}$

Double Pice, or 20 Cash.

65.   *O* :   The company's bale-mark, 1791 under it.

      R :   A balance, with *Adel* (= Justice) between the scales.

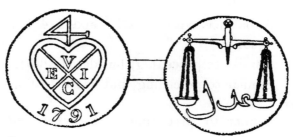

Fifteen Cash.

66.   Similar, excepting in size and value.

67.   Similar to last, excepting that the line of bale-mark is a thick single line, whereas all the others are fine double lines.

68.   There is another variety, evidently a pattern, with much smaller scales.

Ten Cash.

69.   Similar to No. 65, excepting in size and value.

Five Cash.

70.   Similar to No. 65, excepting in size and value.

Twenty Cash.

71.   Similar to No. 65, excepting date, which is 1794.

Fifteen Cash.

72.   Similar to No. 66, excepting date, which is 1794.

Ten Cash.

73.   Similar to No. 69, excepting date, which is 1794.

Five Cash.

74.   Similar to No. 70, excepting date, which is 1794.

            There are gilt and bronzed proof sets of each date.

Pice.

75.   *O* :   The company's bale-mark, 1791 under.

      R :   A balance, with *Adel* (= Justice) between the scales.

Half Pice.

76.   Similar, excepting in size and value.

              These two pieces are hexagonal, not round coins. They are evidently patterns, and occur only as proofs, never having been issued.

Four Pice.

77. *O*: The company's bale-mark, with the date under 18-02.

    R: A balance, with *"Adel"* and a 4 between the scales.

78.   Similar to preceding, but dated 18-04.

79.   Similar to preceding, but dated 18-09.

Double Pice.

80.   Similar to preceding, a 2 over *"Adel,"* date 18-02.

81.   Similar to last, excepting date, which is 18-03.

82.   Similar to last, excepting date, which is 18-04.

83.   Similar to last, excepting date, which is 18-08.

84.   Similar to last, excepting date, which is 18-09.

85.   Similar to last, excepting date, which is 18-12.

86.   Similar to last, excepting date, which is 18-13.

87.   Similar to last, excepting date, which is 18-16.

88.   Similar to last, excepting date, which is 18-25.

89.   Similar to last, excepting date, which is 18-26.

90.   Similar to last, excepting date, which is 18-27.

91.   Similar to last, excepting date, which is 18-29.

Pice.

92.   Similar, excepting size and value, date 1802. *"Adel"* only between scales.

93.   Similar to last, excepting date, which is 18-03.

94.   Similar to last, excepting date, which is 18-04.

95.   Similar to last, excepting date, which is 18-08.

96.   Similar to last, excepting date, which is 18-10.

97.   Similar to last, excepting date, which is 18-13.

98.   Similar to last, excepting date, which is 18-15.

99.   Similar to last, excepting date, which is 18-16.

100.   Similar to last, excepting date, which is 18-18.

101.	Similar to last, excepting date, which is **18-19.**
102.	Similar to last, excepting date, which is **18-21.**
103.	Similar to last, excepting date, which is **18-25.**
104.	Similar to last, excepting date, which is **18-26.**
105.	Similar to last, excepting date, wbich is **18-27.**
106.	Similar to last, excepting date, which is **18-28.**
107.	Similar to last, excepting date, which is **18-29.**

Half Pice.

108.	Similar, dated 18-02.
109.	Similar, dated 18-03.
110.	Similar, dated 18-05.
111.	Similar, dated 18-08.
112.	Similar, dated 18-16.
113.	Similar, dated 18-18.
114.	Similar, dated 18-21.
115.	Similar, dated 18-25.
116.	Similar, dated 18-27.
117.	Similar, dated 18-29.

Quarter Pice.

| 118. | Similar, dated 18-21. |
| 119. | Similar, dated 18-25. |

These pieces from No. **77** to **119** are thick ill-shaped coins, and of very rude workmanship. It is quite possible that there are other dates than those given.

Double Pice.

120. *O*: The company's arms, supporters, &c. EAST INDIA COMPANY, 1804.

R: A balance with *"Adel"* between the scales and the Hegira date under ١٢١٩ (= 1219.)

Pice.

121.   Similar, excepting in size and value.

Half Pice.

122.   Similar, excepting in size and value.
     There are gilt, bronzed, and copper proofs of this set.

Pice.

123.   *O:*   The company's bale-mark, with the date 18-20 under.

    R: A balance with ज्ञा ञ्जा (= *paissa* or pice) between the scales, ।v२९ under.

124.   Similar to last, excepting date, which is 18-21.

Half Pice.

125.   Similar, dated 18-20.

126.   Similar, dated 18-21.
     These four pieces are evidently of Native workmanship, and the characters on the *R:* under the balance are intended doubtless for the date in Persian and English figures mixed.

Half Anna.

127.   *O:*   The company's arms, supporters, &c. EAST INDIA COMPANY, 1834.

    R: A balance with *"Adel"* between the scales, HALF ANNA above ।r۴۹ (= 1249) below.

128.   Similar to preceding, but the legend on *R:* is in smaller letters HALF ANNA.

129.   Similar to preceding, but the letters smaller still HALF ANNA

Quarter Annas.

130. O: The company's arms, supporters, &c. EAST INDIA COMPANY, 1830.

R: The balance, &c., as before, QUARTER ANNA in medium size letters ١٢۴٦ (= 1246) under.

131. Similar to last, date on O: 1832, on R: ١٢۴٦ (= 1246), legend on R: in small letters.

132. Similar to last, date on O: 1832, on R: ١٢۴٧ (= 1247), legend in medium size letters.

133. Similar to last, date on O: 1833, on R: ١٢۴٩ (= 1249), legend in large size letters.

134. Similar to last, date on O: 1833, on R: ١٢۴٩ (= 1249), legend in small letters.

One Pie or One-Twelfth Anna.

135. O: The company's arms, supporters, &c., the date under, 1831.

R: The balance as before, PIE over in small letters, ١٢۴٦ (= 1246) under.

136. Similar to last, date on O: 1833, on R: ١٢۴٨ (= 1248), legend on R: in small letters PIE.

137. Similar to last, but legend on R: in larger letters PIE.

LEAD COINS.

Two Cash.

138. O: Shield of arms between two wreaths, similar to No. 11, Æ.

R: **2** above 75. (1675?) *See* Neumann, No. 19801. This piece is exceedingly rare.

Double Pice.

139. O: A crown, G-R above, BOMB under.

R: AUSPICIO | REGIS ET | SENATUS | ANGLIÆ in four lines, with an ornament above and below.

10 *

Pice.

140.   Similar, excepting in size and value.

                There are several varieties of these two
                pieces differing in size, shape, and arrange-
                ment of letters, &c.

Double Pice.

141.   Similar to No. 139, but with date in place of
                bottom ornament **1717**.

142.   Similar to last, excepting date, which is **1732**.

143.   Similar to last, excepting date, which is **1741**.

144.   Similar to last, excepting date, which is **1742**.

145.   Similar to last, excepting date, which is **1748**.

146.   Similar to last, excepting date, which is **1761**.

147.   Similar to last, excepting date, which is **1771**.

Pice.

148.   Similar, excepting in size and value, dated **1717**.

149.   Similar, excepting in size and value, dated **1741**.

150.   Similar, excepting in size and value, dated **1743**.

151.   Similar, excepting in size and value, dated **1771**.

                There may be dates other than those given.

Half Pice.

152.   *O* :   The company's bale-mark.

        O : $\frac{1}{2}$ | PICE in two lines.

Quarter Pice.

153.   Similar excepting in size and value.

THE only gold coins are the old and new standard 19th sun or " Sicca " Mohurs or " gold Rupees " as they are sometimes called, they are similar to the silver Rupees, and most probably from the same dies.

The old standard have oblique milled edges, and weigh 190 grs.

The new standard have an upright milled edge, and weigh 204 grs., but being of a lower degree of fineness, are worth no more than the old; that is 16 *sicca* Rupees.

Of the silver Rupees there are many varieties. The earliest are very rude coins struck in the Dacca, Moorshedabad, and Patna mints, they show a part only of the legend and are difficult to distinguish with precision from the native issues, these were struck from 1757 to 1773.

An improvement was effected in the latter year, and one date only appears on all struck afterwards—viz. the 19th sun; these are called " *Sicca*," that is "current" Rupees, as they were declared to be the only ones to be allowed to pass.

In 1792 improvements were introduced in the mint at Calcutta, and the legend is now, for the first time, found entire, and an oblique milling is introduced; this in 1818 gave way to the straight milling which was in use until 1832, from which time to 1835 the edges are plain.

Coins for the western provinces were struck at the mint of Furruckabad from 1803 to 1819 with oblique milled edge, from 1819 to 1832 with a straight milling, and from the latter year to 1835 the edge is plain.

The Furruckabad coins, however, were struck from 1825 to 1835 at Benares and Sagur, and not at the former mint which was abolished in 1825.

The coins struck at Sagur prior to 1825 have the name of the place on them in small Roman capitals.

The Benares coins from 1813 to 1819 have an oblique milled edge, those from 1795 to 1812 have the same rude character as the other early issues. From 1819 Furruckabad coins were struck at the Benares mint until 1830, in which year the mint was abolished.

GOLD COINS.

Old standard Mohur. The following is the legend in Persian and its translation :—

1. *O :* حا مي دين محمد سايهٔ نضل‌الله سكه زد بوهفت كشر
و شاه عالم بادشاه

> Defender of the Mohammedan faith, Reflection of Divine excellence, the Emperor Shah Aulum has struck this coin to be current throughout the seven climes.

R : ضرب مرشدآباد سنه ١٩ حلوس ميمنت مابوس

> Struck at Moorshedabad in the year 19 of his fortunate reign.
>
> This has an oblique milled edge and weighs 180 grains, and its half and quarter in proportion.

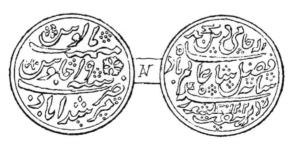

Half Mohur.

2.   Similar, excepting in size and value.

Quarter Mohur.

3.   Similar, excepting in size and value.

New Standard Mohur.

4.   Similar to No. 1, but with an upright milled edge
            and weighing 204 grains. The half and quarter
            in proportion.

Half Mohur.

5.   Similar, excepting in size and value.

Quarter Mohur.

6.   Similar, excepting in size and value.

SILVER COINS.

Patna.

7.   Rupee of the Patna mint. Contains a small
            portion of the above legend, see No. 1, but
            may be known by its mint-mark, a variety of
            the *Tirsool* or trident.

Half Rupee.

8.   Similar to last, excepting in size and value.

Quarter Rupee.

9.   Similar to last, excepting in size and value.

Moorshedabad.

10.   The Moorshedabad Rupee is similar to No. 7,
            and may be distinguished from it by its mint-
            mark, a sun. This was struck with several
            years of the Hegira date, from 1757 to 1773.

Half Rupee.

11.   Similar, excepting in size and value.

Quarter Rupee.

12.   Similar, excepting in size and value. There are
            also pieces of two and one Annas, which are
            very scarce.
            These pieces were also struck at the Dacca
            mint, but so far as I know, without any distin-
            guishing mark by which they can be identified.

Rupee.

13.   Similar to No. 10, but being the 19th sun only,
            this was adopted by the company as the
            standard (*Sicca*) rupee in 1773, and continued
            to be coined in this rude fashion until 1792.
            The mint-mark is a variety of the *Phool*, or
            star. (*See illustration to No.* 21.)

Half Rupee.

14.   Similar, excepting in size and value.

Quarter Rupee.

15.   Similar, excepting in size and value.

Two Annas.

16.   Similar, excepting in size and value.

One Anna.

17.   Similar, excepting in size and value.

          These smaller pieces of the Moorshedabad
          mint with the date of the 19th sun are
          exceedingly rare.

Rupee.

18.   The Sicca Rupee of 1792-1818 has the entire
          legend and an oblique milled edge, and bears
          on its obverse the date ۱۲۰۲ (1202).

19.   Similar to last, but a wide toothing round the rim.

Half Rupee.

20.   Similar to No. 16, excepting in size and value,
          and no date on obverse.

Quarter Rupee.

21.   Similar but with the legend abbreviated and
          date on obverse ۱۲۰۴ (1204).

          Nos. 18, 20, and 21, form a proof set without
          the rings of dots which appeared afterwards
          on the current coin. There is also a proof set
          with oblique milling, but the milling slants
          in the opposite direction.

Rupee.

22.   As above struck for ordinary currency.

Half Rupee.
23.   As last, excepting in size and value.
Quarter Rupee.
24.   Similar.
Rupee.
25.   The Sicca Rupee of 1818-1832 has an upright
             milled edge; it is otherwise similar to No. 18,
             excepting that it has no date on obverse.
Half Rupee.
26.   Similar, excepting in size and value.
Quarter Rupee.
27.   Similar, has the legend abbreviated and date as
             No. 21.
Rupee.
28.   The Sicca Rupee of 1832-1835 is just similar in
             all respects to No. 25, excepting that it has a
             plain edge and a beaded rim.
Half Rupee.
29.   Similar, excepting in size and value.
Quarter Rupee.
30.   Legend and date as No. 21.
             This set also occurs as proofs.

Rupee.   *Benares.*
31.   The Benares Rupee of 1795-1812 is a rudely
             formed coin, it bears part of the legend of the
             Moorshedabad coins and may be distinguished
             from them by its mint-mark, a *Rooee,* or fish.
Half Rupee.
32.   Similar, excepting in size and value.
Quarter Rupee.
33.   Similar, excepting in size and value.
Two Annas.
34.   Similar, excepting in size and value.
             The Benares Rupee of 1813-1819 has an
             obliquely milled edge and has the following
             legend in Persian. The mint-marks are a fish,
             and a kind of flower, or knot, and it is dated
             ırr٩ (= 1229). (*See illustration.*)

35.   *O* :   Same as No. 1.

  R :   مر بنارس سنه ۴۹ حلوس میمنت مانوس

        Struck at Benares in the 49th year of his
        fortunate reign.

Half Rupee.

36.   Similar, excepting in size and value.

Quarter Rupee.

37.   Similar but with the legend abbreviated.
        There are proof sets of Nos. 35, 36, and 37.

Furruckabad.

        The Furruckabad Rupee may be known
        from its bearing the 45th sun (۴۰). It was
        struck from 1803 to 1819, with an obliquely
        milled edge, and has the following legend in
        Persian :—

38.   *O* :   Same as No. 1.

  R :   ضرب فرخ آباد سنه ۴۰ حلوس میمنت مانوس

        Struck at Furruckabad in the year 45 of his
        prosperous reign.

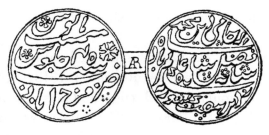

Half Rupee.

39.   Similar, excepting in size and value.

Quarter Rupee.

40. Similar, but the legend is abbreviated, and it bears date ۱۲۰۴ (= 1204).

Rupees with upright milled edges were struck at Furruckabad from 1819 to 1824, at the Benares mint from 1819 to 1830, and at the Sagur mint from 1825 to 1832. There is no means of assigning any special pieces to any particular mint.

Rupee.

41. Similar in all respects to No. 38, but with an upright milled edge.

Half Rupee.

42. Similar to last, excepting in size and value.

Quarter Rupee.

43. Similar, but with legend abbreviated and bearing date ۱۲۰۴ = (1204).

Rupee.

44. Similar to No. 38 in all respects, but with a plain edge.

This was coined at the mints at Calcutta and Sagur from 1832 to 1835.

45. Same as last, excepting a small crescent to the left on the top line of reverse.

This is most likely a mint-mark to distinguish between the two mints, but I am not confident as to its being so.

Half Rupee.

46. Similar to last, excepting in size and value.

Quarter Rupee.

47. Similar, but having the crescent on the obverse, the legend on both sides is abbreviated as before, and it is dated same as No. 43.

These are found as proofs.

The two following rupees I suspect to be patterns, as I have only seen one of each; they are in the cabinet of H. Montagu, Esq.

48. *O* : Similar to the Sicca Rupee, but dated ١١٩٨ (1198) and having a small star as mint-mark. This is the mark of the Moorshedabad mint.

R : Similar to the "Sicca," but with the ٢٦ (26th) year instead of the 19th. The edge is inscribed UNITED * EAST * INDIA * COMPANY * 1784 *

49. *O* : Shield of arms within a circle AUSPICIO . REGIS . ET . SENATUS . ANGLIÆ *

R : CALCUTTA | RUPEE | ضرب کا پکته in three lines within a wreath of palm.

Four Annas or Quarter Rupee.

50. *O* : The value in Persian کۀ بلو within a garter, inscribed FOUR . ANNAS·

R : The value in Telugi within a ribbon with forked ends, which is inscribed with the value in Tamuli; there is a five-pointed star between the forks.

Two Annas.

51. *O* : The value in Persian within a circle, inscribed in script character *Two Annas.*

R : The value in Telugi in a circle, the value in Tamuli round outside circle.

These two are doubtless patterns, and judging from their similarity in type to the Five and Two Fanams pieces coined at Madras in the year 1811, they were most likely fabricated about that same time. The latter I believe to be unique. It is in the cabinet of J. G. Murdoch, Esq.

COPPER COINS.

Two Annas.

52. *O* : Patna | Poft | Two Ann^s | 1774. in four lines.

R : The value in Persian سیم راسبی روپای

One Anna.

53.　　　Similar, excepting in size and value.

Half Anna.

54.　O:　Persian characters; بار ۱۱۹۵ شاه عای = The Emperor Shah Aulum 1195 (= 1780).

　　R:　Persian Characters حلوٯ ۲۲ * س = In the 22nd year of his reign.

Quarter Anna.

55.　　　Similar, excepting in size and value.

Pie.

56.　　　Similar, excepting in size and value.

These pieces vary much in size and weight, and there are possibly four denominations instead of three.

Half Anna.

57.　O:　Persian characters, ضرحلوس ۳۷ شاه عالم بادشاه = In the 37th year of the Emperor Shah Aulum.

　　R:　The value (*One Pai Sicca*) in Bengalee, Persian, and Nagree characters এক পাই সিকা یک پای এক পাइ सीका s_ে in three lines.

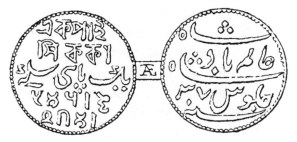

Quarter Anna.

58.　　　Similar, excepting in size and value.

Pie.

59.　　　Similar, excepting in size and value.

These three pieces were struck by Messrs. Boulton and Watt, at their Soho Works, Birmingham, in 1782. They are struck in collar, and there are bronzed proofs of each, they weigh at the rate of 52 grs. to the *pysa* or Quarter Anna.

Half Anna.

60.   As No. 57, but not struck in collar.

Quarter Anna.

61.   Similar to last, except in size and value.

One Pie.

62.   Similar.

These were coined at Calcutta from the year 1795 to 1817, with several reductions in weight from time to time, beginning at the rate of 180 grs. to the *pysa* or quarter anna in 1795, which was reduced to 135 grs. from 1796 to 1809, when it was again reduced to 101 grs., at which it remained. The Half Anna and Pie are in similar proportion.

Half Anna.

63.   Similar to last, but coarser work and with a trident as mint-mark.

Quarter Anna.

64.   Similar, excepting in size and value.

One Pie.

65.   Similar, excepting in size and value.

These pieces struck at the Benares mint were intended at first for circulation in the province of Benares only and were distinguished with a trident or *tirsool*, the symbol of Siva. They were made current through the Bengal provinces at par with the Calcutta and Furruckabad *pysa* in 1817.

Half Anna.

66.   Persian characters as before, but date of year ٤٥ (45).

Quarter Anna.

67.   Similar, excepting in size and value.

One Pie.

68.   Similar, excepting in size and value.

These are the coins of the Furruckabad mint.

One Pie.

69. *O* : The company's arms, supporters, etc. : ONE PIE
above, 1809 below.

R : The value (" *One Pai Sicca* ") in Nagree, Persian,
and Bengalee. (*See illustration.*)

Half Pie.

70. Similar, excepting in size and value.

These are only met with as proofs, in gold,
silver, and copper, and were patterns for a
coinage which was never issued.

Quarter Pice.

71. *O* : C . G . (? For Calcutta Government) 1813.

R : PI ¼ CE

Four Pie.

72. *O* : The company's arms, supporters, &c. 1824.

R : Persian characters چا پاي ١٢٤٠ سسـ = "*Four Pai*
1240." **4** above, within a palm wreath.

73. Similar to preceding excepting the date on *O* :
which is 1825.

Two Pie.

74. Similar to last, excepting in size and value.

One Pie

75. Similar to last, excepting in size and value.

One Pie.

76.   Similar, excepting date which is 1833.

           There are several slight variations in the
           dies of these pieces.

Half Anna.

    O :   The value in English and Bengalee HALE |
           ANNA | অর্দ্ধ আনা in three lines.

    R :   The same in Persian انه يغم and Nagree আধা আনা

Pie.

78.   *O* :   ONE PIE in two lines, the same under in
             Bengalee এক পাই

    R :   The same in Persian پاي ايک and Nagree ऎक पाई

           These were coined at the Calcutta mint in
           1831.

Half Anna.

79.   *O* :   The company's arms, supporters, &c. 1833.

    R :   HALF ANNA in two lines within a wreath
             روپاي (*Two Pai*) over, EAST INDIA
             COMPANY.

√ 80.   Similar to last, excepting date, which is 1835.

81.   Similar to last, excepting date, which is 1845.

           There are bronzed proofs of Nos. 77-81, and
           a silver proof of No. 80.

Quarter Anna.

✓82. *O* : The company's arms, supporters, &c. 1835.

    R : ONE QUARTER ANNA in three lines, within a wreath یک پای (*one Pai*) above, EAST INDIA COMPANY.

        This also occurs as a bronze proof.

        There are several variations in the dies of this piece, principally on the reverse where considerable differences will be observed in the size of letters and shape of wreath.

83. Similar to last, excepting date, which is 1857.

✓84. Similar to last, excepting date, which is 1858.

        There are slight varieties in the dies of the two latter pieces, and both occur as proofs.

One-Twelfth Anna.

✓85. *O* : The company's arms, supporters, &c. 1835.

    R : $\frac{1}{12}$ | ANNA in two lines پلپ پای (*one-third Pai*) under, the whole within a wreath; EAST INDIA COMPANY.

✓86. Similar to last, excepting date, which is 1848.

Half Pice.

87. *O* : The company's arms, supporters, &c. 1853.

    R : $\frac{1}{2}$ | PICE in two lines, within a wreath; EAST INDIA COMPANY.

TOKENS.

Copper.

88. *O* : Bust of Queen to left, with coronet, neck bare, VICTORIA QUEEN.

    R : A round hole in the centre, ONE above, RUPEE below, surrounded with a wreath of palm. ANDAMAN TOKEN 1861.

        This token was most probably struck for use at the convict establishment, on Andaman Island.

11

Brass.

89. *O* : A large round hole in centre, within a circle.

GRAIN TOKEN | ONE RUPEE |

R : FAMINE ✣ 1874 ✣

For the use of relief fund during the famine in Bengal in 1874.

Both the monetary systems of India appear to have been in use in this presidency at the same time, and we find Mohurs and Pagodas in gold, and Rupees, half and quarter Pagodas and Fanams in silver, being struck apparently at the same place and passing side by side.

According to the catalogue of the Fonrobert collection, a quarter Real was sent out from England as early as the reign of James I. for this place; and again in Charles II.'s time double and single Fanams were issued, although by some these pieces are assigned to Bombay, but this I think exceedingly improbable.

The first Rupees were copies of the rude native work of the "*Arcot*" mint and were struck most probably from 1758 (which agrees with the Mahomedan date ١١٧٢ (1172) upon the coins) to 1811, from which year, to 1818, double as well as single rupees were struck with an oblique milled edge which, after that year, was altered to an indented cord milling which continued until 1835, these all have, as a distinguishing mark, the "*Pudune*" Lotus (or trefoil). During the years 1823-5 "*Arcot*" rupees with their halves and quarters were struck at the Calcutta mint for the Dacca and Cuttack districts, having an upright milled edge, and bearing a rose as mint-mark. Half and quarter pagodas together with pieces of five, two, and one fanams were coined from Spanish dollars in 1811.

GOLD COINS.

Star Pagoda.
1. *O* :   The god Swami.
   R :   A five-pointed star within a triple row of dots.
   This weighs 52 grains.

11 *

Double Pagoda.

 2. *O :* A Pagoda, with nine stars on each side, within a
    garter, with a square buckle, inscribed with
    the value, in English and Persian, TWO
    PAGODAS.

  R : The god Swami, within a triple row of dots. The
    value in Tamuli, and Telugi, on a ribbon with
    forked ends, a star between the forks.

 3. Similar to preceding, but with an oval buckle on
    obverse.

    These double pagodas weigh 90 grains.

Pagoda.

 4. *O :* A Pagoda, with five stars on each side, within a
    garter as before, with square buckle.

  R : The god Swami as before, within a single row of
    dots.

 5. Similar to last, but with oval buckle on obverse.

Mohur.

 6. *O :* The company's arms, supporters, &c. ENGLISH
    EAST INDIA COMPANY.

  R : Persian characters = "One Mohur of the Honour-
    able English Company." (*See illustration to
    No. 7.*)

Half Mohur.

 7. *O :* The company's crest, &c. ENGLISH EAST
    INDIA COMPANY.

  R : Persian characters = "Half Mohur of the Honour-
    able English Company."

One-third Mohur.

8. *O* :   The company's shield and crest, legend as before.

   R :   Persian characters = "Five Rupees of the Honourable English Company."

One-quarter Mohur.

9.   Similar to No. 7, excepting in size and value.

           Mohurs with their halves and quarters were also struck from dies similar to the Arcot rupee, of which the following is the Persian legend and its translation :—

Mohur.

10. *O* :   سكة مبارك بادشاه غازي عزيز الدين محمد عالمگير

           "The lucky coin of the noble Monarch Azeezudeen Muhammed Aulumgeer." (He was the father of Shah Aulum.)

   R :   ضرب ارکات سنه ٦ جلوس ميمنت مانوس

           "Struck at Arcot in the 6th year of his propitious reign."

Half Mohur.

11.   Similar, excepting in size and value.

Quarter Mohur.

12.   Similar, excepting in size and value.

           These mohurs weigh 180 grains and their legal value is fifteen rupees, the half and quarter in due proportion.

SILVER COINS.

Double Fanam.

13. *O* :   Two Cs interlinked.

   R   The god Swami.

Fanam.

14.   Similar, excepting in size and value.

There are a number of slight variations in these
pieces in the size and shape of the god, and in
having or not having pellets on the reverse
between the Cs.

Three Fanams.

15.   *O* :   An orb and cross inscribed $^C{}_E{}^C$ within a beaded
circle.

·*R* :   Indian characters within a beaded circle. (*See
illustration.*)

The date of this is assigned to about the year
1720.   Its weight is 50 grains and that of the
two following in proportion.

Double Fanam.

16.   Similar to last excepting in size and value.

Fanam.

17.   Similar, excepting in size and value.

Rupee.

18.   The old " *Arcot* " Rupee is a very rudely made
and ill-shaped coin.   It may be recognized at
once by its mint-mark, a lotus flower (*see
illustration*), and has a portion of the legend
as on No. 10.   The company issued this piece
first about the year 1758, and it most probably
continued in circulation until the year 1811.

Half Rupee.

19.   Similar to preceding, excepting in size and value.

Quarter Rupee.

20.   Similar to preceding, excepting in size and value.

Two Annas.

21.   Similar to preceding, excepting in size and value.

One Anna.

22.   Similar to preceding, excepting in size and value.

In the year 1811 a coinage took place of pieces of half and quarter pagodas, together with five, two and one fanams as follows :—

Half Pagodas.

23. *O:*   A Pagoda, with nine stars on each side, within a garter, inscribed in English and Persian HALF . PAGODA . .ـ يـ پو هون يم

    R: The god Swami, in a three-fold border of dots, the whole surrounded by a forked-end ribbon inscribed with the value in Tamuli and Telugi, a star between the forks.

24. *O:*   A Pagoda with twelve stars on each side, within a forked-end ribbon, inscribed in English and Persian as before.

    R: The god Swami, within a five-fold border of dots, legend as before but no ribbon.

These were struck from Spanish dollars, and traces of the former impression may be seen on some pieces.

25.   Similar to last, but with fifteen stars on each side of Pagoda.

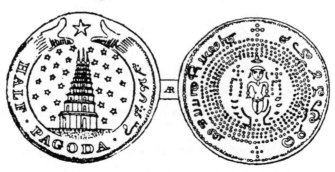

Quarter Pagoda.

26. O : A Pagoda with nine stars on each side within a
          garter with oval buckle, inscribed in English
          and Persian QUARTER . PAGODA باوهون
          بو يـ

     R : The god Swami, within a two-fold border of dots,
          surrounded by a forked-end ribbon as on
          No. 23.

27.   Similar to last, excepting the buckle, which is
          square at one end.

28. O : A Pagoda as before, surrounded by forked-end
          ribbon inscribed in English and Persian as
          No. 26.

     R : The god Swami, within a three-fold border of
          dots, the legend not on ribbon.

29.   Similar to last, but with thirteen stars on each
          side of pagoda, and four-fold border of dots
          round the god.

Five Fanams,

30. O : The value in Persian نلو پنج within a garter with
          square buckle, inscribed FIVE FANAMS.

     R : The value in Telugi within a forked-end ribbon,
          inscribed with the value in Tamuli. A five-
          pointed star between forks of ribbon.

31.   Similar to last, but the buckle is square at one
          end, and round at the other.

32.   Similar, but with an oval buckle showing a cross
          tongue.

33.   Similar, but oval buckle has no cross tongue, and
          there is a dot between FIVE . FANAMS.

34.   Similar, but oval buckle is formed of small beads.

35.   Similar, there is no buckle, but a cross band in its place.

36.   *O*:   The value in Persian within a circle. FIVE .
          FANAMS ❖ outside circle.

      R: The value in Telugi within a circle, and in Tamuli outside circle.

Double Fanam.

37.   *O*:   The value in Persian ورنلم within a garter with square buckle, inscribed DOUBLE FANAM.

      R: The value in Telugi within a forked-end ribbon inscribed with the value in Tamuli. A five-pointed star between the forks.

38.   Similar to last, but the buckle is oblong and smaller.

39.   Similar, square buckle with no tongue, but with a dot in the centre.

40.   Similar, but with a round buckle.

41.   Similar, buckle round at one end and square at the other.

42.   Similar, there is no buckle but a cross fold of the garter in its place.

43.   *O*:   The value in Persian within an inner circle.
          DOUBLE . FANAM ❖ within an outer circle.

      R: The value in Telugi in the centre, the same in Tamuli above and below.   There are no circles but a dot, and ❖ divide the upper and under portions of the Tamul legend.

44.   *O*:   Similar to last, but the letters of legend are coarser and there is neither outer circle nor dots.

      R: The value in Telugi in the centre, the same in Tamuli above and below.   There is the trace of a line (not a circle) around the Telugu legend, there are no dots.

          This is a thick coarse coin, as is also No. 43, and I suspect they were struck prior to the other pieces of this denomination.

45.   *O* :   The value in Persian ڨل within a garter with a
              round buckle, inscribed FANAM.

      R :   The value in Telugi within a forked-end ribbon,
              inscribed with the same in Tamuli, a star
              between forks.

46.   Similar to last, but the buckle square at one end
             and round at the other.

47.   Similar, but with the buckle square.

48.   Similar, but a round buckle formed of beads.

             There are many other minor variations both
             of shape of buckle, position of dots, &c. in
             this series.   I have only mentioned the most
             prominent.

49.   *O* :   A five-pointed star in centre, FANAM above, and
              two small branches crossed below.

      R :   A five-pointed star in centre, within a circle, the
              value in Telugi and Tamuli outside circle.

50.   Similar to last, but no branches under star on
             the obverse.

             These have the appearance of being of
             earlier work also.   There is a *Fanam Token*
             classed by some with this series, but which
             was struck for Ceylon.

             About this same time (1811) a coinage of
             double and single Rupees with their divisions
             also took place, which continued until 1822,
             of the "*Arcot*" type with an oblique milled
             edge.   There are many slight variations in the
             shape of the lotus flower mint-mark.

Double Rupee.

51. Similar to No. 10, but bearing the date of the
year ٢ (2) on the reverse.

This is most likely an error on the part of
the die sinker or engraver, as all the other
coins of this series have the year ٦ (6).

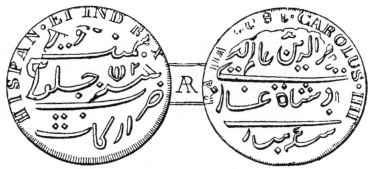

52. Similar to last, but with the date of the 6th year
correct. These pieces being struck over
Spanish dollars usually show traces of the
former impression.

Rupee.

53. Similar to No. 10, bearing date on obverse
١١٨٢ (= 1182).

Half Rupee.

54. Similar to last, except in size and value.

Quarter Rupee.

55. Similar, but the legend is abbreviated.

Two Annas.

56. Similar, the legend still more abbreviated.

One Anna.

57. Similar. Nos. 53-57 have a plain circle around
the outer rim.

During the years 1823-5 "*Arcot*" rupees
with their divisions were struck at the Calcutta
mint for Madras, having an upright milled
edge and bearing a rose mint-mark in place of
the lotus flower, and have a dotted rim.

Rupee.

58. Legend as No. 10.

Half Rupee.

59. Similar, excepting in size and value.

Quarter Rupee.

60.   Similar, but the legend is abbreviated.

Two Annas.

61.   Similar, but the legend is still more abbreviated
             and oblique milled edge.

One Anna.

62.   Similar to last.

             All these occur as proofs.

             From 1825 to 1835 "*Arcots*" were coined
             at Madras, with an indented cord milling and
             a beaded rim, with a lotus flower mint-mark.

63.   Rupee with legend as No 10 and above charac-
             teristics.

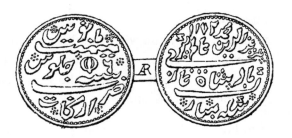

             A pattern of this occurs with an upright
             milled edge.

Half Rupee.

64.   As last, excepting in size and value.

Quarter Rupee.

65.   Similar, but with legend abbreviated.

             These also occur as proofs.

COPPER COINS.

Dudu or Faluce.

66. O :   An orb and cross inscribed $^C E^C$ within a beaded
             circle.

     R :   Native characters as on No. 15 Æ

             This may possibly be from the same dies as
             No. 15. It was quite usual in the early days of
             the East India Company to use the same dies
             for two different metals.

Faluce = 20 *Cash.*

67. *O :*   Orb and cross inscribed ^{C}E^C within a border of rays.

      R :   The date 1693 with a wavy line above and below, within a beaded circle.

68.   Similar to last, excepting date, which is 1695.

69.   Similar to last, excepting date, which is 1702.

70.   Similar to last, excepting date, which is 1703.

71.   Similar to last, excepting date, which is 1705.

72.   Similar to last, excepting date, which is 1706.

73.   Similar to last, excepting date, which is 1709.

74.   Similar to last, excepting date, which is 1716.

75.   Similar to last, excepting date, which is 1720.

76.   Similar to last, excepting date, which is 1722.

77.   Similar to last, excepting date, which is 1726.

78.   Similar to last, excepting date, which is 1741.

79.   Similar to last, excepting date, which is 1744.

80.   Similar to last, excepting date, which is 1748.

81.   Similar to last, excepting date, which is 1750.

82.   Similar to last, excepting date, which is 1752.

83.   Similar to last, excepting date, which is 1755.

84.   Similar to last, excepting date, which is 1756.

85.   Similar to last, excepting date, which is 1761.

86.   Similar to last, excepting date, which is 1765.

87.   Similar to last, excepting date, which is 1768.

88.   Similar to last, excepting date, which is 1769.

89.   Similar to last, excepting date, which is 1774.

90.   Similar to last, excepting date, which is 1777.

91.   Similar to last, excepting date, which is 1780.

92.   Similar to last, excepting date, which is 1784.

93.   Similar to last, excepting date, which is 1787.

94.   Similar to last, excepting date, which is 1790.

95.   Similar to last, excepting date, which is 1800.

96.   Similar to last, excepting date, which is 1801.

97.   Similar to last, excepting date, which is 1806.

Half Faluce.

98.   Similar to preceding, excepting in size and value, date **1702.**

99.   Similar to last, excepting date, which is 1705.

100.   Similar to last, excepting date, which is 1720.

101.   Similar to last, excepting date, which is 1742.

102.   Similar to last, excepting date, which is 1755.

103.   Similar to last, excepting date, which is 1758.

104.   Similar to last, excepting date, which is 1784.

105.   Similar to last, excepting date, which is 1782.

106.   Similar to last, excepting date, which is 1786.

107.   Similar to last, excepting date, which is 1802.

108.   Similar to last, excepting date, which is 1804.

            There are most likely other dates than these in both sizes.

Double Faluce = 40 *Cash.*

109. *O :*   The value in Persian and English ببن عليد كاس
          XL CASH with two lines between, dividing the legends, thus ═══════

     R :   The value in Telugi and Tamuli.

110.   Similar, but legends on obverse divided by
          oooooo ✿ oooooo

111.   Similar, but legends on obverse divided by
          ooo   ooo

Faluce = 20 *Cash.*

112. *O :*   The value in Persian, and English **XX . CASH** divided by ‹ ⟨ ⟨ ⟨ ⟨ ✽ ⟩ ⟩ ⟩ ⟩ ›

     R :   The value in Telugi and Tamuli.

113.   Similar to last, but legends on obverse divided by ‹ ooo ⟨ ✽ ⟩ ooo ›

✓ 114.   Similar to last, but legends on obverse divided by ‹ o o ⟨ ✽ ⟩ o o ›

115.   Similar to last, but legends on obverse divided by ‹ oooo ✿ oooo ›

Half Faluce or 10 *Cash.*

116. The value in Persian, and English X . CASH
      divided by ═══
      This is larger than the varieties which
      follow, and has the double line on both sides.

117. Similar to last, but legends on obverse divided
      by < ooo ✿ ooo >

✓118. Similar to last, but legends on obverse divided
      by ooooOoooo

119. Similar to last, but legends on obverse divided
      by oooOooo

Quarter Faluce or 5 *Cash.*

120. Similar, legends on obverse divided by
      ooooOoooo

Two-and-a-half Cash.

121. 2½ CASH and value in Persian above, nothing
      dividing the two.

Cash.

122. *O :* A cross within a circle, with $E^V I$ in the angles.
      R : The date in Persian numerals |ırı·| (1210)
            within a square.

123. Similar to last, excepting date, which is ırıı
      (1211=1796).

124. Similar to last, excepting date, which is ırır
      (1212=1797).

In the following series an attempt has evidently been
made to assimilate the Mohammedan with the Hindu
monetary systems, as the 48th part of a Rupee is just equal
to the Faluce or piece of 20 Cash. They were struck for
the Circars, a large district on the Coast of the Bay of
Bengal to the north of the Carnatic country, and thus in a
measure connecting Madras with Bengal.

One-Forty-eighth Rupee.

125.   O :   The company's bale-mark. On a broad rim
              incuse, the legend UNITED EAST INDIA
              COMPANY 1794.

       R :   The company's arms, supporters, etc.: **48** TO
              ONE RUPEE under, the legend incuse upon a
              broad rim AUSPICIO REGIS ET SENA-
              TUS ANGLIÆ. The edge is inscribed in
              incuse characters ENGLISH . UNITED .
              EAST . INDIA . COMPANY.

126.   O :   As last.
       R :   The company's crest only in centre, otherwise
              as last.

127.   Similar to No. 125, excepting date, which is
              1797.

128. $\frac{1}{96}$ Rupee similar to No. 125, excepting in size
              and value.

129.   Similar to last, excepting date, which is **1797**.

130.   O :   An elephant, **48** TO ONE RUPEE under. BY
              WISDOM & FORCE incused on a broad
              rim.

       R :   As No. 125. I suspect this is a *mule*, as the
              obverse is found joined with the reverse of
              No. 64 in the Ceylon series, where it seems
              much more appropriate. All these pieces,
              from No. 125 onwards, occur as proofs in
              copper, bronzed, and gilt.

Faluce.

131. *O*: The company's arms, supporters, etc.: EAST INDIA COMPANY 1803.

    R: The value in Persian and English, XX . CASH.

132. Similar to last, excepting date, which is 1808.

Half Faluce.

133. X . CASH piece similar, date 1803.

134. Similar to last, excepting date, which is 1808.

Quarter Faluce.

135. V . CASH piece similar, date 1803.

136. Similar to last, except date, which is 1808.

Cash.

137. *O*: The company's crest only, under it the date 1803.

    R: The value in Persian and English, I . CASH.

These pieces, Nos. 131-137, occur as proofs in silver, bronzed, and gilt. They were made in England by Messrs. Boulton and Watt, and it is said that No. 137 is the smallest coin ever struck in collar.

Double Faluce, or Forty Cash.

138. *O*: Persian legend = " Double Faluce of the Honourable Company. In the year of Christ 1807." Although the date is the Christian era, the numerals used are the Arabic

    R: The value in Telugi and Tamuli.

Faluce.

139. *O*: Persian legend = " This is a little Fanam or Faluce of the Honourable Company. In the year of Christ 1807."

    R: The value in Telugi and Tamuli.

Half Faluce.

140. Similar to No. 138, excepting in size and value.

Double Faluce or Forty Cash.

141.   Similar to No. 138 excepting date, which is
                 ıʌ.ʌ (1808).

Faluce.

142.   Similar to last, excepting in size and value.

Half Faluce.

143.   Similar to last, excepting in size and value.

Dub.

144.   *O :*   Persian legend, = "In the year of Christ
                 1808.   Faluce of the Honourable Company."

        R :   The value in Telugi, in three lines.   Under
                 1 DUB

Half Dub.

145.   Similar to last, but $\frac{1}{2}$ **DUB.**

NOTE.

It must be understood that the dates of the various
coinages, for the three presidencies given here, are only
to be considered as being approximately correct.   Those
wishing to study the subject deeper, will find a mass of
conflicting evidence, in the Transactions of the Asiatic
Society, in Prinsep's Tables, Kelly's Cambist, Marsden,
Ruding, &c. &c.

INDIA (GENERAL).

UNDER this title will naturally come those early pieces which cannot with certainty be assigned to either of the presidencies, and then the coins issued from 1834 and onwards to circulate through the whole country.

Crown or Piece of Eight Reals or Ryals.

1. *O:* The English shield crowned; E - R, also crowned, at sides of shield; O: ELIZABETH D: G: ANG: FRA: ET . HIB REGINA.

   R: A portcullis crowned, O: POSVI . DEVM ADIVTOREM . MEVM.

2. Half-crown or piece of 4 *Reals,* similar excepting HIBER: on obverse.

3. Shilling or piece of 2 *Reals,* similar to last.

4. Sixpence or *Real,* similar to last. Legend on *O:* ends: REGIN. or REGI.

5. *O:* In Persian characters (*see illustration*)—" Sicca of the Company 1793." within a broad, thick rim incused, ENGLISH EAST INDIA COMPANY.

   R: Exactly the same as the obverse. The edge is inscribed ENGLISH UNITED EAST INDIA COMPANY *

12 *

This also occurs with plain edge.

6.   *O* :   The crest of the company, under it **48** TO ONE
            RUPEE, the latter upon a label. AUSPICIO
            REGIS ET SENATUS ANGLIÆ incused
            upon a thick rim. (*See illustration on page*
            176.)

     R :   As last.

7.   *O* :   The company's bale-mark 1794. *See* Bombay,
            No. 65.

     R :   Native legend and date as before, but with no
            broad rim or English legend.

            Nos. 5, 6 and 7 all occur as proofs in
     copper and bronze, and are doubtless patterns.

GOLD COINS OF INDIA.

Two Mohurs.

8.   *O* :   Bust to right, WILLIAM IIII KING 1835.

     R :   Lion and palm-tree, TWO MOHURS دومهر
            beneath. EAST INDIA COMPANY.

Mohur.

9.   Similar to last, excepting in size and value.

There are proofs of these two coins in
silver and copper.

10. *O*: Bust to left, VICTORIA QUEEN 1841.
   R: As the preceding.
11. *O*: Bust to left crowned, and the shoulders robed, VICTORIA QUEEN.
   R: ONE | MOHUR | INDIA | 1862' in four lines within a handsome scroll border.
12. Similar to last, excepting date, which is 1870.
13. Similar to last, excepting date, which is 1871.
14. Similar to last, excepting date, which is 1872.
15. Similar to last, excepting date, which is 1873.
16. Similar to last, excepting date, which is 1874.
17. Similar to last, excepting date, which is 1875.
18. Similar to last, excepting date, which is 1877, and EMPRESS instead of QUEEN.
19. Similar to last, excepting date, which is 1879.
20. Similar to last, excepting date, which is 1880.
21. Similar to last, excepting date, which is 1881.
22. Similar to last, excepting date, which is 1882.
23. Similar to last, excepting date, which is 1884.
24. Similar to last, excepting date, which is 1885.

Proofs exist of Nos. 11, 12, 17 and 18, with milled edges, and of Nos. 11 and 12 with plain edges.

Ten Rupees.

25. Similar to No. 11 except in size and value, date as before, 1862.
26. Similar to last, excepting date, which is 1870.
27. Similar to last, excepting date, which is 1872.
28. Similar to last, excepting date, which is 1875.
29. Similar to last, excepting date, which is 1879, and EMPRESS instead of QUEEN.

Five Rupees.

30. Similar to No. 11 excepting in size and value, date 1862.
31. Similar to last, excepting date, which is 1870.
32. Similar to last, excepting date, which is 1872.

33.　　Similar to last, excepting date, which is 1873.
　　　　There are proofs of Nos. 25, 26, 30, 31, and
　　　32 with plain edges, and of Nos. 26, 27, 28,
　　　31, 32, and 33 with a milled edge.

SILVER COINS.

Rupees.

34.　*O :*　Bust to right, GULIELMUS IIII D . G .
　　　　BRITT . ET IND . REX.　A wavy line
　　　　surrounds legend.

　　R :　ONE | RUPEE in two lines, with a lotus flower
　　　　above and the date 1834 below, the whole
　　　　within a wreath of palm, EAST INDIA
　　　　COMPANY, and the value in Bengalee,
　　　　Persian, and Nagree characters around out-
　　　　side of wreath.　A wavy line surrounds
　　　　legend.

35.　*O :*　Bust as before, GULIELMUS IIII D : G :
　　　　BRITANNIAR : REX F : D :

　　R :　As preceding.

36.　　Similar in all respects to last, but a thicker and
　　　　smaller coin.

37.　*O :*　Bust as before, WILLIAM IIII. KING.

　　R :　As before, a wavy line surrounds legend on both
　　　　sides.

38.　*O :*　As last, a wavy line on obverse only.

　　R :　A Lion and Palm-tree, BRITISH INDIA.

39.　*O :*　As the reverse of the preceding.

　　R :　As the reverse of No. 34.

40.　　Similar to No. 37, excepting date, which is 1835.
　　　　The value on reverse in Persian only, and
　　　　there is no wavy line around outside legend
　　　　on either side.
　　　　These are evidently patterns for a coinage
　　　which was afterwards brought out as fol-
　　　lows :—

41 O: Bust to right, WILLIAM IIII, KING. The initials R . s on truncation of neck.

    R: The value in English and Persian, ONE | RUPEE | یکپ روک in three lines within a palm wreath, EAST INDIA COMPANY ✳ 1835 ✳

42. Similar to last, but various small differences in size of letters, &c. and the initial F. on the truncation of neck.

43. Similar, but with no initial on neck.

Half Rupee.

44. Similar to No. 42, excepting in size and value, both with and without the initials.

Quarter Rupee.

45. Similar, both with and without initials.

    All these pieces occur as proofs.

Rupee.

46. O: Bust to left, filleted, VICTORIA QUEEN.

    R: Similar to No. 41, excepting date, which is 1840.

Half Rupee.

47. Similar, excepting in size and value.

Quarter Rupee.

48. Similar, excepting in size and value.

Rupee.

49. Similar to No. 46, but with the legend divided = VICTORIA —— QUEEN, and with the initials w w on the truncation of neck.

Half Rupee.

50.   Similar to last, excepting in size and value, and
             that the initials on neck are incused, whereas
             those on No. 49 are raised.

Quarter Rupee.

51.   Similar, excepting in size and value.

Two Annas.

52.   With continuous legend as No. 46 and with
             the initial s on the truncation of neck, and
             dated 1841.

53.   With divided legend as No. 49, but dated 1841.
             There are proofs of all these pieces.

Rupee.

54.   Similar to No. 49, but dated 1849.

Half Rupee.

55.   Similar to No. 50, but dated 1849.

Quarter Rupee.

56.   Similar to No. 51, but dated 1849.

Two Annas.

57.   Similar to No. 53, but dated 1849.
             I have only seen these as proofs, and, from
             their rarity, suspect them to be patterns.
             They have plain and milled edges.

Rupee.

58. *O*:   Bust of queen to left, crowned and robed,
             VICTORIA—QUEEN.
     R: ONE | RUPEE | INDIA | 1860 in four lines,
             within a handsome scroll border.

Half Rupee.

59.   Similar, excepting in size and value.

Quarter Rupee.

60.   Similar, excepting in size and value.

Two Annas.

61.   Similar, excepting in size and value.

Rupee.

62.   Similar to No. 58, but dated 1861.

Half Rupee.

63.   Similar to last, excepting in size and value.

Quarter Rupee.

64.   Similar, excepting in size and value.

Two Annas

65.   Similar, excepting in size and value.

          These only occur as proofs, and are patterns
          for the coinage issued in the following year,
          as follows :—

Rupee.

66.   As No. 58, excepting date, which is 1862.

For some reason, with which I am unacquainted, there
was no alteration in the date for several years after 1862,
the pieces bearing date 1864-1872 being very rarely met
with, and, as I suspect, patterns only. Upon the reverse of
the Rupee, however, immediately above a shell-like ornament,
which forms the centre of the scroll-work border, and just
under the date, will be found small dots numbering from
one to ten, which denote the year of the issue. These dots
do not occur upon the smaller pieces.

Half Rupee.

67.   Similar, excepting in size and value.

Quarter Rupee.

68.   Similar, excepting in size and value.

Two Annas.

69.   Similar, excepting in size and value.

          Proofs of these occur struck in gold, silver,
          and copper.

Rupee.

70.   Similar to No. 58, excepting date, which is 1864.

71.   Similar to last, excepting date, which is 1867.

72.   Similar to last, excepting date, which is 1870.

73.   Similar to last, excepting date, which is 1871. .

74.   Similar to last, excepting date, which is 1872.

75.	Similar to last, excepting date, which is 1873.
76.	Similar to last, excepting date, which is 1874.
77.	Similar to last, excepting date, which is 1875.
78.	Similar to last, excepting date, which is 1876.
79.	Similar to last, but dated 1877, EMPRESS instead of QUEEN.
80.	Similar to last, but dated 1878.
81.	Similar to last, but dated 1879.
82.	Similar to last, but dated 1880.
83.	Similar to last, but dated 1881.
84.	Similar to last, but dated 1882.
85.	Similar to last, but dated 1883.
86.	Similar to last, but dated 1884.
87.	Similar to last, but dated 1885.
88.	Similar to last, but dated 1886.

Half Rupee.

89.	Similar to No. 59, dated 1864.
90.	Similar to last, excepting date, which is 1867.
91.	Similar to last, excepting date, which is 1870.
92.	Similar to last, excepting date, which is 1871.
93.	Similar to last, excepting date, which is 1872.
94.	Similar to last, excepting date, which is 1873.
95.	Similar to last, excepting date, which is 1874.
96.	Similar to last, excepting date, which is 1875.
97.	Similar to last, excepting date, which is 1876.
98.	Similar to last, excepting date, which is 1877. EMPRESS instead of QUEEN.
99.	Similar to last, excepting date, which is 1878.
100.	Similar to last, excepting date, which is 1879.
101.	Similar to last, excepting date, which is 1880.
102.	Similar to last, excepting date, which is 1881.
103.	Similar to last, excepting date, which is 1882.
104.	Similar to last, excepting date, which is 1883.
105.	Similar, but dated 1884.
106.	Similar, but dated 1885.
107.	Similar, but dated 1886.

Quarter Rupee.

108. Similar, excepting in size and value, but dated 1864.
109. Similar, but dated 1867.
110. Similar, but dated 1870.
111. Similar, but dated 1871.
112. Similar, but dated 1872.
113. Similar, but dated 1873.
114. Similar, but dated 1874.
115. Similar, but dated 1875.
116. Similar, but dated 1876.
117. Similar, but dated 1877, EMPRESS instead of QUEEN.
118. Similar. but dated 1878.
119. Similar, but dated 1879.
120. Similar, but dated 1881.
121. Similar, but dated 1882.
122. Similar, but dated 1883.
123. Similar, but dated 1884.
124. Similar, but dated 1885.
125. Similar, but dated 1886.

Two Annas.

126. Similar, excepting in size and value, dated 1864.
127. Similar, dated 1867.
128. Similar, dated 1868.
129. Similar, dated 1870.
130. Similar, dated 1872.
131. Similar, dated 1873.
132. Similar, dated 1874.
133. Similar, dated 1875.
134. Similar, dated 1876.
135. Similar, dated 1877, EMPRESS instead of QUEEN.
136. Similar, dated 1878.
137. Similar, dated 1879.
138. Similar, dated 1880.

139.   Similar, dated 1881.
140.   Similar, dated 1882.
141.   Similar, dated 1883.
142.   Similar, dated 1884.
143.   Similar, dated 1885.
144.   Similar, dated 1886.

I have seen proof sets of the years 1867, 1875, 1877, 1878, 1882 and 1885. There are in all probability proofs of each year.

COPPER COINS.

Half Anna.
145.   *O*:   Bust to left, crowned and robed, VICTORIA QUEEN.

    R: HALE ANNA INDIA 1861, in four lines, within an elegant scroll border.

146.   Similar to last, excepting date, which is 1862.
147.   Similar to last, excepting date, which is 1864.
148.   Similar to last, excepting date, which is 1867.
149.   Similar to last, excepting date, which is 1870.
150.   Similar to last, excepting date, which is 1871.
151.   Similar to last, excepting date, which is 1872.
152.   Similar to last, excepting date, which is 1873.
153.   Similar to last, excepting date, which is 1874.
154.   Similar to last, excepting date, which is 1875.
155.   Similar to last, excepting date, which is 1876.
156.   Similar to last, excepting date, which is 1877, and EMPRESS instead of QUEEN.
157.   Similar to last, excepting date, which is 1878.
158.   Similar to last, excepting date, which is 1879.
159.   Similar to last, excepting date, which is 1880.
160.   Similar to last, excepting date, which is 1881.
161.   Similar to last, excepting date, which is 1882.
162.   Similar to last, excepting date, which is 1883.
163.   Similar to last, excepting date, which is 1884.
164.   Similar to last, excepting date, which is 1885.

165.   Similar to last, excepting date, which is 1886.

Quarter Anna.

166.   Similar, excepting in size and value, dated 1861.
167.   Similar, excepting in size and value, dated 1862.
168.   Similar, excepting in size and value, dated 1864.
169.   Similar, excepting in size and value, dated 1867.
170.   Similar, excepting in size and value, dated 1870.
171.   Similar, excepting in size and value, dated 1871.
172.   Similar, excepting in size and value, dated 1872.
173.   Similar, excepting in size and value, dated 1873.
174.   Similar, excepting in size and value, dated 1874.
175.   Similar, excepting in size and value, dated 1875.
176.   Similar, excepting in size and value, dated 1876.
177.   Similar, excepting in size and value, dated 1877,
              and EMPRESS instead of QUEEN.
178.   Similar to last, excepting date, which is 1878.
179.   Similar to last, excepting date, which is 1879.
180.   Similar to last, excepting date, which is 1880.
181.   Similar to last, excepting date, which is 1881.
182.   Similar to last, excepting date, which is 1882.
183.   Similar to last, excepting date, which is 1883.
184.   Similar to last, excepting date, which is 1884.
185.   Similar to last, excepting date, which is 1885.
186.   Similar to last, excepting date, which is 1886.

One-twelfth Anna.

187.   Similar, excepting in size and value, dated 1861.
188.   Similar, excepting in size and value, dated 1862.
189.   Similar, excepting in size and value, dated 1864.
190.   Similar, excepting in size and value, dated 1867.
191.   Similar, excepting in size and value, dated 1870.
192.   Similar, excepting in size and value, dated 1871.
193.   Similar, excepting in size and value, dated 1872.
194.   Similar, excepting in size and value, dated 1873.
195.   Similar, excepting in size and value, dated 1874.
196.   Similar, excepting in size and value, dated 1875.
197.   Similar, excepting in size and value, dated 1876.

198.   Similar, excepting size and value, dated 1877, and EMPRESS instead of QUEEN.

199.   Similar to last, excepting date, which is 1878.

200.   Similar to last, excepting date, which is 1879.

201.   Similar to last, excepting date, which is 1880.

202.   Similar to last, excepting date, which is 1881.

203.   Similar to last, excepting date, which is 1882.

204.   Similar to last, excepting date, which is 1883.

205.   Similar to last, excepting date, which is 1884.

206.   Similar to last, excepting date, which is 1885.

207.   Similar to last, excepting date, which is 1886.

There are bronzed and copper proof sets of 1861; gold, bronzed, and copper of 1862; there are also bronzed proof sets of 1864, 1870, 1875, 1877, 1879, 1880, and 1883, and in all probability of other years as well.

Half Pice.

208. *O:*   Bust of Queen to left crowned and robed, VICTORIA QUEEN.

    R: ½ PICE INDIA 1861 in four lines, within a scroll border as before.

209.   Similar to last, but dated 1862.

Copper proofs occur of both these pieces.

MISCELLANEOUS INDIAN COINS.

SILVER.

Alwar Rupee.

210. *O:*   Bust to left crowned and robed, VICTORIA EMPRESS.

    R: Persian inscription, *Máhá Ráo Rája Sewaï Mongul Singh Bihádur* . 1877 . within a circle, ALWAR STATE below, ONE RUPEE above, divided by two sprigs of palm.

Tellichery Double Fanams.

211. *O* : A balance, with T between the scales, 1805 under.
    R : Persian inscription.
212. *O* : Persian inscription, with T and a star at the top.
    R : Persian inscription.

COPPER.

213. *O* : The crest of the East India Company within a
         circle. AUSPICIO REGIS ET SENATUS
         ANGLIÆ 1824.
    R : The value ⅓ Cent. in English, Persian, Chinese,
         and Malay in the form of a cross. (*See illus-*
         tration.)

This is an exceedingly rare piece, and as it only occurs in
proof condition was most probably only a pattern, and never
issued. From the value being the fraction of a cent, and
being expressed in Chinese and Malay as well as Persian, it was
doubtless intended to circulate either in one of the Straits
Settlements or in some portion of the Eastern Archipelago.

214. *O* : A balance, " *Adel*" between the scales.
    R : Native characters the Hegira date ١٢٢٦
         (= 1226). This is equivalent to A.D. 1811.
215. *O* : A balance, "*Adel*" between the scales, the
         Hegira date under ١٢٥٨ (= 1258). Two
         four-pointed stars above the balance.
    R : Two arrows crossed, above them the Hegira date
         as before (this is equivalent to A.D. 1842), above
         the date زرىم between two four-pointed stars.
216. *O* : A crown within a wreath.
    R : Native characters. (Cabul ?)

CEYLON.

The first intercourse of the English with Ceylon began in the year 1713. In 1782 a large portion of the island was taken by them from the Dutch, who then held it, but it was restored to them again in 1783. However, in 1795 the Dutch settlements were again seized upon, and the entire island was finally ceded to Great Britain at the Peace of Amiens in the year 1802.

We learn from Ruding that on November 14th, 1812, there was ordered to be executed in the island, and again in 1814, an issue of both silver and copper, amounting in value to 300,000 rix-dollars. On October 19th, 1821, there was another issue of rix-dollars to the value of £400,000, and in 1828 half-farthings were first coined for Ceylon. Three-halfpenny pieces were ordered to be coined in 1834, and have been continued since.

Silver Coins.

1. *O* :   An elephant with the date under **1803**.

   R : $\frac{96}{S\underline{T}}$ within a beaded circle, CEYLON GOVERN-
MENT ⁖

2.   Similar to last, excepting date, which is **1808**.
3.   Similar to last, excepting date, which is **1809**.

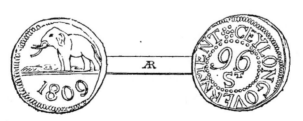

4. *O* : An elephant facing left with the date under it **1803.**

   R : $\frac{48}{S^{\underline{T}}}$ within a beaded circle, CEYLON GOVERN-MENT ∴

5. Similar to preceding, but the Elephant faces the right.

6. Sim lar to No. 4, excepting date, which is **1804.**

7. Similar to No. 4, excepting date, which is **1805.**

8. Similar to No. 4, excepting date, which is **1808.**

9. Similar to No. 4, excepting date, which is **1809.**

10. *O* : Elephant facing left with the date under **1803.**

    R : $\frac{24}{S^{\underline{T}}}$ within a beaded circle, CEYLON GOVERN. MENT ∷

11. Similar to last, excepting date, which is **1804.**

12. Similar to last, excepting date, which is **1808.**

13. Similar to last, excepting date, which is **1809.**

Fanam.

14. *O* : A small circle in centre with F A N A M round it.

    R : A similar circle with T O K E N . round it.

Double Rix Dollar.

15. *O* : An elephant with the date under 1812.

    R : In an oblong compartment, TWO RIX DOL-LARS. A crown above and a ribbon under inscribed " *Honi soit qui mal y pense.*" CEY-LON CURRENCY.

Rix Dollars.

16. Rix Dollar similar, excepting in size and value. These are very rare, are only met with as proofs, and were, I suspect, patterns for a coinage which was not issued.

17. *O* : Bust to right laureated, T . W . on the truncation of neck. GEORGIUS III D : G : BRITANNIARUM REX.

    R : An elephant within an oak wreath, over it CEYLON ONE RIX DOLLAR, the date 1815 below.

18. *O :*   Bust to left laureated, B . P . under neck.
           GEORGIUS IV D : G : BRITANNIAR :
           REX F : D :

     R :   Similar to last, excepting date, which is 1821.

           Proofs are met with of both these elegant pieces.

Three Halfpence.

19. *O :*   Bust to right, GULIELMUS IIII D : G :
           BRITANNIAR . REX F : D :

     R : $1\frac{1}{2}$ in the centre, with a crown above and the
           date 1834 below, within a wreath.

20.   Similar to last, excepting date, which is 1835.
21.   Similar to last, excepting date, which is 1836.
22.   Similar to last, excepting dàte, which is 1837.

23. *O :*   Bust to left, VICTORIA D : G : BRITAN-
           NIAR . REGINA F : D :

     R :   As before, date 1838.

24.   Similar to last, excepting date, which is 1839.
25.   Similar to last, excepting date, which is 1840.
26.   Similar to last, excepting date, which is 1841.
27.   Similar to last, excepting date, which is 1842.
28.   Similar to last, excepting date, which is 1843.
29.   Similar to last, excepting date, which is 1860.
30.   Similar to last, excepting date, which is 1862.

COPPER COINS.

One-Twelfth Rupee.

31. *O :*   An elephant, with the date 1801 under, within
           a beaded circle.

     R :   **12** within a circle, CEYLON GOVERNMENT
           surrounded by a beaded circle.

32.	Similar to last, excepting date, which is 1802.
33.	Similar to last, excepting date, which is 1803.
34.	Similar to last, excepting date, which is 1804.
35.	Similar to last, excepting date, which is 1805.
36.	Similar to last, excepting date, which is 1806.
37.	Similar to last, excepting date, which is 1809.
38.	Similar to last, excepting date, which is 1810.
39.	Similar to last, excepting date, which is 1811.
40.	Similar to last, excepting date, which is 1812.
41.	Similar to last, excepting date, which is 1814.
42.	Similar to last, excepting date, which is 1815.

One Twenty-fourth Rupee.

43. **24** Similar to No. 31, excepting in size and value, date 1801.
44. Similar to last, excepting date, which is 1802.
45. Similar to last, excepting date, which is 1803.
46. Similar to last, excepting date, which is 1805.
47. Similar to last, excepting date, which is 1809.
48. Similar to last, excepting date, which is 1811.
49. Similar to last, excepting date, which is 1812.
50. Similar to last, excepting date, which is 1813.
51. Similar to last, excepting date, which is 1815.

One Forty-eighth Rupee.

52. **48** Similar to No. 31, excepting in size and value, date 1801.
53. Similar to last, excepting date, which is 1802.
54. Similar to last, excepting date, which is 1803.
55. Similar to last, excepting date, which is 1805.
56. Similar to last, excepting date, which is 1806.
57. Similar to last, excepting date, which is 1809.
58. Similar to last, excepting date, which is 1810.
59. Similar to last, excepting date, which is 1811.
60. Similar to last, excepting date, which is 1812.
61. Similar to last, excepting date, which is 1813.
62. Similar to last, excepting date, which is 1814.

13 *

63.   Similar to last, excepting date, which is 1815.

           These are rudely struck, ill-shapen pieces, rarely showing the entire legend or date; there are possibly other dates than those given.

One Forty-eighth Rupee.

64.   *O*:   The company's bale - mark VNITED EAST INDIA COMPANY 1794.

    R: An elephant **48** TO ONE RUPEE under BY WISDOM AND FORCE.

65.   Similar to preceding, dated 1797.

           These are most probably patterns, as they are rare and only occur as proofs.

66.   *O*:   An elephant with the date under 1801, within a border of annulets.

    R: **48** in a circle CEYLON . GOVERNMENT ✻ within a border of annulets.

67.   Similar to last, excepting date, which is 1802.

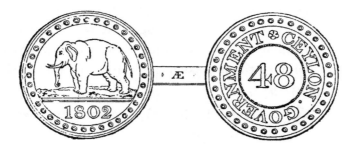

68.   Similar to last, excepting date, which is 1803.
69.   Similar to last, excepting date, which is 1804.

One Ninety-sixth Rupee.

70.   **96** Similar to No. 66, excepting in size and value, and dated 1802.

One Hundred and ninety-second Rupees.

71.   **192** Similar to No. 66 excepting in size and value, and dated 1802.

72.   Similar to last, excepting date, which is 1804.

Although of the same date as the series Nos. 31-63 these are well-made coins and may be met with as proofs. There are also gilt and bronzed proof sets of 1802, and the *R* : of No. 64 occurs as a pattern, joined to the *R* : of Madras No. 125, of which the *O* : is used for No. 64 of this series.

Two Stivers.

73. *O* : Bust to right laureated, GEORGIUS III D : G : BRITANNIARUM REX.

R : An elephant, above it CEYLON TWO STIVERS, the date below 1815.

One Stiver.

74.   Similar to last, excepting in size and value.

Half Stiver.

75.   Similar to last, excepting in size and value.

There are proof sets of these three pieces in gilt, bronze, and copper.

One-twelfth Fanam.

76. *O* : An elephant with the date under 1815, above it CEYLON GOV : the whole within a circle.

R : $\frac{1}{12}$ within a circle, surrounded by the word F A N A M . An outer circle surrounds the whole.

This excessively rare piece is a pattern, never having been circulated.

Half Farthings.

77.   *O* :   Bust to left, GEORGIUS IV DEI GRATIA 1827.

      R :   Britannia seated holding trident, rose, thistle, and shamrock in exergue, BRITANNIAR . REX FID : DEF :

78.   Similar to last, excepting date, which is 1828.

79.   Similar to last, excepting date, which is 1830.

         There are proofs of the two latter dates.

80.   *O* :   Bust to right, GULIELMUS IIII DEI GRATIA. 1837.

      R :   As before.

         This also occurs as a proof in copper and bronze.

81.   *O* :   Bust to left, VICTORIA D : G : BRITAN- NIAR : REGINA F : D :

      R :   HALF | FARTHING | 1839 in three lines, with a crown above, and rose, thistle, and shamrock below.

82.   Similar to last, excepting date, which is 1842.

83.   Similar to last, excepting date, which is 1843.

84.   Similar to last, excepting date, which is 1844.

85.   Similar to last, excepting date, which is 1847.

86.   Similar to last, excepting date, which is 1851.

87.   Similar to last, excepting date, which is 1852.

88.   Similar to last, excepting date, which is 1853.

89.   Similar to last, excepting date, which is 1854.

90.   Similar to last, excepting date, which is 1856.

91.   Similar to last, excepting date, which is 1868.

         Proofs occur of Nos. 81, 82, 86, 87, and 91, and possibly of all other dates.

Five Cents.

92. *O* : Coroneted bust to left within a key border, on which is inscribed VICTORIA QUEEN.

   R : A palm-tree with Cingalese characters at its sides within a beaded circle, CEYLON . FIVE . CENTS . 1870 . within another beaded circle.

One Cent.

93.   Similar to last, excepting in size and value.

Half Cent.

94.   Similar to last, excepting in size and value.

Quarter Cent.

95.   Similar to last, excepting in size and value.
       Proofs occur of this set in gold and in copper.

COPPER TOKENS.

96. *O* : An elephant, CEYLON . COMPANY LIMITED.

   R : C in an inner circle, ST. SEBASTIAN MILLS.

97.   Similar to last, but a smaller piece and with B on reverse.

98.   Similar to last, but still smaller and with A on reverse.
       These may be intended for penny, halfpenny, and farthing.

99. *O* : A bust. COFFEE PICKERS CHIT.

   R : $4\frac{1}{2}^{1d}$ in the centre PILO FERNANDO . COLOMBO.

100. $2\frac{1}{2}$ otherwise the legend as before, this is a square piece whereas the former is round.

101.   There is a halfpenny of George III. countermarked with an elephant and WB Co. which I considered should be included in this series, although nothing definite can be discovered concerning it.

SUMATRA.

THE English had possessions in this island at a very early date, having formed a settlement at Fort Marlborough or Bencoolen in 1685. There were no coins however struck either there or in England for Sumatra until the year 1783. A large number of patterns were executed, some of which are very elegant in design, principally in the year 1787. Possession of the island was finally given up by the English to the Dutch by exchange for other places in 1824, since which time our connection with it has ceased.

SILVER.

Two Sookoo picu.

1.   *O*:   Malay characters. (*See illustration to No.* 2.) = " Money of the company. 2 Sookoos— 1197."

     R: 2 | FORT | MARLBRO' | 1783 . in four lines.

2.   Similar to last, excepting date, which is 1784.

HALF DOLLAR TOKEN.

3.   *O*:   ½ DOLLAR.

     R: FORT MARLBRO'.

       This was struck in copper and issued in 1797 by Governor Bruff.

COPPER.

Two Kapangs.

4.   *O* :   The company's bale-mark J 7:∴:83.

     R :   Malay characters, ٢ كڤڠ ١٩٦ ١١٩٧ = 2 Kapangs 1197.

         There are proofs of this coin in both gold and silver.

5.   Similar to last, but dated 17:∴:86.

Three Kapangs.

6.   *O* :   The company's bale-mark 17:∴:86.

     R :   Malay characters ٣ كڤڠ تيݢ ١٢٠٠ = 3 Kapangs 1200. "*Tiga Kapangs.*"

Two Kapangs.

7.   Similar = ٢ كڤڠ ٩٦ ١٢٠٠ "*Dua Kapangs.*"

One Kapang.

8.   Similar = ١ سكڤڠ ١٢٠٠ "*Sata Kapang.*"

         There are gilt and bronze proofs of Nos. 6-8, and No. 7 occurs with an oblique milling as the other two, or with an engrailed edge.

Two Kapangs.

9.   *O* :   The company's shield radiated, UNITED EAST INDIA COMPANY 1787.

     R :   In Malay characters—" 2 Kapang 1200." Within a border of converging rays.

         This is an oval coin, and the only one of the kind in the entire colonial series.

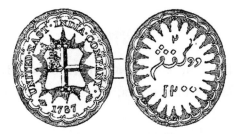

10.   A round coin similar in all respects.

11.   *O* :   The company's arms, supporters, &c. : a ribbon
                  under inscribed UNITED EAST INDIA COMPANY,
                  under the ribbon the date 1787.

         R :   In Malay characters—"2 Kapang 1200."
                  Within a border of converging rays.

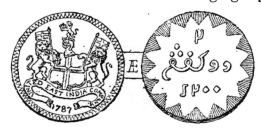

12.   *O* :   The company's bale-mark in a beaded circle,
                  with the date under 17⚘87.

         R :   As last.

One Kapang.

13.   Similar to preceding, excepting in size and value.

Two Kapangs.

14.   *O* :   As No. 12.

         R :   In Malay characters—"2 Kapangs 1202."
                  Within a wreath.

These pieces, Nos. 9-14, are all patterns,
and are all exceedingly rare.

Three Kapangs.

15. *O*: The company's bale-mark, with the date under 17 ❋ 87.

R: The value and date in Malay characters = "Three Kapangs 1200."

Two Kapangs.

16. Similar, excepting in size and value.

One Kapang.

17. Similar, excepting in size and value.

These three pieces have obliquely milled edges, and Nos. 16 and 17 are met with having upright milling. There are gilt and bronzed proofs of all.

Three Kapangs.

18. *O*: The company's bale-mark with the date under 1798.

R: The value and date (۱۲۱۳) in Malay characters = "3 Kapangs 1213."

Two Kapangs.

19. Similar, excepting in size.

One Kapang.

20. Similar, excepting in size.

These pieces are all marked on *R*: with the Persian numeral ۳ = 3, evidently a mistake of the artist in cutting the dies. There are copper, bronze, and gilt proofs of each size.

Four Kapangs.

21. *O*: The company's arms, supporters, &c., EAST INDIA COMPANY 1804.

R: Malay characters ۱۲۱۹ امڤت کڤڠ ۴ = "4 Kapangs 1219." (*Ampat Kapangs.*)

Two Kapangs.

22. Similar, excepting in size and value.

One Kapang.

23. Similar, excepting in size and value.

√ 24.   *O* :   The company's arms, supporters,&c.: ISLAND OF SUMATRA 1804.

      R :   Malay characters as last excepting that the 1 is made thus ρ

    Both gilt and bronzed proofs occur of all these pieces.

PULU-PENANG, or PRINCE OF WALES' ISLAND.

This colony is usually called by its shorter name of Penang, and now forms a portion of the Straits Settlements. It was originally ceded to the Indian Government in the year 1786 by one of their officers, Captain F. Light, who received it as a marriage portion with the daughter of the Rajah of Kedah.

The coins struck for Penang by the East India Company are not numerous, but form an interesting, although small, collection.

SILVER.

Rupee.

1. *O :*   The company's bale-mark, under it the date $J7 \star 87$

   R :   Legend in Persian covers the field = "*Prince of Wales Island*" (*see illustration to No. 4*).

Half Rupee.

2.   Similar, excepting in size and value.

Quarter Rupee.

3.   Similar, but the Persian legend is abbreviated.

Rupee.

4.   As before, but dated $J7 \ast 88$.

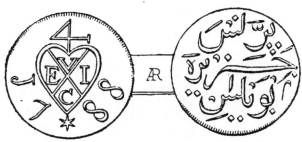

Half Rupee.

5.   Similar, excepting in size and value.

Cent.

7. *O* :   The company's bale-mark within a circle.

   R :   Blank.

8. *O* :   The company's bale-mark with the date under
       *J*7 ::: 87

   R :   Legend in Persian as No. 1.

9.   Similar to preceding, but a star divides the date
       thus *J*7 ✳ 87.

Half Cent.

10.   Similar to No. 8, excepting in size and value.

Half Cent.

11.   Similar to No. 9, excepting in size and value.

Quarter Cent.

12. *O* :   The company's bale-mark, the date under *J*787.

   R :   Persian legend abbreviated as before.

Cent.

✓ 13. *O* :   The company's arms, supporters, &c. the ribbon
       inscribed AUSPICIO—REGIS ET SENATUS—ANGLIÆ
       the date under in small figures 1810, the
       whole within a beaded circle some distance
       from the edge.

   R :   Persian characters ڤولوڤينݢ = *" Pulu-Penang "*
       within a wreath of lilycups and leaves, the
       whole within a beaded circle some distance
       from the edge.

14. *O* : Arms, &c. as before, ribbon inscribed AUSPICIO
            REGIS—ET—SENATUS ANGLIÆ date in larger
            figures 1810, and beaded circle quite close to
            the edge of the coin.

     R : Persian legend as before, within a close wreath
            of lilycups only (?) and beaded circle close to
            the edge.

15. *O* : Similar to No. 13, but with a circle of strokes
            close to the edge, and no beaded circle.

     R : Persian legend as before, with an open wreath of
            lilycups only proceeding in opposite direction
            to last, a circle of strokes near the edge as on
            obverse.

Half Cent.

16.   Similar to No. 13, excepting in size and value.
                These pieces were coined in England, there
            are bronzed and copper proofs of each.

Two Cents.

17. *O* : Arms, supporters, &c. as No. 13, date under 1825.

     R : Similar to No. 13.   Although several years later
            this is not nearly such fine work as those preced-
            ing, and is most probably of colonial fabrication.

Cent.

18.   Similar, excepting in size and value.

Half Cent.

19.   Similar, excepting in size and value.

Two Cents.

20.   Similar, but dated 1828.

One Cent.

21.   Similar, but dated 1828.

√ *Half Cent.*

22.   Similar, but dated 1828.

MALACCA.

MALACCA, on the west coast of the Malay Peninsula, was exchanged with the Dutch for Bencoolen on the Island of Sumatra in 1824. It was placed under the government of the Bengal Presidency until the year 1853, when, together with Prince of Wales' Island and Singapore, it was constituted a separate colony under the title of the Straits Settlements.

There were but few coins struck for this settlement and those of little consideration, and in copper only.

Two Kapangs.

✓ 1. *O*: A cock with Malay characters over it. تانه ملايو = "Malayan Land."

    R: Persian characters ۲ روكڤع ۱۲۴۷ = 2 Kapangs 1247 = (1835).

One Kapang.

  2. *O*: As before.

    R: Persian characters ۱ سات كڤع ۱۲۴۷ = 1 Kapang 1247.

  3. *O*: As last.

    R: Malay characters, as on *O*: of No. 1 ۱۴۱۱ = Malayan Land 1411.

       This is a strange piece, as the date would place it to about the end of the twentieth century, but what is more strange is that this same reverse is used for the reverse of one of the Kapangs of the island of Labuan, so this is doubtless a *mule*.

       There are bronze proofs of each of these pieces.

THE Straits Settlements are so called from being situated on the Straits of Malacca, and they include Pulu-Penang, Malacca, and Singapore. They were secured to Great Britain in 1824, and were made a dependency in 1853, under the Governor-General of India. In the year 1867 they were separated from India and constituted an independent colony.

SILVER COINS.

Twenty Cents.

1. O: Coroneted bust to left, VICTORIA QUEEN.

   R: **20** within a beaded circle, STRAITS SETTLEMENTS · TWENTY CENTS 1871.

2. Similar to last, but dated 1872, and with initial H. under bust.

3. Similar to last, but dated 1873. No initial.

4. Similar to last, but dated 1874. H under bust.

5. Similar to last, but dated 1876. H under bust.

6. Similar to last, but dated 1877. No initial.

7. Similar to last, but dated 1878. No initial.

8. Similar to last, but dated 1879. H. under bust.

9. Similar to last, but dated 1880. H. under bust.

10. Similar to last, but dated 1881. No initial.

11. Similar to last, but dated 1882. H. under bust.

12. Similar to last, but dated 1883. H. under bust.

13. Similar to last, but dated 1883. Without initial.

14. Similar to last, but dated 1884. Without initial.

15. Similar to last, but dated 1885. Without initial.

16. Similar to last, but dated 1886. Without initial.

14

Ten Cents.

17. **10** Similar to No. 1 excepting in size and value, dated 1871.

18. As last, but dated 1872. H under bust.
19. As last, but dated 1873. Without initial.
20. As last, but dated 1874. H. under bust.
21. As last, but dated 1876. H. under bust.
22. As last, but dated 1877. Without initial.
23. As last, but dated 1878. Without initial.
24. As last, but dated 1879. H. under bust.
25. As last, but dated 1880. H. under bust.
26. As last, but dated 1881. Without initial.
27. As last, but dated 1882. H. under bust.
28. As last, but dated 1883. H. under bust.
29. As last, but dated 1883. Without initial.
30. As last, but dated 1884. Without initial.
31. As last, but dated 1885. Without initial.
32. As last, but dated 1886. Without initial.

Five Cents.

33. **5** Similar to No. 1 excepting in size and value, date 1871.

34. As last, but dated 1872. H. under bust.
35. As last, but dated 1873. Without initials.
36. As last, but dated 1874. H. under bust.
37. As last, but dated 1876. H. under bust.
38. As last, but dated 1877. Without initial.
39. As last, but dated 1878. Without initial.
40. As last, but dated 1879. H. under bust.
41. As last, but dated 1880. H. under bust.
42. As last, but dated 1881. Without initial.
43. As last, but dated 1882. H. under bust.
44. As last, but dated 1883. H. under bust.
45. As last, but dated 1883. Without initial.
46. As last, but dated 1884. Without initial.
47. As last, but dated 1885. Without initial.
48. As last, but dated 1886. Without initial.

COPPER AND BRONZE COINS.

Cent.

✓49. *O :* Coroneted bust of the Queen facing to the left, VICTORIA QUEEN.

R : ONE CENT within a laurel wreath, EAST INDIA COMPANY 1845.

✓ *Half Cent.*

50. Similar, excepting in size and value.

✓ *Quarter Cent.*

51. Similar.

Cent.

✓ 52. *O :* As No. 49.

R : ONE | CENT | INDIA | STRAITS | 1862 in five lines, within a laurel wreath.

Half Cent.

53. Similar to last, excepting in size and value.

Quarter Cent.

54. Similar.

Cent.

55. *O :* Bust to left, with open crowned VICTORIA QUEEN. There is a small H. under bust.

R : **1** within a beaded circle, STRAITS SETTLE- MENTS . ONE CENT 1872 .

56. Similar to last in all respects, but without the initial under bust.

57. Similar to last, excepting date, which is 1873.

58. Similar to last, excepting date, which is 1874.

59. Similar to last, excepting date, which is 1875.

60. Similar to last, excepting date, which is 1875, w. under bust.

61. Similar to last, excepting date, which is 1876, without initial under bust.

62. Similar to last, excepting date, which is 1883.

63. Similar to last, excepting date, which is 1884.

64. Similar to last, excepting date, which is 1885.

14 *

Half Cent.

ᐯ 65. $\frac{1}{2}$ similar to No. 55, except in size and value, date 1872.

66.   As last, but without initial under bust.

67.   Similar to last, but dated 1873. Without initial.

68.   Similar to last, but dated 1874. Without initial.

69.   Similar to last, but dated 1875.

70.   Similar to last, but dated 1875, and with initial under bust.

71.   Similar to last, but dated 1884, without initial.

72.   Similar to last, but date 1885.

Quarter Cent .

✓ 73. $\frac{1}{4}$ similar, excepting in size and value, dated 1872. H. under bust.

74.   Similar to last, but without the initial under bust.

75.   Similar to preceding, dated 1873, and without initial.

76.   Similar to preceding, dated 1875, with initial under bust.

77.   Similar to preceding, dated 1875, without initial.

78.   Similar to preceding, dated 1884.

79.   Similar to preceding, dated 1885.

There are proof sets of 1872, with and without initials, also of 1873, and the Cent and Half Cent of 1874 and of 1875, both with and without initial.

JAVA.

JAVA was held by the Dutch from 1619 (in which year they built the capital city, Batavia) until the year 1811, when it was taken by the English, who retained it until the treaty of Paris in 1814, after which it was restored to the Dutch, who still possess it. During the English occupation of the island coins in gold, silver and copper were struck for them at the Surabaga mint by the late Dutch official Johan Anton Zwekhert, whose initial appears on most of the coins.

Sir Stamford Raffles, who was appointed Governor, sent out, or favoured the sending out of an expedition under the command of an English agent and adventurer named Alexander Hare. He made a settlement on the southern coast of Borneo, and obtained a grant of land from the Sultan of Bandarmassin, where he struck small copper coins (*Doits*) between the years 1812-14.

GOLD COINS OF JAVA.

Mohurs.

1. *O* : Persian inscription="Money of the English Company. Struck in the year 1229."

   R : Javanese inscription = "English Company. Struck at Surabaga 1741." (*See illustration to No.* 4.) The English date is above this legend, 1814, and below the initial Z.

2. Similar to last, but dates 1230=1743=1815.

3. Similar to last, but dates 1230=1743=1816.

   The first of these dates is the Hegira, the second is the Java "*Aki Saka*," and the third is the Christian era.

SILVER COINS.

Rupee.

4. *O* :   Persian inscription similar to No. 1, but the
            Hegira date is ١١٦٨ (1668) which is a mistake
            for ١٢٢٨ (1228).

    R :   Javanese inscription similar to No. 1, but with a
            star in place of English date, and the Javan
            date is 1740.

5.   Similar to last, but Hegira date is ١٢٢٩ (1229)
            and Java date 1741.

6.   Similar to last, but Hegira date is ١٢٣٠ (1230)
            and Java date 1743.

7.   Similar to last, but Hegira date is ١٢٣٢ (1232)
            and Java date 1744.

Half Rupee.

8.   Similar, except in size and value, 1668 (? 1228)
            =1740=1813.

9.   Similar, except in size and value, 1229=1741
            =1814.

            No. 8 has the same mistake in the Hegira
            date as Rupee No. 4.

COPPER COINS.

Stiver.

10. *O* : The East India Company's bale-mark, B above it,

            1–St at sides.

    R :   JAVA | 1814 in two lines, a six-pointed star
            above, the initial z below.

11.   Similar to last excepting date, which is 1815.

Half Stiver.

12.   Similar, dated 1811.

13.   Similar to last, dated 1812.

14.   Similar to last, dated 1813.

15.   Similar to last, dated 1814.

Doits.

16.   Similar to No. 10 excepting in size and value, dated 1811.

17.   Similar to No. 10 excepting in size and value, dated 1812.

18.   Similar to No. 10 excepting in size and value, dated 1813.

LEAD COINS.

Doits.

19.   *O*:   A large **V** surrounded by E^{I}c the date under 1813.

    R: ° 1 ° | DOIT | JAVA in three lines, a pellet under.

20.   Similar to last excepting date, which is 1814.

THE following are the Doits struck by Hare for

BANDARMASSIN.

1. *O* :   A fan-shaped star. The date under ۱۲۲۸.
   R :   ٭1٭ يت ۹٦ (1 Doit).

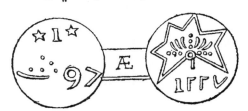

2. *O* :   A wreath enclosing the date ۱۲۲۸ with three stars over it.
   R :   ٭I٭ يت ۹٦ (1 Doit) a quatrefoil and two five-pointed stars under.

        Nos. 1 and 3 are usually found counter-marked with something resembling a wheel . It has been suggested that it may be intended for the Union Jack.

3 *O* :   A pointed shield inscribed يت ۹۸۹ مصر (Trade Doit).
   R :   A pointed shield with the date in English and Persian 1813

4. *O* :   A running flower spray.
   R :   A rude imitation of the company bale-mark inscribed يت ۹٦ | ۱۲۲۸ (Doit 1228.=1813).

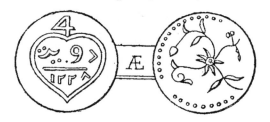

Hong Kong, an island at the mouth of the Canton river, was taken from the Chinese by Capt. Elliot on August 23rd, 1839, and was formally ceded to Great Britain in 1841. Its chief town is called Victoria, it was built in 1842. Sometimes the whole colony is called by that name. Considering the time it has been established, its coins, both silver and bronze, are numerous, and there are also a very large number of patterns, some of which must be considered as " *mules*," or simply varieties created for that purpose.

SILVER COINS.

Pattern Dollars.

1. *O* : Bust of Queen to left, crowned, and wearing a robe. VICTORIA . QUEEN.

   R : Chinese characters, 仙香港一 within a beaded circle, surrounded by a wreath of oak, the whole within a tressure of outward curves.

2.   Similar to last, but with HONG-KONG above, and ONE DOLLAR 1863 below.

3.   Bust of Queen to left, crowned, neck bare, within a beaded circle, VICTORIA QUEEN HONG KONG.

   R : As No. 2.

4. *O* : As No. 1.

   R : Chinese characters 圓香港壹 within a beaded circle, HONG KONG above, ONE DOLLAR 1864 below, the whole within a tressure of inward curves.

5.   *O*:   As No. 1.

     R: Four small blank shields crosswise, in the angles oak and laurel branches, and in the centre a star, ONE DOLLAR above, and HONG KONG 1864 below.

6.   Similar to last, but with Chinese characters of No. 4 on the shields.

7.   *O*:   As No. 1.

     R: ONE DOLLAR 1864 in the centre, four shields . bearing Chinese characters as No. 4 arranged round, and in the spaces between, a mallet and club, an anchor, T . G and H . K . both in monogram.

8.   *O*:   Bust as before with bare neck. *See* No. 3.

     R: As No. 1.

9.   *O*:   As last.

     R: Chinese characters as No. 1, within a beaded circle, ONE DOLLAR above, HONG KONG 1864 incuse; the whole within a tressure of inward curves.

10.   Similar to No. 8, but the tressure is of inward curves.

11.   *O*:   As last.

     R: As No. 9, but HONG KONG above, ONE DOLLAR 1864 below.

12.   Similar to last, but the legend is frosted.

13.   *O*:   As last.

     R: As No. 4.

14.   *O*:   Small bust of the Queen crowned and robed within a beaded circle, VICTORIA . QUEEN . HONG . KONG . ONE . DOLLAR.

     R: As No. 9. The legends on both sides are incuse, and there is a flaw in the die running through the Queen's bust.

15.   *O*:   As last, showing flaw in die.

     R: As No. 4. Incuse legend on obverse only.

16.   Similar to No. 14, but the legend in raised letters and without flaw in die on obverse.

17.   *O* :   Similar to No. 14, but the beaded circle is smaller.

     R :   Chinese characters as No. 1 within a beaded circle, surrounded by a wreath of oak, the whole within a tressure of inward curves, each containing a pellet.

18   *O* :   Queen's bust as No. 14 within a small circle. VICTORIA—QUEEN separated by a tressure of inward curves each containing a pellet.

     R :   As No. 5.

19.   *O* :   As last.

     R :   As No. 7.

20.   *O* :   Queen's bust with a coronet, neck bare, within **a** key border VICTORIA QUEEN.

     R :   Chinese characters as on No. 4, within scroll-work, ONE DOLLAR HONG KONG 1865, the whole within a key border.

21.   The same as last, but struck in copper and with the word TRIAL behind bust.

        This was the pattern that was ultimately adopted for currency.

Dollars.

22.   Similar to No. 20, excepting date, which is 1866.

23.   Similar to No. 20, excepting date, which is 1867.

24.   Similar to No. 20, excepting date, which is 1868.

        There are proofs of these dollars with plain and milled edges.

Half Dollars.

25.   *O* :   Coroneted bust of the Queen, neck bare. VICTORIA QUEEN and key border.

     R :   Chinese characters 圓 香港 羊 within scroll-work, HALF DOLLAR HONG 1865, the whole within a key border.

26.   Similar to last, excepting date, which is 1866.

There are proofs of Nos. 25 and 26.

27.   Similar, excepting date, which is 1867.
28.   Similar, excepting date, which is 1868.

Twenty Cents.

29. *O* : Coroneted bust of Queen to left, neck bare,
             VICTORIA QUEEN.

     R : Chinese characters 毫香貳港 within a beaded circle,

             HONG—KONG＊TWENTY CENTS 1866＊
30.   Similar to last, excepting date, which is 1867.
31.   Similar to last, excepting date, which is 1868.
32.   Similar to last, excepting date, which is 1872.
33.   Similar to last, excepting date, which is 1873.
34.   Similar to last, excepting date, which is 1874.
35.   Similar to last, excepting date, which is 1875.
36.   Similar to last, excepting date, which is 1876.
37.   Similar to last, excepting date, which is 1877.
38.   Similar to last, excepting date, which is 1879.
39.   Similar to last, excepting date, which is 1880.
40.   Similar to last, excepting date, which is 1881.
41.   Similar to last, excepting date, which is 1883.
42.   Similar to last, excepting date, which is 1884.
43.   Similar to last, excepting date, which is 1885.
44.   Similar to last. excepting date, which is 1886.
45.   Similar to last, excepting date, which is 1887.

46.   Similar to last, excepting date, which is 1888.

           Nos. 29, 30, 38, and 40 occur as proofs; and Nos. 34, 35, 36, 37, 39, and 40 have a small H under the bust showing they were struck by Messrs. Heaton of Birmingham.

Ten Cents.

47. *O* :   Bust of Queen to left, crowned and robed. VICTORIA QUEEN.

    R :   10 | CENTS | 1862 in three lines, within a beaded circle, surrounded by scrollwork.

48. *O* :   As last.

    R :   TEN CENTS within a laurel wreath. HONG-KONG above 1862 below.

49. *O* :   As last excepting that the robe is slightly different.

    R :   A plain circle with a dot in the centre surrounded by Chinese characters 一香港亳

50. *O* :   As reverse of No. 48.

    R :   As last. This is manifestly a *mule*.

        These pieces, Nos. 47-50, are patterns and never circulated and are very rare, this latter remark applying to all the patterns of this series.

51. *O* :   As No. 47.

    R :   Chinese characters as No. 49 within a beaded circle, a dot in the centre, HONG-KONG * above. TEN CENTS 1863 * below.

52.   Similar to last, excepting date, which is 1865.

53.   Similar to last, excepting date, which is 1866.

54.   Similar to last, excepting date, which is 1867.

55.   Similar to last, excepting date, which is 1868.

56.   Similar to last, excepting date, which is 1872.

57.   Similar to last, excepting date, which is 1873.

58.   Similar to last, excepting date, which is 1874.

59.   Similar to last, excepting date, which is 1875.

60.	Similar to last, excepting date, which is 1876.
61.	Similar to last, excepting date, which is 1877.
62.	Similar to last, excepting date, which is 1879.
63.	Similar to last, excepting date, which is 1880.
64.	Similar to last, excepting date, which is 1881.
65.	Similar to last, excepting date, which is 1883.
66.	Similar to last, excepting date, which is 1884.
67.	Similar to last, excepting date, which is 1885.
68.	Similar to last, excepting date, which is 1886.
69.	Similar to last, excepting date, which is 1887.
70.	Similar to last, excepting date, which is 1888.

Five Cents.

71. *O* : Coroneted bust of Queen to left, neck bare. VICTORIA QUEEN.

   R : Chinese characters 仙香港五 within a beaded circle HONG-KONG . FIVE CENTS 1866.

72.	Similar to last, excepting date, which is 1867.
73.	Similar to last, excepting date, which is 1868.
74.	Similar to last, excepting date, which is 1872.
75.	Similar to last, excepting date, which is 1873.
76.	Similar to last, excepting date, which is 1874.
77.	Similar to last, excepting date, which is 1875.
78.	Similar to last, excepting date, which is 1876.
79.	Similar to last, excepting date, which is 1877.
80.	Similar to last, excepting date, which is 1879.
81.	Similar to last, excepting date, which is 1880.
82.	Similar to last, excepting date, which is 1881.
83.	Similar to last, excepting date, which is 1883.
84.	Similar to last, excepting date, which is 1884.
85.	Similar to last, excepting date, which is 1885.
86.	Similar to last, excepting date, which is 1886.
87.	Similar to last, excepting date, which is 1887.
88.	Similar to last, excepting date, which is 1888.

The same remarks as to proofs and also the initial H will apply to the same dates on the ten and five cent pieces as to the twenty cents.

Cents.

89. *O* : Laureated bust as on English penny VICTORIA
D : G : BRITT : REG : F . D .

R : A small circle surrounded by Chinese characters

仙．一
香
港

90. *O* : As last.

R : A small circle, ONE above, CENT below, within
a wreath HONG KONG ✿ 1862 ✿. A quatrefoil on either side between the legend and date.

92. Similar to No. 90, but with a small lion on either
side of date.

91. Similar to No. 90, but with 𝕮𝕲 and 𝕽𝕱 instead
of quatrefoils.

93. Similar to No. 90, but with a club and mallet
crossed to left and a small lion to right of
date.

94. Similar to No. 90, but with an anchor to left,
and a lion to right of date.

95. Similar to No. 94, but with a crown in centre of
circle.

96. Similar to No. 90, but with a crown to left and
a dragon to right of date.

97. Similar to No. 96, but with a crown in centre of
circle.

98. *O* : As before.

R : A lion, an anchor 𝕮𝕲 and 𝕽𝕱 in the angles of
Chinese characters. *See* No. 89.

99. *O* : As before.

R : ONE CENT | HONG KONG | 1862, in three
lines, within a circle, with a border composed
of two dragons issuing from wreaths, a scroll
above.

100. *O* : Small bust of the Queen to left, crowned and
robed. VICTORIA QUEEN.

R : As last.

101.   *O* :   As last.
    R :   As No. 91.

102.   *O* :   As last.
    R :   As No. 94.

103.   *O* :   As last.
    R :   As No. 98.

104.   *O* :   Larger bust of Queen, showing more of the robe, otherwise as No. 100. L.C. WYON under bust.
    R :   As No. 89.

105.   *O* :   As last.
    R :   As No. 90.

106.   *O* :   As last.
    R :   As No. 93.

107.   *O* :   As last.
    R :   As No. 94.

108.   *O* :   As last.
    R :   As No. 99.

In addition to these numerous patterns the various reverses are joined together to make other varieties, which will not require describing, being simply *mules*.

109.   *O* :   Laureated bust as No. 89.
    R :   Chinese characters as No. 89 within a beaded circle, HONG-KONG above ✿ ONE CENT 1862 ✿ below, a small dot in the centre.

110.   Similar to last, excepting date, which is 1863.

111.   *O* :   Large bust as No. 104.
    R :   As No. 109.

112.   *O*:   Smaller bust crowned and robed as No. 100.

      R: As No. 109.

          This last piece was the type which was afterwards in the succeeding year adopted for permanent use, although in a smaller size than the patterns, they being $\frac{19}{16}$ of an inch, whereas the following are only $\frac{17}{16}$ of an inch.

113.   *O*:   Bust as No. 100.

      R: Chinese characters in a beaded circle, HONG-KONG ✿ ONE CENT 1863 ✿.

114.   Similar to last, excepting date, which is 1865.

115.   Similar to last, excepting date, which is 1866.

116.   Similar to last, excepting date, which is 1875.

117.   Similar to last, excepting date, which is 1876.

118.   Similar to last, excepting date, which is 1877.

119.   Similar to last, excepting date, which is 1879.

120.   Similar to last, excepting date, which is 1880.

121.   Similar to last, excepting date, which is 1881.

          Nos. 113, 115, 117 and 120 occur as proofs, and Nos. 117 and 120 have a small H for Heaton.

Cash.

122.   *O*:   A square in centre HONG-KONG. ONE CASH.

      R: A square in centre surrounded by Chinese characters 文 香港 一

123.   Similar to last, but with a round hole in centre of square.

124.   Similar to No. 124, but with a crown above square and Ɏ Ⓑ under, and date at sides 1863.

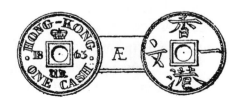

125.   Similar to last, but no square on either side.
            This and the following four pieces although
            called "Cash" are smaller than the preced-
            ing, and just the size of the Mil which follows.

126.   Similar to last, but with no hole in centre.

127.   Similar to last, square on obverse only and a
            dot in centre of reverse.

128.   Similar to last, circle in place of square on
            either side.

129.   Similar to last, neither circle or square but a
            dot in centre on both sides.
                These are only met with as proofs and
            were never issued.

Mil.

130. *O :* A square pierced with round hole, a crown
            above, v r below, date at sides 18—63.
            HONG-KONG ONE MIL.

      R : A square surrounded by Chinese characters
            千香港一,

131.   Similar to last, excepting date, which is 18—64.
132.   Similar to last, excepting date, which is 18—65.
133.   Similar to last, excepting date, which is 18—66.
                There are proofs of Nos. 130, 131 and 133.

White Metal.

134. *O :* A square pierced with round hole, ROYAL
            MINT ✳ 1862 ✳

      R : A rose, shamrock and thistle issue from three
            sides of square, a lion under.

Nickel Token.

135. *O :* A round hole in centre, E^d SMITH . HONG-
            KONG.

      R : A round hole in centre, VALUE . II . CENTS.
                The following are patterns only, never
            having been issued, and are very rare.

PATTERNS.

One Tael.

136. *O:*   Coroneted bust of Queen, to left . VICTORIA QUEEN.

   R: Chinese characters 兩紋銀壹 with a dot in the centre and the word TRIAL above the dot, 986 under.   ONE . TAEL . HONG - KONG ✻ 1867 ✻

137. *O:*   Arms in garter crowned 982 and 366 under ⌃ONE TAEL SHANGHAI ʜᴏɴɢ 1867 ᴋᴏɴɢ.

   R:·   The Chinese dragon within a garter, Chinese characters 兩壹色上 round outside garter.

Two Mace.

138. *O:*   A crown within a beaded circle, TWO MACE . SHANGHAI ✻ 1867 ✻

   R: An eight-pointed star in a beaded circle, surrounded by Chinese characters.

SARAWAK (NORTH BORNEO).

SARAWAK in North Borneo was founded by Sir Jas. Brooke, who was appointed Rajah in 1841, and through his instrumentality the Island of Labuan or Sultana and the adjacent dependencies became incorporated with the British Empire, and were formally taken possession of in the presence of the Bornean chiefs, December 2nd, 1846. Previously to this, so long ago as 1804, the East Indian Company had struck small coins (Kapangs) for Labuan similar to those struck for Sumatra.

A company trading to Borneo had a charter granted to them as the North Borneo Company, and cents and half cents were coined for them by Messrs. Heaton and Sons in 1882 and following years.

SARAWAK.

Cent.
1. *O*:   Bust to left. J BROOKE RAJAH.
   R: ONE CENT in a wreath. SARAWAK over it. Date under 1863.

Half Cent.
2.   Similar to No. 1, excepting in size and value.

Quarter Cent.
3.   Similar to No. 1, excepting in size and value.

Cent.
4. *O*:   Bust to left. C BROOKE RAJAH.
   R: Similar to Rev : of No. 1. Date 1870.
5.   Similar to last, excepting date, which is 1879.
6.   Similar to last, excepting date, which is 1880.
7.   Similar to last, excepting date, which is 1882.
8.   Similar to last, excepting date, which is 1884.

Half Cent.

✓ .9.   Similar to No. 4, excepting in size and value, date 1870.

Quarter Cent.

10.   Similar to No. 4, excepting in size and value, date 1870.

There are proofs of Nos. 1-3, also 5 and 9.

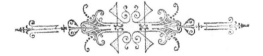

LABUAN OR ISLAND OF SULTANA.

1. *O* :   Arms, supporters, &c., of the East India Company.
             ISLAND OF SULTANA 1804.

    R :   Malay characters ρ جفك سانت‌ ١٢١٩ "One Kapang
             1219."

2. *O* :   As last.

    R :   The rev: of a Kapang of Molucca (Celebes)
             having a 16-rayed star in centre and legend
             in Malayan characters round = "Land of
             Buggi, One Kapang." 1250.

3. *O* :   Shield with two unicorns as supporters, a castle
             for crest between two flags. ISLAND OF
             SULTANA 1835.

    R :   Malay characters, = "Malay Island, 1411." *See*
             note to No. 3 Malacca.

4.   Similar to preceding, but with a single flag in
             place of crest.

5.   Similar to last, but the flag hangs in a different
             direction, and there is no legend on obverse.

BRITISH NORTH BORNEO COMPANY.

1. *O*:   Arms, supporters, &c., PERGO ET PERAGO on a ribbon, date under 1882, a small н above date.

     R: ONE CENT 洋一元分 within a wreath BRITISH NORTH BORNEO Co. ساتوسين

2.   Similar to last, excepting date, which is 1884.
3.   Similar to last, excepting date, which is 1886.

4. *O*:   Ornamental shield of arms, date under 1885, a small н above date (for Heaton).

     R: HALF CENT 洋半元分 within a wreath, BRITISH NORTH BORNEO Co. تڠه سيت

5.   Similar to last, excepting date which is 1886.

       All these pieces may be met with in proof condition.

MAURITIUS.

Mauritius, or the Isle of France, was discovered by the Portuguese in 1505. It was taken by the Dutch in 1598 and was named by them after Prince Maurice. It afterwards came into the possession of the French, who held it till 1810, when it was taken by the English and has since been retained by them. Ruding informs us that on April 24th, 1820, half dollars, with the quarter, eighths and sixteenths, were ordered to be struck. In 1821-2 there were pieces of 50 and 25 Cents in white metal struck at the Calcutta mint for Mauritius of the value of Rs. 116.477.—*Prinsep's Tables*, p. 57.

Silver Coins.

Half Dollar.

1. *O :*   Ornamental shield of arms GEORGIUS IV D : G : BRITANNIARUM F : D :

    R :   An anchor crowned, between II-II, COLONIAR : BRITAN : MONET : 1820.

    I have described this coin from a similar one dated 1822 which was struck for the West Indies (*which see*). I doubt the existence of a half dollar of 1820, but as it ought to exist I have included it, hoping it may turn up some day.

Quarter Dollar.

2.   Similar, but with IV-IV at sides of anchor.

Eighth Dollar.

3.   Similar, but with VIII-VIII at sides of anchor.

Sixteenth Dollar.

4.   Similar, but with XVI - XVI at sides of anchor.

    There are proofs of Nos. 2, 3 and 4.

Twenty Cents.

5. *O*: Coroneted bust of Queen to left, neck bare, a small н under bust, VICTORIA QUEEN.

   R: **20** within a beaded circle, MAURITIUS ◦ TWENTY CENTS 1877 ◦

6. Similar to last, excepting date, which is 1878, and there is no initial under bust.

7. Similar to last, excepting date, which is 1882, and there is no initial under bust.

8. Similar to last, excepting date, which is 1882, and initial н under bust.

9. Similar to last, excepting date, which is 1883, no initial under bust.

10. Similar to last, excepting date, which is 1886.

Ten Cents.

11. *O*: Bust as before with initial н under.

    R: **10** within a beaded circle MAURITIUS ◦ TEN CENTS 1877 ◦

12. Similar to last, excepting date, which is 1878, and without initial under bust.

13. Similar to last, excepting date, which is 1880, and without initial under bust.

14. Similar to last, excepting date, which is 1882, with initial н under bust.

15. Similar to last, excepting date, which is 1883, no initial under bust.

16. Similar to last, excepting date, which is 1886.

17. Five Cents, similar to preceding, excepting in size and value, dated 1877. This is a pattern, and was not issued for circulation, and is, necessarily, scarce.

    There are proofs of the 20 and 10 Cents for 1877, 1878, 1883 and 1886, and possibly for the other years, which I have not seen.

White Metal Coins.

18.　*O*:　A palm (?) within a double circle, inscribed GOUV : DE MAURICE ET DEP : the whole surrounded by a zigzag border.

　　R:　*pour* | **50** | Sous. in three lines within a double circle, inscribed RECU AU : BUR : DU TRES : the whole surrounded by a zigzag border as before.

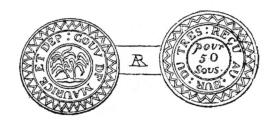

19.　*O*:　RECU | *au* | TRESOR in three lines within a circle surrounded by a zigzag border.

　　R:　*pour* | **25** | Sous in three lines within a circle surrounded by a zigzag border.

Bronze Coins.

Five Cents.

20.　*O*:　Coroneted bust to left, neck bare . VICTORIA QUEEN.

　　R:　**5** within a dotted circle, MAURITIUS ✳ FIVE CENTS 1877 ✳

21.　　　Similar to last, but with a small H under bust.

22.　　　Similar to No. 20, except date, which is 1878, no initial.

23.　　　Similar to last, excepting date, which is 1882, and with initial H under bust.

24.　　　Similar to last, excepting date, which is 1883, no initial.

25.　　　Similar to last, excepting date, which is 1884.

26. Similar to last, excepting date, which is 1888.

Two Cents.

27. *O* : Similar to No. 20.

    R : **2** within a beaded circle MAURITIUS ✳
TWO CENTS 1877 ✳

28. Similar to last, but with a small ʜ under bust.

29. Similar to No. 27, excepting date, which is 1878, no initial.

30. Similar to No. 27, excepting date, which is 1882, and with initial under date.

31. Similar to No. 27, excepting date, which is 1883, no initial.

32. Similar to No. 27, excepting date, which is 1884.

33. Similar to No. 27, excepting date, which is 1888.

One Cent.

34. *O* : Similar to No. 20.

    R : **1** within a beaded circle, MAURITIUS ✳
ONE CENT 1877 ✳

35. Similar to last, but with a small ʜ under bust.

36. Similar to No. 34, excepting date, which is 1878, no initial.

37. Similar to No. 34, excepting date, which is 1882, and with initial under bust.

38. Similar to No. 34, excepting date, which is 1883, no initial.

39. Similar to No. 34, excepting date, which is 1884.

40. Similar to No. 34, excepting date, which is 1888.
There are proofs of each denomination of 1877 with and without the initial, and also of 1878, there may be others which I have not seen.

COINS AND TOKENS

OF THE BRITISH POSSESSIONS

IN

AFRICA,

INCLUDING

GOLD COAST,
SIERRA LEONE,
ST. HELENA,

CAPE COLONY,
GRIQUA TOWN,
AND NATAL.

COINS OF THE AFRICAN COMPANY ON THE GOLD COAST.

THE African Company arose out of an association formed in London in 1588. A charter was granted to a joint stock company in 1618, a second company was created in 1631, a third in 1662; another in 1672 was formed by letters patent which was remodelled in 1695. In 1750 the African Company, which struck the following coins, was constituted by Act of Parliament.

It was abolished in 1821, and its forts and settlements were transferred to the Crown.

SILVER COINS.

Ackey or Crown.

1. O: *G R* in monogram within a wreath, a crown above divides the date, which is 17—96.

   R: Shield of arms with supporters and crest, FREE TRADE TO AFRICA . BY ACT OF PARLIMENT . 1750.

2. A bronze proof of the above has the spelling of PARLIAMENT corrected.

Half Ackey.

3. Similar to No. 1, excepting in size and value, and that there are no supporters on obverse.

Quarter Ackey.

4. Two Takoe piece, similar excepting in size and value.

One Takoe Pieee.

5. Similar, but without legend on reverse.

Ackey.

6. *O*: Bust to right, laureated, GEORGIUS III D : G : BRITANNIAR : REX F : D : Upon the truncation of the neck there is a small H . and under the bust 1 ACKEY TRADE 1818.

    R: Arms, supporters, &c. as before, FREE . TRADE . TO . AFRICA . BY . ACT . OF . PARLIAMENT . 1750.

Half Ackey.

7. $^1/_2$ ACKEY TRADE similar to last excepting in size and value.

There are silver, pewter, and bronze proofs of all these pieces.

There is a small copper token which is usually assigned to the West Coast of Africa, which I will place here although the grounds for doing so are very slight, it is as follows:—

8. *O*: LAIRD at the top, SPERO IMLIOLA upon a ribbon issuing from a staff which divides $\frac{1}{8}$ PENNY and $\frac{1}{400}$ DOLLAR, the date 1858 at the bottom.

    R: A three-masted steamer, $\frac{1}{F..}$ = $(\frac{1}{400})$ above, and ı ɾvɼ = (1274) below.

SIERRA LEONE.

THE first settlement of Sierra Leone took place in 1776, when a great number of Negroes and about sixty women of bad character were sent out from London at the expense of the British Government to form the Colony. The project, however, did not succeed; and a number of persons, interested in the abolition of the slave trade, took the affair in hand. A capital was raised amongst several subscribers and they became incorporated as the Sierra Leone Company in October, 1791.

SILVER COINS.

1. *O*: A lion preparing to spring. SIERRA LEONE COMPANY AFRICA.

   R: Black and white hands clasped, **100** above and below, ONE DOLLAR PIECE 1791.

2. Half Dollar similar, except in size and value, **50** above and below.

3. "Twenty Cent Piece" similar, **20** above and below.

4. "Ten Cent Piece" similar, **10** above and below.

5. Similar to last, excepting date, which is 1796

6. Similar to last, excepting date, which is 1805.

   There are gilt and bronze proofs of all these pieces, and there is a copper proof of No. 2.

COPPER.

Penny.

7. *O* : As No 1.

    R : Two hands clasped, **1** above and below them
    ONE PENNY PIECE 1791.

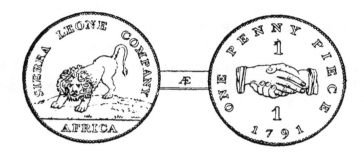

8. Similar to last, but from smaller dies.

Cent.

9. *O* : As before.

    R : As before, but ONE CENT PIECE 1791.

10. Similar to last, but dated 1796.

    There are bronze proofs of all these pieces.

ST. HELENA.

An island in the South Atlantic Ocean, was discovered by the Portuguese under Juan de Nova Castilla on St. Helena's Day, May 21st, 1502. The Dutch afterwards held it till they were expelled by the English in 1600. The British East India Company settled here in 1651, and the island was held alternately by the Dutch and English till 1673, when Charles II. assigned it to the Company once more. St. Helena was the place of Napoleon's captivity and here he died, May 5th, 1821. The population of the island in 1871 was 6241.

SILVER.

1. O: Arms, supporters, &c. of the East India Company.

   R: S^T HELENA | HALFCROWN | 1823 . in three lines within a wreath.

2. Shilling similar, excepting in size and value, and dated 1833.

3. Sixpence similar.

   These are patterns for a coinage which was never issued, they are usually met with as bronze or copper proofs.

COPPER.

4. O: As No. 1.

   R: S^T HELENA | HALFPENNY | 1821, in three lines within a wreath.

5. *O*: *S D T* in the centre, ONE HALFPENNY ❋

R: BY | SOLOMON | DICKSON | AND | TURNER in five lines in the centre, PAYABLE AT ST HELENA ❋

Bronze proofs are met with of No. 4.

CAPE COLONY.

The Cape of Good Hope was occupied by the Dutch in 1600, reduced by the English in 1795, and restored to Holland by the peace of Amiens in the year 1802.

It was again taken by the English in January, 1806, and finally confirmed to them at the Congress of Vienna, 1814· There are no coins struck for this Colony, and the following are the only known tokens.

Copper Tokens.

Halfpenny size.

1. *O* : MARSH & SONS IMPORTERS CAPETOWN.
   R : A three-masted steamer, HALFPENNY TOKEN . to facilitate trade.

2. *O* : J. W. IRWIN in centre. TEA MERCHANT & GROCER . CAPETOWN.
   R : Arms, supporters, &c. CAPE of GOOD HOPE 1879.

3. *O* : WHYTE & Co. TEA MERCHANTS & GROCERS . CAPE TOWN .
   R : A female seated on the ground leaning against an anchor, CAPE OF GOOD HOPE 1861.

GRIQUA TOWN.

GRIQUA LAND West, in the diamond-fields of South Africa. It seems to have been acquired in the usual manner about 1850, when it had about four hundred white inhabitants. It was annexed to the British dominions in November, 1871.

"Boyne" supposes the following tokens to have been issued by the London Missionary Society for the Griquas, a mixed breed of Dutch, Hottentots, and Kaffirs, who settled near the Colony of Natal. I have made inquiries of the Society's agents, but have learned nothing to justify this supposition.

SILVER.

Shilling size.

1.   *O* :   A dove flying, with an olive branch in its mouth.
       R :   **10** in the centre, GRIQUA above, TOWN under. (? Ten pence.)

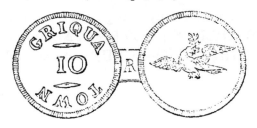

Sixpenny size.

2.   *O* :   As before.
       R :   **IIIII** in the centre, legend as before. (? Five pence.)

COPPER.

Halfpenny.

3.   *O* :   As before.
       R : $\frac{1}{2}$ in the centre, legend as before.

An attempt was made to colonize this district in 1823 by Lieut. Farewell and some emigrants. A number of discontented Boers from Cape Colony settled here in 1837, and it was declared a Colony in 1843, and in 1856 was formed a separate Colony.

Boyne in his " Silver Tokens " says that in 1860 so great was the scarcity of small change here as to occasion the striking in thin brass of the token for sixpence described below.

Sixpence.

1. *O* :   SIXPENCE | 1860 | NATAL.   In three lines.
    R :   Blank.   Struck on a thin piece of brass about the size of a farthing.

    Probably Boyne was mistaken about this, and that the thin piece of brass he speaks of was only a trial of the obverse die of the following token which is struck in white metal, a copy being in the British Museum.

2. *O* :   SIXPENCE | 1860 | NATAL.   In three lines.
    R :   DURBAN | 6$\underline{D}$ | CLUB.   In three lines.

COINS AND TOKENS

OF THE BRITISH POSSESSIONS

IN

AMERICA,

EMBRACING

EARLY AMERICAN.

NEWFOUNDLAND.

NEW BRUNSWICK.

NOVA SCOTIA.

PRINCE EDWARD'S ISLAND.

MAGDALEN ISLAND.

BRITISH COLUMBIA.

CANADA.

THE WEST INDIES.

BRITISH HONDURAS.

BRITISH GUIANA.

UNDER this head we class all coins struck by, or for, our possessions in what are now the United States, prior to their Declaration of Independence in the year 1776, the very earliest of which is in all probability the following jeton or token, which is supposed to have been issued by Sir Walter Raleigh for the settlement made by him in Virginia, 1584. It is in brass, and as follows :—

1.   *O* :   A boy seated under a tree, his head resting on his right hand, and holding a skull in his left. By his left foot is a rose bush.

       R :   A rose with two leaves, within a double circle inscribed, AS . SOONE : AS WEE . TO . BEE . BEGVNNE ✤ WE . DID . BEGINNE : TO . BE . VNDONE : ✤

MASSACHUSETTS, OR NEW ENGLAND.

This was the first of the American colonies to establish a mint of its own, and prior to 1651 silver coins were in circulation as follows :—

Shilling for New England.   A silver planchet bearing on an indent :—

2.   *O* :   ΛE being initials of New England.

       R :   XII for value ; one shilling.

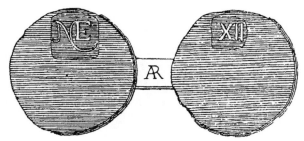

Sixpence.

3.   Similar excepting in size and value, marked **VI**.

Threepence.

4.   Similar, marked **III**.

In the year 1652 a regular coinage of silver was commenced, consisting of shillings, sixpences, and threepences, of two distinct types, the one bearing an oak-tree and the other a pine-tree.

These were continued for thirty years without any alteration of date, which is 1652.

There are also twopences of the oak-tree type dated 1662. There are many varieties in the dies of these pieces, differing not only in the form of tree and disposition of branches, but also in number and size of beads, forming an inner circle on both obverse and reverse, as well as in the letters of the legends, and the punctuation thereof. These variations will best be shown by the following table, which is abridged from a valuable work by Dr. Crosby issued by the New England Numismatic and Archæological Society, to which I would refer those wishing to more fully investigate this subject.

PINE-TREE SERIES.

O : A pine-tree in a circle of dots . MASATHV-
  SETS . IN .

R : Value and date in a circle . of dots. NEW
  ENGLAND . AN . DOM .

  The varieties of this series will best be distinguished by the differences in legend and in number of branches and of points at top of tree, which in the following table will be marked as 7$\frac{3}{}$7, which means, seven branches on each side and three points to top of tree.

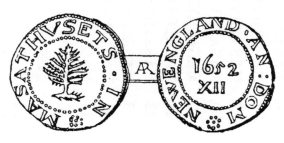

SHILLINGS.

No.	Legend on O:	Branches.	Legend on R:
5.	MASATHVSETS . IN .	737 All pairs	NEWENGLAND . AN . DOM .
6.	MASATVSETS . H .	837 Lower five pairs	NEWENGLAND : AN : DOM :
7.	MASATHVSETS . IN .	827 Lower five pairs	NEWENGLAND . AN . DOM .
8.	MASATHVSETS . IN .	738 Alternate	NEWENGLAND . AN . DOM .
9.	MASATHVSETS . IN .	827 Mostly alternate	NEW . ENGLAND . AN . DOM .
10.	MASATHVSETS ❖ IN ❖	627 Top three pairs	NEW ❖ ENGLAND ❖ AN ❖ DO :
11.	MASATHVSETS . IN .	818 Mostly alternate	As No. 9.
12.	MASATHVSETS . IN .	414 All pairs	NEW ENGLAND . AN . DOM .
13.	MASATHVSETS . IN .	646 Alternate	NEW ENGLAND . AN . DOM .
14.	MASATHVSETS . IN .	636 Mostly pairs	NEW ENGLAND . AN . DO .
15.	MASATHVSETS . IN ❖	727 Alternate and irregular	NEWENGLAND : AN : DOM ❖
16.	MASATHVSETS . IN ❖	637 Alternate	NEWENGLAND : AN : DOM ❖
17.	As No. 10	444 All pairs	NEW . ENGLAND . AN : DO :
18.	As No. 10	535 Four pairs	NEW : ENGLAND : AN : DO :
19.	MASATHVSETS ❖ IN ❖	515 Four pairs	NEVVENGLAND . AN . DO
20.	MASATHVSETS ❖ IN ❖	525 All pairs	NEVVENGLAND . AN . DO
21.	MASATHVSETS ❖ IN ❖	515 Lower four pairs	NEWENGLAND . AN . DO

SHILLINGS—*continued.*

No.	Legend on O:	Branches.	Legend on R:
22.	MASATHVSETS ∷ IN ∷ .	617 Alternate .	NEWENGLAND . AN . DO .
23.	MASATHVSETS ∷ IN ∷ .	515 All pairs .	NEWENGLAND . AN . DO .
24.	MASATHVSETS ∷ IN ∷ .	535 Lower four pairs .	NEWENGLAND . AN . DO .
25.	MASATHVSETS ∷ IN ∷ .	635 Three pairs .	NEWENGLAND . AN . DO .
26.	MASATHVSETS ∷ IN ∷ .	725 Mostly alternate .	NEWENGLAND . AN . DO .
27.	MASATHVSETS ∷ IN ∷ .	737 Mostly alternate .	NEWENGLAND . AN . DO .
28.	MASATHVSETS . ∷ IN . ∷	736 Three pairs, 1 lower, 2 upper	NEWENGLAND . AN . DO .
29.	MASATHVSETS . IN .	525 All pairs .	NEW ENGLAND .

SIXPENCES.

No.	Legend on O:	Branches.	Legend on R:
30.	MASATHVSETS : IN .	424 All pairs .	NEW ENGLAND . ANO .
31.	MASATHVSETS : IN : ∷ :	424 (?) Worn .	NEW ENGLAND . ANO .

THREEPENCES.

No.	Legend on O:	Branches.	Legend on R:
32.	MASATHVSETS . . .	424 All pairs .	NEWENGLAND ∷
33.	MASATHVSETS ∷	334 Second branch on R. hand double	NEWENGLAND . ANO .

OAK-TREE SERIES.

O :   An oak-tree in a circle of dots . MASATHV-
SETS . IN .

R :   Value and date in a circle of dots. NEW
ENGLAND . AN . DOM .

The date of all with the exception of the
twopence is 1652, the latter is 1662.

The varieties will best be distinguished by
the number of beads forming inner circle, and
by differences of legend and punctuation.

SHILLINGS.

| | OBVERSE. | | REVERSE. | |
No.	Legend.	Beads in inner circle.	Legend.	Beads in inner circle.
34.	MASATHVSETS IN	51. Medium size	NEWENGLAND . AN DOM .	68. ⚚ close at top
35.	MASATHVSETS . IN	64. Small .	NEWENGLAND . AN DOM .	68. Medium, close at top
36.	MASATHVSETS . IN	67. ...cted	NEWENGLAND . AN DOM .	68. Medium, close at top
37.	MASATHVSETS . IN	73. ...cted	NEWENGLAND . AN DOM .	79. Large
38.	MASATHVSETS . IN	64. Large .	NEWENGLAND . AN DOM	61. Medium, irregular
39.	MASATHVSETS . IN	48. Large .	As No. 34	52. Large
40.	MASATHVSETS : IN :	66. Medium, on thread .	NEWENGLAND . AN . .	67. m...ll, connected
41.	MASATHVSETS : IN :	66. Medium, on thread .	NW ENGLAND : AN . DOM . NEWENGLAND	69. Medium, connected
42.	MASATHVSETS : IN :	66. Medium, on thread .	NWENGLAND . AN . DO ⦂	70. Med. many conn.

SIXPENCES.

No.	Legend.	Beads in inner circle.	Legend.	Beads in inner circle.
43.	MA 2 ATHVSETS . IN	43. Irregular .	NEW ENGLAND . ANO .	42. Large
44.	MASATHVSETS . IN	46 (?). Large, connected	NEW ENGLAND . AN .DOM .	Large, connected
45.	MASATHVSETS IN	57. Medium, close	IN NEWENGLAND : ANO :	57. Medium

SIXPENCES—continued.

No.	Obverse Legend	Beads in inner circle	Reverse Legend	Beads in inner circle
46.	MASATHVSETS : IN :	Small, connected	NEW : ENGLAND : AN : DOM :	Small, connected
47.	MASATHVSETS . IN ⁛	Medium, connected	As No. 44	Medium, connected
48.	MASATHVSETS ⁛	50. Medium	IN NEWENGLAND . ANO ⁛	52. Medium

THREEPENCES.

No.	Obverse Legend	Beads in inner circle	Reverse Legend	Beads in inner circle
49.	MA ? ATHV ? ET ? . IN ⁛	45. Small, connected	NEWENGLAND ⁛	43. Small
50.	MA ? ATHVSETS ⁖	36 (?). Large, connected	NEWENGLAND ⁛	43. Small
51.	MASATHVSETS ⁛	36. Large and small	NEWENGLAND ⁛	38. Medium
52.	MASATHVSETS ⁛	36 (? Medium	NEWENGLAND ⁛	38. Medium
53.	MASATHVSETS ⁛	30. Large	NEWENGLAND ⁛	36. Some double
54.		Mm		30. Large

TWOPENCE.

No.	Obverse Legend	Beads in inner circle	Reverse Legend	Beads in inner circle
55.	MASATHVSETS . IN :	26. Large	NEWENGLAND ⁛	26. Large

BALTIMORE, OR MARYLAND.

The next in order are the coins struck in England for Lord Baltimore in 1660, and consist of shillings, sixpences, and groats in silver, and a penny in copper, only one specimen of which latter coin is known to exist; this was sold at the sale of Rev. J. Martin for the large sum of £75, and went to America.

Shilling.

56. *O*:   Bust to L. CÆCILIVS : DN̄S : TERRÆ-MARIÆ & C.ᵗ ✠

      R: A shield crowned between **X-II**. CRESCITE : ET : MVLTIPLICAMINI .

Sixpence.

57.   Similar to last, except in size and value, **V—I**.

Groat.

58.   Similar to last, except in size and value, **I—V**.

Penny.

59. *O*:   Bust to L. CÆCILIVS : DN̄S : TERRÆ-MARIÆ & C . ✠

      R: Two flags issuing from a ducal crown. DE-NARIVM : TERRÆ-MARIÆ ✠

          A proof of the sixpence exists struck in copper.

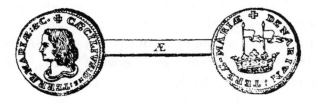

Tɪɴ Pɪᴇᴄᴇ ꜰᴏʀ ᴛʜᴇ Pʟᴀɴᴛᴀᴛɪᴏɴꜱ.

The next piece which falls under our observation is a very curious one in an economical point of view. It recognizes a Spanish currency as generally prevalent in the American plantations, and offers the means of small change in the terms of the Spanish mint.

17

60. *O* :   Figure of James II. on horseback. JACOBUS .
             II . D . G . MAG . BRI . FRAN . ET .
             HIB . REX.

     R :   Four shields crosswise crowned. The shields,
             which are joined with chains, bear the arms
             of England, Scotland, France, and Ireland.
             Legend in four quadrants VAL . 24 .
             PART . REAL . HISPAN . .

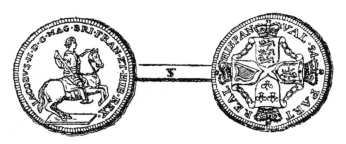

There is no date to this coin, but being during the
reign of James II. it must have been issued between 1685
and 1688.

NEW YORK TOKEN.

The token next to be considered is one about which
nothing can be said but what is founded entirely upon
conjecture. By some it has been thought to be of Dutch
origin, but there is little room for such an opinion, as
the legend is English, such as it is. Again, it is very
difficult to assign a date to it, but it was most likely struck
late in the 17th century, say between 1667, when New
York was confirmed to England by the Peace of Breda,
and 1710, after which date the name was rarely spelt with
an E.   It is found in brass and lead.

61. *O* :   An eagle displayed. ✳ NEW . YORKE . IN
             AMERICA ✳ ∾

     R :   A group of five palm-trees, Venus on the right-
             hand side, and Cupid with his bow in his
             hand, running, on the left-hand side.

THE "ST. PATRICK" OR "MARK NEWBY" COPPERS.

Upon the 19th of November, 1681, there arrived in New Jersey a party of Irish emigrants, Mark Newby and his family being among them. He brought with him a quantity of the pieces known as St. Patrick's halfpence, which, in consequence of the scarcity of small change there, were in the ensuing May made current in that State under certain conditions expressed in the act by which they were authorized. This act is found in the "Grants, Concessions and Original Constitutions of the Province of New Jersey," under date of May 8th, 1682.

62. *O*: David playing the harp. FLOREAT ✠ REX.
    R: S. Patrick surrounded by the people. ECCE . GREX.

> There are several varieties of this piece, but as they belong rather to the Irish series than the Colonial it is not thought necessary to further describe them.

CAROLINA AND NEW ENGLAND HALFPENNIES.

We have next the two pieces with the above title which were issued in 1694. These appear to have been private speculations, and to have had no very extensive currency. They are both extremely rare and command high prices. They are of English manufacture, and the obverse is not only similar to, but absolutely from, the same die as the "London" halfpenny; but whereas the London halfpenny weighs from 210 to 240 grains, the heaviest of these do not exceed 160 grains.

17 *

CAROLINA HALFPENNY.

63.   *O* :   An elephant to the left.

     R :   GOD | PRESERVE | CAROLINA AND |
           THE LORDS | PROPRIETORS | 1694.   In
    six lines.

NEW ENGLAND HALFPENNY.

64.   *O* :   An elephant to the left.

     R :   GOD | PRESERVE | NEW | ENGLAND |
           1694.   In five lines.

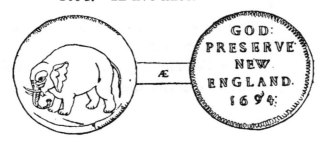

ROSA AMERICANA SERIES.

We now come to the consideration of these interesting but unfortunate coins. Struck in brass or bronze, beautiful as works of art, and presenting a remarkably fine portrait of the king (George I.), and infinitely superior to any other coins in circulation as regards intrinsic value, they were yet exceedingly unpopular, and, practically speaking, were never in any quantity circulated in America. It is usual to denominate these as the penny, halfpenny, and farthing; but they were, in fact, twopenny pieces, pennies, and halfpennies. Of this coinage there are several types, as follows :—

Twopenny Pieces.

65. *O*:   Bust to right, GEORGIVS . D : G : M : B : FR ·
       ET . H : REX :

   R: **II** crowned . 1717 over . MAG : BRIT . FRA .
       ET . HIBER . REX.

66. *O*:   Bust to right, GEORGIUS . D : G : MAG :
       BRI : FRA : ET . HIB : REX.

   R: A full-blown rose. ROSA AMERICANA ·
       UTILE DULCE.

67.   Similar to last, but with UTILE DULCI on a
       label.

68.   Similar to last, but with date 1722 following
       legend on reverse.

69. *O*:   As No. 66.

   R: A full-blown rose crowned . ROSA . AMERI-
       CANA . 1723.   UTILE . DULCI . on label.

70. *O*:   Bust to left, GEORGIUS . II . D . G . REX.

   R: Rose branch bearing seven leaves, rose and bud.
       ROSA AMERICANA 1733 . UTILE . DULCI.
       on label.

PENNIES.

71. *O* :   Bust to right. GEORGIUS : D : G : M : BRI :
FRA : ET . HIB : REX.

   R :   **I** crowned . DAT . PACEM . ET . NOUAS .
PREBET . ET . AUGET . OPES.

72. *O* :   As last.

   R :   **I** crowned, within a wreath . BRUN : ET . LUN :
DUX : SA : ROM : MI : (IM ?) ARC=THE :
ET . PR : ELECT.

73. *O* :   Bust to right, GEORGIUS . DEI . GRATIA .
REX.

   R :   A full-blown rose. ROSA . AMERICANA .
UTILE . DULCI . 1722 ✻

74.   As last, but ROSA . AMERICANA ✻ UTILE .
DULCI . 1722 ✻

75.   As No. 73 but no rose after date.

76. *O* :   As No. 73.

   R :   Rose crowned. ROSA . AMERICANA . 1723.
On a label UTILE . DULCI.

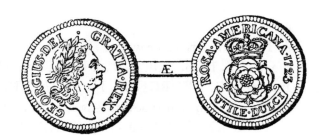

There is a variety of this piece having the
A.^{S} spread out very wide.

77. *O* :   As No. 73.

Rose crowned. ROSA AMERI 1724. UTILE
DULCI.

This is given on the authority of the Rev.
H. Christmas. I have not seen it.

HALFPENNIES.

78. *O* :   Bust to right, GEORGIUS REX.

   R $\frac{1}{2}$: crowned. DAT . PACEM . ET . AUGET . OPES.

79. *O* :   Bust to right, GEORGIUS . D : G : REX.

   R :   Rose. ROSA . AMERI : UTILE : DULCI . 1722.

80. *O* :   Bust to right, GEORGIUS : DEI . GRATIA . REX.

   R :   Rose. ROSA . AMERI : UTILE . DULCE . 1722.

81. *O* :   As No. 73.

   R :   Rose. ROSA . AMERICANA . UTILE . DULCE . 1722 ✱

82. *O* :   As No. 73.

   R :   Rose. ROSA . AMERICANA ✱ UTILE DULCE . 1723 ✱

83. *O* :   As No. 73.

   R :   Rose crowned. ROSA . AMERICANA . 1723. Upon a label under UTILE . DULCE.

The following piece is described, not because I consider it as strictly belonging to this series, but because it bears a considerable resemblance to the twopence of 1733, and might be confounded with it.

84. *O* :   Bust to right, GEORGIUS . DEI . GRATIA . REX.

   R :   A rose bush, bearing one full-blown rose, two buds closed, and two partly open. ROSA : SINE : SPINA.

     It is about the penny size of this series.

THE GRANBY OR HIGLEY TOKENS.

These pieces are said to have been struck by a blacksmith named John Higley, of Granby, in the State of Connecticut.

The authorities appear to have taken no notice of his issues
of coin, which seem to have continued for about three years
—from 1737 to 1739—specimens being extant bearing these
dates, though I have not seen or heard of any dated 1738.
The following is a description of the principal varieties, the
different sides being mixed or *"muled"* to make more :—

85.　*O:*　A deer standing facing left. ☞ THE.VALVE.
　　　　　OF.THREE.PENCE.
　　R:　Three banners, each crowned. ✻ CONNEC-
　　　　　TICVT.1737.
86.　*O:*　As last. ☞ VALVE.ME.AS.YOU.
　　　　　PLEASE. ✻ **III** with a crescent under it
　　　　　beneath the deer.
　　R:　As last. ☞.I.AM.GOOD.COPPER.
　　　　　⠿ ⠿ ⠿ 1737.
87.　*O:*　As before, but a crescent on field above deer.
　　　　　☞ VALUE.ME.AS.YOU.PLEASE. ✻
　　R:　A broad axe. ☞ J.CUT.MY.WAY.
　　　　　THROUGH.
88.　　　As No. 87, but the date 1739 follows legend on
　　　　　R:
　　　　　They are all extremely rare.

THE PITT PENNY.

The history of this piece is better known than most
American tokens.　The Stamp Act was passed March 22nd,
1765, and repealed, principally by the agency of Mr. Pitt,
March 18th, 1766.　This coin, or rather medalet, was struck
to commemorate this event by Mr. Smithers, of Phila-
delphia, from the designs of Colonel Revere, of Boston.
Although doubtless originally intended for this purpose
only, it soon became, in consequence of the dearth of small
change, converted into currency.

89. *O:* Bust of Pitt to left. THE RESTORER OF
          TRADE AND COMMERCE . 1766. NO.
          STAMPS.
     R: Three-masted ship. THANKS TO THE

FRIENDS OF LIBERTY AND TRADE.

VIRGINIA HALFPENNY.

There is much doubt whether the coin now to be described
was ever really an authorized issue, for although bearing
the bust, arms, and title of the king, there is no record
concerning it, and most likely it was a private speculation.

90. *O:* Bust to right, GEORGIUS . III . REX.
     R: Shield of arms crowned, the crown divides date
          17-73 VIRGINIA.

91.   A variety has no dot after GEORGIUS, and
          there are several other minor differences.

A few specimens are struck on thicker and larger pieces
of metal, and are sometimes called, without good reason,
pennies. They are extremely rare. A silver proof exists
dated 1774, and, on the authority of the Rev. H. Christmas,
I believe, a bronze proof of the same date, but these too
are exceedingly rare.

This exhausts the list of the pre-revolutionary coins and
tokens of the American colonies, which, in 1776, declared
themselves "free, sovereign, and independent," which independence was recognized by the mother-country in 1783.

COINS AND TOKENS OF NEWFOUNDLAND.

NEWFOUNDLAND, an island situate on the N.E. side of the Gulf of St. Lawrence, was discovered by Sebastian Cabot in 1497, who called it *Prima Vista*. It was formally taken possession of for the English by Sir Humphrey Gilbert in 1583, and the fisheries which were soon after commenced became of so much importance that in the year 1625 more than 150 ships were employed in them, from the Devonshire ports alone. The sovereignty of England was recognized in 1713, and in 1832 Newfoundland obtained the privilege of a colonial legislature, and at the present time it is the only North American colony which returns its independence, all the others being merged in the Dominion of Canada.

Although politically and commercially of much less importance than the latter colony, from the numismatic point of view Newfoundland claims precedence, as being the only place to issue gold coins, which precedence it also deserves by the order of seniority.

GOLD COINS.

1. *O :*   Laureated bust to left. VICTORIA D : G : REG : NEWFOUNDLAND.

   R :   2 | DOLLARS | 1865 in three lines within a beaded circle. TWO HUNDRED CENTS above, ONE HUNDRED PENCE below.

   This is a pattern, the form ultimately adopted being very similar, the only difference being in the shape and size of the letters of the value in the centre of R: A pattern also exists in copper, the O: of which is similar to No. 1, and the R: TWO | DOLLARS | 1864 in three lines within a wreath of maple, similar to that used for the 10 cents of Canada, and surmounted by a crown. This is in the cabinet of H. Montagu, Esq., and I believe unique.

2. Similar to No. 1, but 2 | DOLLARS | 1865 in Roman capitals.

3. Similar to last, excepting date, which is 1870.

4. Similar to last, excepting date, which is 1872.

5. Similar to last, excepting date, which is 1873.

6. Similar to last, excepting date, which is 1874.

7. Similar to last, excepting date, which is 1876.

8. Similar to last, excepting date, which is 1880.

9. Similar to last, excepting date, which is 1881.

10. Similar to last, excepting date, which is 1882, and there is a small H under the date.

11. Similar to last, excepting date, which is 1885, but without the H.

There are proofs of each date.

SILVER COINS.

Fifty Cents.

12. O: Laureated bust to left, VICTORIA DEI GRATIA REGINA NEWFOUNDLAND.

   R: 50 | CENTS | 1870 in three lines, within an ornamental border.

13. Similar to last, excepting date, which is 1872, and with a small H under bust.

14. Similar to last, excepting date, which is 1873, but without the H.

15. Similar to last, excepting date, which is 1876, with the H.

16.   Similar to last, excepting date, which is 1880, without the н.

17.   Similar to last, excepting date, which is 1881.

18.   Similar to last, excepting date, which is 1882.

19.   Similar to last, excepting date, which is 1885.
             There are proofs of Nos. 12 and 16, with milled edges.

Twenty Cents.

20. *O* :   Bust as before, VICTORIA D : G : REG : NEW-FOUNDLAND.

     R :   20 | CENTS | 1865 in three lines within an ornamental border.

21.   Similar to last, excepting date, which is 1870.

22.   *v* Similar to last, excepting date, which is 1872, and with a small н under bust.

23.   Similar to last, excepting date, which is 1873, but without the н.

24.   Similar to last, excepting date, which is 1874.

25.   Similar to last, excepting date, which is 1876, with the н.

26.   Similar to last, excepting date, which is 1880, without the н.

27.   Similar to last, excepting date, which is 1881.

28.   Similar to last, excepting date, which is 1882.

29.   Similar to last, excepting date, which is 1885.
             Proofs occur of No. 20 with plain and milled edge, also of No. 26 with milled edge.

Ten Cents.

30.   Similar excepting in size and value, dated 1865.

31.   Similar to last, excepting date, which is 1870.

32.   Similar to last, excepting date, which is 1872, and with a small н under bust.

33.   Similar to last, excepting date, which is 1873, but without the н.

34.   Similar to last, excepting date, which is 1874.

35.   Similar to last, excepting date, which is 1876, with the н.

36.   Similar to last, excepting date, which is 1880, without the н.

37.   Similar to last, excepting date, which is 1881.

38.   Similar to last, excepting date, which is 1882.

39.   Similar to last, excepting date, which is 1885.

           There are milled edge proofs of Nos. 30, 36, and 39.

Five Cents.

40.   Similar excepting in size and value, dated 1865.

41.   Similar to last, excepting date, which is 1870.

42.   Similar to last, excepting date, which is 1872, and small н under bust.

43.   Similar to last, excepting date, which is 1873, but without the н.

44.   Similar to last, excepting date, which is 1874.

45.   Similar to last, excepting date, which is 1876. with the н.

46.   Similar to last, excepting date, which is 1880, without the н.

47.   Similar to last, excepting date, which is 1881.

48.   Similar to last, excepting date, which is 1882.

49.   Similar to last, excepting date, which is 1885.

Proofs of No. 40 with both plain and milled edges, and also with milled edges of Nos. 46 and 49. There are patterns of the 20 and 5 cent pieces, the *O* : of which is similar to that of this series, and the *R* : resembles that of New Brunswick, which are dated 1864.

These are proofs in copper. The 10 cent piece is most likely in existence, but I have not yet seen it.

BRONZE COINS.

50.   *O* :   Laureated bust to left. **VICTORIA D : G : REG :**

     R :   The date, 1864, with a crown above it, within a beaded circle, surrounded with a wreath. **ONE CENT** above, **NEWFOUNDLAND** below.

51.   Similar to last, excepting date, which is 1865.

52.   Similar to last, excepting date, which is **1872**, and a small н under the tie of the wreath on *O*:

53.   Similar to last, excepting date, which is **1873**, but without the н.

54.   Similar to last, excepting date, which is **1876**, with the н.

55.   Similar to last, excepting date, which is **1880**, without the н.

56.   Similar to last, excepting date, which is **1885**.

There is a pattern cent dated 1864, which differs from No. 50 in the legend on *O*: which is **VICTORIA QUEEN**.

TOKENS.

Halfpenny size.

57.· *O* : Shield of arms, supporters, &c. of the Rutherford family.

  R : A fleece suspended, R & I . S . RUTHERFORD Sᵀ JOHN'S ✳ NEWFOUNDLAND ✳

58.   Similar to the preceding, but with date on *O*: below the shield, 1841.

59. *O* : As No. 57.

  R . A fleece as before.   RUTHERFORD BROs HARBOUR GRACE NEWFOUNDLAND.

60.   Similar to preceding, but with date on *O*: below the shield, 1846.

There is a variety of this token slightly differing in position of letters, &c.

61. *O* : RESPONSIBLE GOVERNMENT . AND |
FREE | TRADE the latter portion in three
lines in the centre.

R : The date, 1860, in the centre within a circle,
FISHERY RIGHTS FOR NEWFOUND-
LAND.

Farthing size.

62. *O* : PETER | M^c AUSLANE | S^T JOHN'S |
 | NEWFOUNDLAND in five lines.

R : SELLS | ALL SORTS | OF SHOP & | STORE
GOODS in five lines.

COINS AND TOKENS OF THE DOMINION OF CANADA.

UNDER this head we shall include all the coins and tokens struck in or for the British possessions in North America which have since been incorporated under this title. The principal part of the currency until quite recently consisted of tokens, many of which were issued by banks or private individuals, while some were designed and executed in England, as a matter of speculation, and were sold in bulk to the merchants during the seasons of scarcity of change. Others again are the work of native artists, the number of the latter, however, being very small. There are but few silver coins to describe and no gold. The first of the Colonies to be mentioned under this heading being :—

NOVA SCOTIA.

NOVA SCOTIA was discovered by Cabot in 1475, visited by Verrazzani and by him named *Acadia* in 1524; settled in 1622 by the Scotch, under William Alexander, in the reign of James I. of England, from whom it received the name of Nova Scotia. Since its first settlement it has more than once changed proprietors, and was not confirmed to England till the peace of Utrecht in 1713. There are no silver and but a very few bronze coins, but there are several copper tokens.

1. *O*: A ship in full sail, NOVA SCOTIA AND NEW BRUNSWICK SUCCESS.
   R: Female seated, holding scales and cornucopia, HALFPENNY TOKEN.

2. *O*: A full-rigged ship, PAYABLE AT THE STORE OF J. BROWN.

   R: A thistle with four leaves, NEMO ME IMPUNE LACESSIT.

3. *O*: ROBERT PURVIS | CHEAP | FAMILY | STORE | °WALLACE° displayed in five lines.

   R: ENCOURAGE | COUNTRY | IMPORTERS in three straight lines.

4. *O*: ONE | FARTHING in two lines in the centre, PAYABLE AT W. L. WHITE'S HALIFAX HOUSE HALIFAX.

   R: CHEAP | DRY GOODS | STORE in three lines. W. L. WHITE'S HALIFAX HOUSE HALIFAX.

5. *O*: A steamboat. HALIFAX STEAMBOAT COMPANY ✳

   R: FERRY TOKEN in two lines.

   This is in brass, farthing size, and is very scarce.

Halfpenny size.

6. *O*: Military bust to left. BROKE HALIFAX NOVA SCOTIA.

   R: Britannia seated holding a trident and palm branch. BRITANNIA 1814.

   There are two varieties of this token which differ in the position of the trident.

18

7. *O* :   A large bust of George III. HALF PENNY
           TOKEN 1814.

   R :   A three-masted ship under sail, PAYABLE
           BY CARRITT & ALPORT HALIFAX.

8. *O* :   A smaller bust of George III. within a circle.
           HALFPENNY TOKEN . 1814.

   R :   View of a house. PAYABLE BY HOSTER-
           MAN & ETTER . HALIFAX.

           A variety shows a slight difference in
           house on *R* :

9. *O* : ✓Larger bust than last, without **the** circle.
           HALFPENNY TOKEN 1815.

   R :   As last.   Although bearing a larger bust this
           token is rather smaller than the last.

10. *O* : As last.

    R : A ship in full sail. PAYABLE BY JOHN
           ALEXᴿ BARRY . HALIFAX.

11.   Small bust on *O* : otherwise same as last.
           There are three varieties of this token,
           differing in the arrangement of ship's sails.

12. *O* : Large bust and legend as No. 9.

    R : A ship in full sail, HALIFAX.

· 13. *O* : An Indian with bow and arrow, a dog by his side.
            STARR & SHANNON HALIFAX . 1815.

    R : A three-masted ship under sail. HALF-
           PENNY TOKEN NOVA SCOTIA.

           . There are three varieties of this, which
           differ in the position of bow and arrow.

14.   Similar to last but the legend on *O* : is
           COMMERCIAL CHANGE . 1815.

15. *O* : A cask, inscribed, SPIKES NAILS &c. within a
           circle. HALFPENNY TOKEN 1815.

    R : PAYABLE | BY | MILES W. | WHITE |
           HALIFAX | N . S . in six lines within a
           circle. IMPORTER OF IRONMONGERY
           HARDWARES &c.

16. *O* : A cask marked NAILS & SPIKES between a scythe blade and sickle, two spades crossed above. PAYABLE AT W. A. & S. BLACK'S . HALIFAX . N . S.

  R : View of a house. WHOLESALE & RETAIL HARDWARE STORE 1816 ✻

17. Similar to last excepting that the legend on *O* : is HALIFAX NOVA SCOTIA.

Penny size.

18. *O* : A laureated bust to left, PROVINCE OF NOVA SCOTIA.

  R : A thistle with two leaves, ONE PENNY TOKEN 1823.

  The bust on this piece is most probably intended for George IV.

19. Similar to last, excepting date, which is 1824.

20. *O* : A similar bust to last.

  R : Similar to last, excepting date, which is 1832.

  Although from the date on this coin the bust should be that of William IV., it is evidently intended to be that of George IV., as it faces to the left, as the preceding, all busts of William IV. facing to the right.

21. *O* : Bust of Queen, facing left, legend as before.

  R : Similar to last, but dated 1840.

22. Similar to last, excepting date, which is 1843.

  There are two varieties of this token, which differ slightly in the bust, although they are of equally inferior workmanship.

Halfpenny size.

23. Similar to No. 18, excepting in size and value, dated 1823.

24. Similar to No. 18, excepting in size and value, dated 1824.

25. Similar to No. 18, excepting in size and value, dated 1832.

26.　　　　　　Similar to No. 21, excepting in size and value,
　　　　　　　　dated 1840.

27.　　　　　　Similar to No. 21, excepting in size and value,
　　　　　　　　dated 1843.

　　　　　　　　There are varieties of Nos. 18 and 23 which
　　　　　　　　differ in the shape of thistle leaves on R:

Penny.

28.　*O*:　Coronetted bust to left. VICTORIA D : G :
　　　　　　BRITANNIAR : REG : F : D : 1856.

　　R:　A branch of mayflower. PROVINCE OF
　　　　　NOVA SCOTIA ONE PENNY TOKEN.

29.　　　　HALFPENNY TOKEN similar excepting in
　　　　　　size and value.

　　　　　　There are bronzed proofs of these two pieces
　　　　　　which are very rarely met, and there are five
　　　　　　varieties differing in various minor points.

Cent.

30.　*O*: ∵ Laureated bust to left, VICTORIA D : G :
　　　　　　BRITT : REG : F : D :

　　R:　A crown in the centre with the date 1861 under
　　　　　it, within a beaded circle, surrounded by a
　　　　　wreath of roses and mayflower. ONE CENT
　　　　　NOVA SCOTIA.

31.　　　　Similar to last, excepting date, which is 1862.

32.　　　　Similar to last, excepting date, which is 1864.

　　　　　　The obverse die appears to be the same as
　　　　　　that of the English halfpenny.

Half Cent.

33.　　　　Similar excepting in size and value, dated 1861.

34.　　　　Similar excepting in size and value, dated 1862.

35.　　　　Similar excepting in size and value, dated 1864.

A very curious and perhaps unique trial piece or pattern
is in the cabinet of H. Montagu, Esq., the *O*: of which is
similar in all respects to No. 30, the *R*: having a crown
within a thick wreath of roses and rose leaves, with 186
under the wreath, the last figure of the date not being

filled in. The legend which extends round on the outside of the wreath is, NOVA SCOTIA ONE CENT.

There is also a pattern cent and half cent, dated 1861, with the bust and letters of legend smaller than on those afterwards issued.

NEW BRUNSWICK.

NEW BRUNSWICK was taken from Nova Scotia and elevated to the dignity of a separate colony in the year 1785. It became incorporated in the Dominion of Canada by an act passed March 29th, 1867. Its interest from a numismatic point of view is small, as there are but few silver and bronze coins, and the tokens are fewer still.

SILVER COINS.

Twenty Cents.

1. *O:*   Laureated bust to left, VICTORIA D : G : REG : . NEW BRUNSWICK .

   R: 20 | CENTS | 1862 in three lines within a wreath of maple leaves. A crown above.

2.   Similar to last, excepting date, which is 1864.

Ten Cents.

3.   Similar to No. 1, excepting in size and value, dated 1862.

4.   · Similar to last, excepting date, which is 1864.

Five Cents.

5.   Similar to No. 1, excepting in size and value, dated 1862.

6.   Similar to last, excepting date, which is 1864.

    All these occur as proofs. There is also a 20 cent of 1871, a 10 cent of 1870, and a 5 cent piece of 1875, but these are made by "*muling*" the *O:* die with the *R:* dies of Canada for those dates.

BRONZE COINS.

Cents.

7. *O :* ✔ Laureated bust to left. VICTORIA D : G :
BRITT : REG : F : D :

   R : The date, 1861, crowned within a beaded circle,
surrounded by a wreath of roses and may-
flowers, ONE CENT NEW BRUNSWICK.
The obverse die of this piece appears to be
identical with that of the English halfpenny.

8. ✔ Similar to last, excepting date, which is 1864.

Half Cents.

9. Similar to No. 7, excepting in size and value,
dated 1861.

10. Similar to last, excepting date, which is 1864.
I have not seen No. 10, but give it upon the
authority of *Sandham.*

COPPER TOKENS.

11. *O :* HALF | PENNY | TOKEN in three lines in
the centre, S? JOHNS NEW BRUNS-
WICK ✻

   R : A frigate sailing, FOR PUBLIC ACCOMMO-
DATION.

12. *O :* E. M? DERMOTT | IMPORTER | OF ENG-
LISH | FRENCH & GERMAN | FANCY
GOODS | KING S? | S? JOHNS N . B in
seven lines.

   R : Ornamented shield of arms, with crest and
ribbon. DEPOSITORY OF ARTS.

13. *O :* ✔ Coronetted bust to left. VICTORIA DEI
GRATIA REGINA . 1843.

   R : ✔ A frigate, NEW BRUNSWICK . ONE PENNY
TOKEN.

14.   HALFPENNY TOKEN similar excepting in size and value.

There are bronzed **and** copper proofs of these two pieces, which are exceedingly rare.

15. *O* : Filleted bust to left, legend as before, date 1854.

   R : A frigate as before, NEW BRUNSWICK . ONE PENNY CURRENCY.

16.   HALFPENNY CURRENCY similar, excepting in size and value.

These two latter pieces occur both with and without w . w incused on the neck.

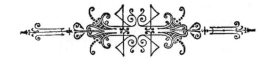

PRINCE EDWARD'S ISLAND.

THIS island was taken from the French by the British in the year 1757, and united with Cape Breton as a colony in 1763, but separated again in 1768. In 1800 it received its present title from Prince Edward, Duke of Kent. Its inhabitants are almost exclusively engaged in agriculture, considerable attention, however, being given to the fisheries. Allusions to these two points are found on most of the few tokens belonging to this colony, which finally became a province of the Dominion of Canada in 1873.

There are but few tokens, and but one coin, and they are all halfpenny size, or *cents*.

1. *O* : A steamship going to the left, HALFPENNY TOKEN.

    R : FISHERIES | AND | AGRICULTURE in three lines.

2. *O* : A plough. SPEED THE PLOUGH.

    R : A split codfish. SUCCESS TO THE FISHERIES.

    There are several varieties of this token, differing chiefly in the plough on *O* :

3. *O* : A wheatsheaf and sickle. PRINCE EDWARD'S ISLAND HALFPENNY 1840.

    R : A plough. COMMERCE & TRADE *

4.   *O* :   ONE | CENT | 1855 in three lines.

     R :   FISHERIES | AND | AGRICULTURE in three lines.

√ 5. *O* :   PRINCE EDWARD ISLAND 1855.

     R :   SELF | GOVERNMENT | AND | FREE | TRADE displayed in five lines.

6.   *O* :   PRINCE EDWARD'S ISLAND 1855.

     R :   As last.

7.   Similar to No. 5, excepting in date, which is 1857.

√ 8. *O* :   Coroneted bust to left, VICTORIA QUEEN ⚘ 1871 ⚘

     R :   Two trees within a beaded circle, PRINCE EDWARD ISLAND °ONE CENT° Under the trees and within the circle is PARVA SUB INGENTI in minute letters.

        This occurs also as a bronze proof.

MAGDALEN ISLAND.

THE Magdalen Islands are a small group near the centre of the Gulf of St. Lawrence, and about equi-distant from Cape Breton and Prince Edward Island. They contain about 2000 inhabitants, who are chiefly supported by the productive cod, herring and seal fisheries of the neighbouring waters. There is but one token, and that bears direct reference to the prevalent industry.

1.   *O* :   A seal, within a circle, MAGDALEN ISLAND TOKEN ⚹ 1815 ⚹

      R :   A split codfish, also within a circle. SUCCESS TO THE FISHERY . ONE PENNY.

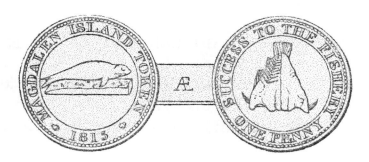

BRITISH COLUMBIA.

UNTIL the year 1858 British Columbia formed a portion of the Hudson's Bay Territory; but in that year large discoveries of gold were made which, attracting a vast immigration of gold-diggers, rendered it necessary for the British Government to take measures for the maintenance of order, and the country was erected into a colony. In 1866 Vancouver's Island was united to it, and in 1871 it became incorporated with the Dominion of Canada. There are no coins of this colony with the exception of the two following pieces, and they can scarcely be more than patterns, as I have only seen one of each, which is in the National Collection at the British Museum, having been presented by F. Seymour, Esq., Governor of British Columbia in 1864.

1. *O*: A Crown. GOVERNMENT OF BRITISH COLUMBIA.

   R: 20 | DOLLARS | 1862 | in three lines within a wreath of oak leaves and acorns.

2. 10 DOLLARS, similar, excepting in size and value.

CANADA.

CANADA was discovered by John and Sebastian Cabot, on June 24th, 1497. In 1524 a French settlement was formed, and called New France, and in 1535 a Breton mariner named Jacques Cartier ascended the St. Lawrence as far as the present site of Montreal; and Quebec was founded about 1608. A raid upon these settlements was made by the English in 1629, but the French regained possession in 1632, which they held until 1759, when Canada was conquered by the English, and their acquisition was confirmed to them by the Treaty of Paris in 1763.

During this period coins of silver and copper were struck by the French king, Louis XIV., for his American dominions, but these pieces, interesting as they be to the Canadian collector, do not come within the scope of the present work.

Since its incorporation with the other colonies of North America, in the year 1867, the whole have been termed " The Dominion of Canada," and silver and bronze coins are now issued for the entire district. These, although later in chronological order, will first be described, and afterwards, the somewhat numerous series of copper tokens, and at the end of these will be placed a number of pence and halfpence, all of which were most probably struck in England, and which would more correctly be described as Non-Local Tokens of the nineteenth century, and which are usually so described, but which are included here as they were used very freely as small change in Canada for many years, and are claimed by Canadian collectors as their own.

Silver Coins.

50 Cents or Half Dollar.

1. *O* :   Coroneted bust to left, VICTORIA DEI
           GRATIA REGINA CANADA. The initials
           L . C . W . are formed in minute characters
           upon the truncation of the neck.

   R :   50 | CENTS | 1870 in three lines within a
           wreath of maple, a crown above.

2.   Similar to last, excepting date, which is 1871.

3.   Similar to last, excepting date, which is 1872,
           and with a small H under the tie of wreath
           on *R* :

4.   Similar to last, but without the initial H.

5.   Similar to last, excepting date, which is 1873.

6.   Similar to last, excepting date, which is 1874.

7.   Similar to last, excepting date, which is 1875,
           with H . as before.

8.   Similar to last, excepting date, which is 1880,
           with H . as before.

9.   Similar to last, excepting date, which is 1881,
           with H . as before.

10.   Similar to last, excepting date, which is 1882,
           with H . as before.

11.   Similar to last, excepting date, which is 1884,
           but without the H.

12.   Similar to last, excepting date, which is 1885,
           but without the H.

13.   Similar to last, excepting date, which is 1886,
           but without the H.

14.   Similar to last, excepting date, which is 1887,
           but without the H.

           Proofs occur of the following dates—1870,
           both plain and milled edge ; 1872, without H . ;
           1874 and 1885.

25 Cents or Quarter Dollar.

15. O: Bust and legend as before.
    R: 25 | CENTS | 1870 in three lines within a wreath of maple, a crown above.

16.   Similar to last, excepting date, which is 1871.

17.   Similar to last, excepting date, which is 1872, and with a small H under the wreath on R:

18.   Similar to last, but without the H.

19.   Similar to last, excepting date, which is 1873.

20.   Similar to last, excepting date, which is 1874.

21.   Similar to last, excepting date, which is 1875, and H as before.

22.   Similar to last, excepting date, which is 1880, and H as before.

23.   Similar to last, excepting date, which is 1881, and H as before.

24.   Similar to last, excepting date, which is 1882, and H as before.

25.   Similar to last, excepting date, which is 1884, but without the H.

26.   Similar to last, excepting date, which is 1885, but without the H.

27.   Similar to last, excepting date, which is 1886, but without the H.

28.   Similar to last, excepting date, which is 1887, but without the H.

        Proofs occur of 1870 with plain edge, also of 1872 without H, and possibly others.

20 Cents.

29. O: Laureated. bust to left. VICTORIA DEI GRATIA REGINA CANADA.
    R: 20 | CENTS | 1858 in three lines, within a wreath of maple, a crown above.

        This coin was only struck in this year, proofs occur with both plain and milled edge.

10 *Cents.*

30.   *O* :   Similar to preceding excepting in size.

     R :   10 | CENTS | 1858 in three lines within a wreath of maple surmounted by a crown.

31.   Similar to last, excepting date, which is 1870.

32.   Similar to last, excepting date, which is 1871.

33.   Similar to last, excepting date, which is 1872, and with a small н as before.

34.   Similar to last, but without the н.

35.   Similar to last, excepting date, which is 1873.

36.   Similar to last, excepting date, which is 1874.

37.   Similar to last, excepting date, which is 1875, and н as before.

38.   Similar to last, excepting date, which is 1880, and н as before.

39.   Similar to last, excepting date, which is 1881, and н as before.

40.   Similar to last, excepting date, which is 1882, and н as before.

41.   Similar to last, excepting date, which is 1884, but without the н.

42.   Similar to last, excepting date, which is 1885, but without the н.

43.   Similar to last, excepting date, which is 1886, but without the н.

44.   Similar to last, excepting date, which is 1887, but without the н.

    Nos. 30, 33, 37, and 41 to 44 occur as proofs.

5 *Cents.*

45.   *O* :   As before.

     R :   5 | CENTS | 1858 in three lines within a maple wreath, surmounted by a crown.

46.   Similar to last, excepting date, which is 1870.

47.   Similar to last, excepting date, which is 1871.

48.   Similar to last, excepting date, which is 1872, and with a small н as before.

49.   Similar to last, but without the H.
50.   Similar to last, excepting date, which is 1873.
51.   Similar to last, excepting date, which is 1874.
52.   Similar to last, excepting date, which is 1875,
            and H as before.
53.   Similar to last, excepting date, which is 1880,
54.   Similar to last, excepting date, which is 1881.
55.   Similar to last, excepting date, which is 1882.
56.   Similar to last, excepting date, which is 1884.
            but without the H.
57.   Similar to last, excepting date, which is 1885.
58.   Similar to last, excepting date, which is 1886.
59.   Similar to last, excepting date, which is 1887.
            There are proofs with both plain and milled
            edge of 1870 and 1875, with plain edge of
            1858 and 1885.

BRONZE COINS.

60.   O :   Laureated bust to left, within a beaded circle, VIC-
            TORIA DEI GRATIA REGINA CANADA.
      R :   ONE | CENT | 1858 in three lines, within a
            beaded circle, and border of maple leaves.
            This is a pattern, and very scarce, the type
            issued being as follows :—
61.   O :   Coroneted bust to left, within a beaded circle,
            legend as before.
      R :   ONE | CENT | 1858 in three lines within a
            beaded circle and scroll border.
            A variety has been made by combining the
            O : of No. 60 with the R : of No. 61, but this
            partakes rather of the nature of a *mule.*
62.   V   As last, excepting date, which is 1859.
63.   As last, excepting date, which is 1876, and with
            a small H on R : under the date.
64.   ✓   As last, excepting date, which is 1881.
65.   ✓   As last, excepting date, which is 1882.

                                                    19

66.   ❧ As last, excepting date, which is 1884, but without the H.

67.   As last, excepting date, which is 1885.

68.   ⌣ As last, excepting date, which is 1886.

69.   As last, excepting date, which is 1887.

TOKENS.

70. ↻O: Female figure seated, her hand resting upon a harp. NORTH AMERICAN TOKEN 1781.

     R: A two-masted ship under sail. COMMERCE.

71.   O: A river god, with trident and urn. FERTILI-TATEM DIVITIAS QUE CIRCUMFERE-MUS 1794.

     R: COPPER | COMPANY | OF UPPER | CANADA in four lines within a circle. ONE HALFPENNY.

72.   O: A female presenting children to a bishop. BRITISH SETTLEMENTS KENTUCKY 1796.

     R: Same as last.

        Nos. 71 and 72 both occur as proofs, the latter usually in silver.

73. *O :*   Coarsely executed bust to left. VEXATOR CANADIN SIS.

    R :   Female figure seated (?) RENUNTER ✳ VISCAPE 1811.

74.   Legend on *O :* VEXATOR CANADIENSIS otherwise similar to preceding.

75. *O :*   Bust as before. VEXATOR CANADIENSIS 1811.

    R :   Female figure as before RENUNILLUS VISCAPE.

      There are at least two other varieties of this, differing in spelling and punctuation, they are all of excessively rude workmanship.

76. *O :*   CANADA | HALF | PENNY | TOKEN displayed in four lines.

    R :   Three-masted ship under sail. FOR PUBLIC ACCOMMODATION.

77. *O :*   T. S. BROWN & C? | IMPORTERS | OF | HARDWARE | UPPER TOWN | QUEBEC displayed in four lines.

    R :   An anvil with two spades crossed above it, between a vice and scythe-blade.

78. *·O :*   UN CENTIM PAYABLE | CHEZ | H. GAGNON & C!E | RUE LA COURONNE | S ROCH QUEBEC in six lines.

    R :   A beaver. MAISON JACQUES CARTIER S? ROCH | QUEBEC.

79. *O :*   LYMBURNER & BROTHER | GOLD | AND SILVER PLATERS | 663 | CRAIG STREET | MONTREAL displayed in seven lines.

    R :   LYMBURNER & FRERE | D'OREURS ET ARGENTEURS | 663 | RUE CRAIG | MONTREAL displayed in five lines.

      The number is in the centre, radiated, on both sides.

19 *

80. *O* :   FRANCIS MULLINS & SON|IMPORTERS|
            OF|SHIP CHANDLERY|&c.|MONTREAL
            in six lines.

     R :   A ship in full sail. COMMERCE TOKEN.

81. *O* :   R. W. OWEN | MONTREAL | ROPERY in
            three lines within a cable border.

     R :   A ship under sail.

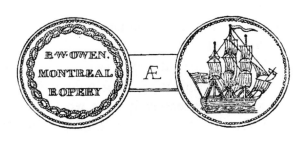

82. *O* :   J. SHAW & C? | IMPORTERS | OF |
            HARDWARES | UPPER TOWN | QUE-
            BEC in six lines.

     R :   A kettle, knife and fork, vice, saw, spade and
            scythe-blade.

83. *O* :   Bust to left. R. SHARPLEY . JEWELLER &
            WATCHMAKER NOTRE DAME S? MONT-
            REAL.

     R :   IMPORTER | OF | SILVERWARE | ᴄʟᴏᴄᴋꜱ |
            ɢᴀꜱᴇʟɪᴇʀꜱ | ʙʀᴏɴᴢᴇꜱ | CABINET-
            WARE | GLASS-WARE | &c &c &c: displayed in
            nine lines.

            This piece is struck in brass **and** is rather
            small for halfpenny size.

84. *O* :   SIR ISAAC | BROCK BART | THE HERO
            OF | UPPER CANADA | WHO FELL AT
            THE | GLORIOUS BATTLE OF | QUEENS-
            TOWN HEIGHTS | ON THE 13TH OCT^R |
            1812 displayed in nine lines.

     R :   A ship in full sail, SUCCESS TO THE COM-
            MERCE OF UPP? & LOW? CANADA.

85. *O*: The date 1816 in the centre, with a radiation above and below it. SUCCESS TO COMMERCE & PEACE TO THE WORLD.

    R: As last.

86. *O*: As last.

    R: Two angels holding a wreath over an urn placed on a pedestal, which is inscribed FELL | OCT.ᴿ 13 | 1812 in three lines. SIR ISAAC BROCK THE HERO OF UPP CANADA. There are two slight variations of this token, and one reading BROOK.

87. *O*: Laureated bust to left, within a circle. HALF PENNY TOKEN 1816.

    R: A ship in full sail. MONTREAL.

88. *O*: Laureated bust to right. TOKEN 1820.

    R: A beaver. NORTH WEST COMPANY.

89. *O*: A sloop under sail. HALFPENNY TOKEN UPPER CANADA.

    R: An Indian with bow and arrow, a dog by his side. COMMERCIAL CHANGE 1815.

90. *O*: As last.

    R: An anvil, with two spades crossed above it. COMMERCIAL CHANGE 1820.

91. *O*: As before.

    R: A cask inscribed UPPER CANADA. COMMERCIAL CHANGE 1821.

92. *O*: As before.

    R: A plough. TO FACILITATE TRADE ✝ 1823.

93. As last, but dated 1833.
    A variety has the bowsprit of sloop projecting over the final A in Canada, and occurs with both plain and milled edges.

94. *O*: As before.

    R: An anvil with two spades crossed over it, between a vice and scythe-blade. COMMERCIAL CHANGE 1833.

Twopence.

95. *O* : Figure of Justice standing, holding balance and
sword. LESLIE & SONS TORONTO &
DUNDASS 1822.

R : A plough, TOKEN above, 2ᴰ ᴄᴜʀʀᴇɴᴄʏ below.
PROSPERITY TO CANADA . LA PRU-
DENCE ET LA CANDEUR.

Halfpenny.

96. *O* : Figure of Justice as before. LESLIE & SONS
YORK KINGSTON & DUNDAS.

R : A plough, TOKEN above, ʜᴀʟꜰᴘᴇɴɴʏ below,
legend as before.

There are several varieties of this token,
differing chiefly in shape of plough.

97. *O* : CANADA . 1830.
R : HALF | PENNY in two lines.

98. Similar to last excepting date, which is 1841.

99. *O* : Laureated bust to left, similar to that on No. 25,
Nova Scotia. PROVINCE OF UPPER
CANADA.

R : Figure of Britannia seated, holding trident and
palm branch. HALFPENNY TOKEN 1832.

100. *O* : A cask between UN — SOU, BREWERS
above, ᴅɪꜱᴛɪʟʟᴇʀꜱ &c &c &c below, within a
circle. THˢ & Wᴹ MOLSON * MON-
TREAL *

R : A still within a circle. CASH PAID FOR
ALL SORTS OF GRAIN * 1837 *

About the year 1837 the following pieces were issued,
which are usually spoken of as the "*Un Sou Series.*"
They are without date, and bear a general resemblance to
each other; the majority of them have a bouquet on *O* :
with the legend TRADE AND AGRICULTURE. Those
easiest to identify will be described first, the remainder
being placed in a table, for the conception of which, I am

indebted to a little work published by Jos. Le Roux of Montreal.

101. *O* : A bouquet. AGRICULTURE & COM-MERCE ✻ BAS-CANADA ✻

    R : An eagle holding a shield, surrounded with thirteen stars. T. DUSEAMAN BUTCHER ✿ BELLEVILLE ✻

102. *O* : A bouquet. TRADE & AGRICULTURE ✿ LOWER CANADA ✻

    R : $\frac{1}{2}$ PENNY within a wreath. BANK TOKEN MONTREAL.

103. *O* : A bouquet. TRADE AND AGRICULTURE LOWER CANADA.

    R : UN | SOUS within a wreath in two lines. BANK TOKEN MONTREAL.

104.   Similar to last, but legend on *R* : is BANK OF MONTREAL TOKEN.

105.   Similar to last, but UN | SOU within wreath on *R* :

106. *O* : Two maple leaves crossed. COMMERCE ✳ BAS-CANADA ✳

    R : UN | SOU in two lines within a wreath. J^H ROY MONTREAL.

107. *O* : A bouquet. AGRICULTURE & COM-MERCE ✿ BAS-CANADA ✿

    R : UN | SOU in two lines, within a wreath formed of five maple leaves, a five-pointed star on one side, and small head wearing the cap of liberty on the other. BANQUE DU PEUPLE . MONTREAL.

108.   *O* :   A bouquet. AGRICULTURE & COMMERCE
               BAS CANADA.

  R :   UN | SOU in two lines, within a thick wreath
          of maple leaves. BANQUE DU PEUPLE .
          MONTREAL .

The remainder of this series all have as legend on *O* :
AGRICULTURE & COMMERCE BAS-CANADA, and
on *R* : TOKEN MONTREAL.   They must therefore be
distinguished by the composition of bouquet on *O* : and in
some instances by the number of leaves forming the wreath
on *R* : This will be done best by the arrangement of the
following table :—

No.	Roses	Buds	Thistle heads	Sham-rocks	Rose leaves	Thistle leaves	Maple leaves	Heads of wheat	Blades of grass	Reverse.
109.	1	1	1	2	3	2	.	3	2	Wreath of 32 small laurel leaves, dot over o. of sou.
110.	1	1	2	5	5	3	.	2	5	Wreath of 35 small leaves, a dot over the ò of sou.
111.	1	1	2	6	5	3	.	2	3	Wreath of 17 leaves, slender triangular bow.
112.	1	1	2	4	3	1	.	2	5	
113.	1	.	1	3	6	2	.	3	5	Same as No. 109.
114.	1	.	1	2	3	1	.	3	2	Same as No. 109.
115.	1	.	2	1	5	2	.	2	5	
116.	1	.	2	1	5	2	.	2	9	Wreath of 18 leaves.
117.	1	.	2	1	7	2	.	2	6	Same as No. 110.
118.	1	.	2	2	4	.	2	2	5	
119.	1	.	2	2	5	.	3	2	5	
120.	1	.	2	2	6	2	1	2	1	This occurs in brass and copper. Wreath of 20 leaves.
121.	1	.	2	2	6	2	.	3	5	
122.	1	.	2	2	7	.	2	3	4	
123.	1	.	2	2	4	.	2	3	6	
124.	1	.	2	3	4	3	.	2	4	Wreath of 16 leaves, very large triangular bow.
125.	1	.	2	3	5	3	.	2	3	Wreath of 18 leaves, dot over ò in sou.
126.	1	.	2	3	6	3	.	2	3	Open wreath of 18 leaves, no bow.
127.	1	.	2	3	6	3	.	2	4	
128.	1	.	2	4	3	.	4	2	9	

No.	Roses	Buds	Thistle heads	Sham-rocks	Rose leaves	Thistle leaves	Maple leaves	Heads of wheat	Blades of grass	REVERSE.
131.	1	.	2	5	3	.	4	2	8	
132.	1	.	2	5	4	.	4	2	4	
133.	1	.	2	5	7	.	.	2	3	Wreath of 16 leaves. This is made of brass and badly struck.
134.	1	.	2	5	8	.	.	2	3	
135.	1	.	2	6	4	.	4	2	.	Wreath of 16 leaves, triangular bow, dot over ȯ of sou.
136.	1	.	2	6	4	.	4	2	4	Wreath of 18 leaves.
137.	1	.	2	7	4	.	3	2	4	
138.	1	.	2	7	4	.	4	2	4	Wth of 18 l was, no , dot oer ȯ in sou.
139.	1	.	2	7	6	.	3	2	2	This token is made of brass.
140.	1	.	2	7	8	2	2	2	2	Wreath of 18 leaves, large bow.
141.	1	.	2	.	4	.	2	3	3	Wth of 18 l was, small triangular bow.
142.	1	.	2	5	6	2	.	4	1	Wreath of 16 leaves, flat triangular bow.
143.	1	.	2	7	4	.	4	2	4	Wreath of 18 leaves, flat triangular bow, dot over ȯ in sou.
144.	1	.	2	7	4	.	4	2	4	Wreath of 16 leaves, large triangular bow, dot over ȯ in sou.
145.	1	.	1	7	10	.	.	2	2	Open wreath of 18 leaves, no bow.
146.	1	.	2	7	4	2	3	2	2	Wreath of 16 leaves, triangular bow, dot over ȯ in sou.
147.	1	.	2	7	4	.	.	2	1	Wreath of 40 small laurel leaves, large open bow.
148.	1	.	1	7	8	2	.	2	2	Open wreath of 18 leaves, no bow.
149.	4	1	2	.	17	.	.	3	.	Open wreath of 18 leaves, no bow.

In addition to these there are several other varieties made by taking the *O*: of one and joining it to the *R* : of another. I have not seen all the pieces described, but am indebted to " Sandham " and " Le Roux " for a few.

Penny size.

150. *O* : A Canadian farmer standing, with a whip in his hand. PROVINCE DU BAS CANADA DEUX SOUS.

R : The Canadian arms within a garter inscribed CONCORDIA SALUS; upon a ribbon is inscribed BANK OF MONTREAL; above is BANK TOKEN and below the date 1837 and ONE PENNY.

151. Similar to last, but the ribbon is inscribed BANK DU PEUPLE.

152. Similar to last, but the ribbon is inscribed CITY BANK.

153. Similar to last, but the ribbon is inscribed QUEBEC BANK.

Halfpenny size.

154. Similar to No. 150, excepting in size and value.

155. Similar to No. 151, excepting in size and value.

156. Similar to No. 152, excepting in size and value.

157. Similar to No. 153, excepting in size and value.

Penny size.

158. *O* : Front view of a house. PROVINCE OF CANADA . BANK OF MONTREAL.

R : Similar to No. 150.

159. Similar to last, excepting date, which is 1842.

160. Similar to last, excepting date, which is 1844.

Halfpenny size.

161. Similar to No. 159, excepting in size and value.

162.   Similar to No. 160, excepting in size and value.
              There are bronze and copper proofs of
              these pieces.

Penny size.

163. *O:*   Corner view of a house. BANK OF MONT-
              REAL 1838.

      R: Similar to No. 150, but without the date.

164.   Similar to last, excepting date, which is 1839.

Halfpenny size.

165.   Similar to No. 163, excepting in size and value.
166.   Similar to No. 164, excepting in size and
              value.

Penny size.

167. *O:*   Female seated by a rock, her hand resting
              upon a shield, a ship in the distance.
              QUEBEC BANK TOKEN above, and
              below the date 1852 and ONE PENNY.

      R: A Canadian farmer as before. PROVINCE
              DU CANADA DEUX SOUS.

Halfpenny size.

168.   Similar, excepting in size and value.

Penny size.

169. *O:*   St. George and the dragon. BANK OF
              UPPER CANADA ✿ 1850 ✿

      R: Sword and anchor crossed over two cornu-
              copias; a crown above and a Union Jack to
              right of the crown. BANK ✿ TOKEN ✿
              ONE . PENNY ✿

170. Similar to last, excepting date, which is 1852.
171. Similar to last, excepting date, which is 1854.
      A variety of this has no cross to bottom stroke of figure 4 in date.
172. Similar to preceding, but dated 1857.

Halfpenny size.

173. Similar to No. 169, excepting in size and value.
174. Similar to No. 170, excepting in size and value.
175. Similar to No. 171, excepting in size and value.
176. Similar to No. 172, excepting in size and value.
      Bronzed proofs also occur of these pieces.
177. *O*: Bust of Queen to left, laureated. DOMINION OF CANADA PROVINCE OF QUEBEC.
      R: USE | DEVINS' | VEGETABLE | WORM | PASTILES | JULY 1ST | 1867 in five lines, within a beaded circle. DEVINS & BOLTON * DRUGGISTS MONTREAL.

The *O*: of this token, or advertising ticket, bears a close resemblance to the cent No. 60, and the issue of it was in consequence forbidden by the colonial authorities.

UNDER this head we shall include a few railway and toll checks and tickets, which although scarcely coming under the head of coins or tokens, are yet usually sought after and prized by Canadian collectors, and also a number of what are probably English nineteenth century non-local tokens, for the same reason. These latter were doubtless, in the absence of small change, imported and used in considerable quantities in Canada, and therefore have acquired in some measure "a local habitation," if not a name, as Canadian tokens.

178. *O* : A steamboat. LAWSON 1821.

    R : FOUR PENCE TOKEN . BON POUR HUIT SOLS.

        This piece is of lead, and was a ferry ticket between Quebec and Point Levi.

179. *O* : A locomotive engine. MONTREAL & LACHINE RAILROAD COMPANY.

    R : A beaver, by a trunk of a tree. THIRD CLASS.

This railway, when first opened, was largely used by the Indians and their squaws, together with the navvies working upon the line. The ordinary cardboard ticket not being sufficiently strong for this class of customers, this metal ticket was introduced and used instead. A hole in the centre of the ticket was used by the conductors to string them upon a piece of wire. Somewhat similar tickets were used upon some of our earliest English lines.

180. *O*: DE L'ISLE | DE MONTRÉAL | À REPEN-TIGUY | ON | LACHESNAYE displayed in five lines.

R: PERSONNE above, and a wreath below.

181. *O*: As last.

R: CHEVAL in the centre, with a scroll above and below.

182. *O*: As last.

R: CALÈCHE in the centre, with a floral ornament above and below.

183. *O*: As last.

R: CHARRETTE in the centre, with two sprigs of laurel above and below.

184. *O*: DE REPENTIGUY | A | L'ISLE DE | MONTRÉAL | . . ✶ . . | ON LACHES-NAYE . displayed in six lines.

185. *R*: PERSONNE, as before.

186. *O*: As last.

R: CHEVAL, as before.

187. *O*: As last.

R: CALÈCHE, as before.

188. *O*: As last.

R: CHARRETTE, as before.

These were toll checks for the bridge known as the *Porteous Bridge,* which was erected in 1808, to connect the island of Repentiguy with that of Montreal.

189. *O*: EVENING GLOBE . GOOD FOR ONE COPY.

R: Same as *O*: This is of brass, with a hole in the centre.

NON-LOCAL TOKENS, PENNY SIZE.

190. *O*: Bust of George III. ONE PENNY TOKEN 1811.

R: Britannia seated. COMMERCE.

191. *O* :   Laureated bust of George III. within a thick
             wreath of oak.

      R :   Female seated holding scales and cornucopia.
             ONE PENNY TOKEN 1812.

192.   As last, but the wreath on *O* : is divided at
             bottom to insert date 1812.

193.   As last, but without date on *R* :

194.   Similar to last, excepting date, which is
             1813.

195. *O* :   Bust of George III.   BON POUR DEUX
             SOUS.

      R :   Female seated as in No. 191.   ONE PENNY
             TOKEN 1813.

196. *O* :   As No. 191.

      R :   Britannia seated.   COMMERCE 1814.

197. *O* :   A Druid's head.   PURE COPPER PREFER-
             ABLE TO PAPER.

      R :   Female seated holding olive branch and
             caduceus.   TRADE & NAVIGATION
             1813.

198. *O* :   ONE | PENNY | TOKEN in three lines
             within a circle. PURE COPPER PREFER-
             ABLE TO PAPER.

      R :   As last.

199. *O* :   ONE | PENNY | TOKEN in three lines within
             a thick wreath of oak.

      R :   A ship under sail. ONE PENNY TOKEN
             1813.

200. *O* :   ONE | PENNY in two lines within a wreath
             of laurel.

      R :   A ship under sail.

201. *O* :   A ship under sail. ONE PENNY TOKEN
             1814.

      R :   *RH* in monogram, within a wreath of oak
             leaves and acorns.

202. *O* : ONE | PENNY | TOKEN in three lines within a thick wreath of oak.

R : A phœnix within a floral wreath.
This piece has been struck over either No. 199 or 200, a portion of the first impression still showing.

203. *O* : ONE | PENNY | TOKEN in three lines within a wreath of oak and laurel.

R : Figure of Justice standing on a pedestal, within a wreath of laurel and palm.

204. *O* : Laureated bust to left, a laurel wreath under. FIELD MARSHAL WELLINGTON.

R : Britannia seated. ONE PENNY TOKEN 1813.

205. Similar to last, but without the date.

206. Similar to No. 204, but with a laurel wreath in place of date on *R* :

207. *O* : Bust to left, not laureated . VIMIERA . TALAVERA . BADAJOZ . SALAMANCA . VITTORIA.

R : As No. 204.

208. *O* : Bust as last. VIMERA . TALAVERA . BUSACO . BADAJOZ . SALAMANCA ✦

R : A Cossack on horseback. COSSACK PENNY TOKEN.

209. *O* : Laureated bust to left, different to No. 204. WELLINGTON & VICTORY 1814.

R : Female seated, holding palm branch and spear, a shield with a harp inscribed upon it by aside (evidently a colourable imitation of Britannia). EDW.D.BEWLEY 1816.

210. *O* : A bust somewhat similar to last. WELLINGTON & ERIN GO BRAGH.

R : A harp crowned EDW.D STEPHENS 1816.

211. *O* : A slightly different bust. WELLINGTON above, ERIN GO BRAGH below.

R : Similar to last.

HALFPENNY SIZE.

212   *O* :   Laureated bust of George III. within a wreath of
            oak leaves and acorns.

      R :   Female seated on bale, holding scales and
            cornucopia.   HALFPENNY TOKEN 1812.
            There are several varieties of this token,
            and it is found in both copper and brass.

213. *O* :   Bust as before, but without the wreath.
            SUCCESS TO TRADE . 1812.

      R :   Figure of Britannia seated, holding palm
            branch and trident.   COMMERCE.   Under
            the figure in exergue is RULES THE MAIN.

214. *O* :   Bust as before.   GENUINE   BRITISH
            COPPER 1815.

      R :   Britannia seated, holding a trident.   HALF-
            PENNY.

215. *O* :   Small bust of George III. to right, laureated.
            HALFPENNY TOKEN 1815.

      R :   Ship under sail. SUCCESS TO NAVIGATION
            & TRADE ✤

216. *O* :   Bust of George III. slightly different to last.
            HALFPENNY TOKEN 1814.

      R :   A ship under sail. FOR THE CONVENIENCE
            OF TRADE.

217. *O* :   Bust as before.   GREAT BRITAIN.

      R :   Female seated, holding a branch of olive and of
            palm.   COMMERCE 1814.

218. *O* :   Bust as before, no legend.

      R :   Britannia seated, holding a trident. GENUINE
            BRITISH COPPER.

219.   Similar to last, but date on *R* : 1820 and no
            legend.

220. *O* :   Laureated and armoured bust to left.

      R :   A harp, 1820.

221. Similar to last, but without date.

These two pieces are made of brass, and the latter is of very inferior workmanship.

222. *O*: Bust in military dress to right, a wreath of laurel under. · VICTORIA NOBIS EST.

R: Female figure seated resembling Britannia holding. olive branch and wand. HALF-PENNY TOKEN.

223. *O*: Female seated holding olive branch and caduceus. TRADE & NAVIGATION 1812.

R: HALF | PENNY | TOKEN in three lines within a circle. PURE COPPER PREFERABLE TO PAPER.

224. *O*: A ship under sail. TRADE & NAVIGATION 1813.

R: As last.

225. Similar to No. 223, excepting date, which is 1813.

226. *O*: Ship in full sail. FOR GENERAL ACCOMMODATION.

R: As last.

227. *O*: Ship as before, but no legend.

R: Female seated, holding scales and cornucopia. HALFPENNY TOKEN 1815.

228. *O*: Female seated resting upon a harp (Hibernia ?) ONE HALFPENNY TOKEN 1820.

R: Ship under sail. TRADE AND NAVIGATION.

229. *O*: Ship under sail to right. SHIPS COLONIES & COMMERCE 1815.

R: ONE | HALFPENNY | TOKEN in three lines.

230. *O*: As last.

R: FOR | PUBLICK | ACCOMMODATION in three lines.

231. *O*: Ship under sail. HALFPENNY TOKEN 1814.

   R: *R H* in monogram, within a wreath of oak leaves and acorns.

232. *O*: Ship under sail, no legend.

   R: SHIPS | COLONIES | & | COMMERCE in four lines.

   There are several varieties of this token, differing in size and form of letters, arrangement of sails, &c.

233. *O*: As last.

   R: Female seated on bale, looking to left, holding scales and cornucopia.

234. *O*: As last.

   R: Female as before. HALFPENNY TOKEN 1812.

235. *O*: As last.

   R: The date only, in the centre of the field 1858.

   Many other varieties are made by joining this obverse with other obverses or reverses together, and so manufacturing *mules*. The same remarks will apply to several other pieces of this series.

236. *O*: A man ploughing with two oxen. SPEED THE PLOUGH HALFPENNY TOKEN.

   R: A man threshing grain. NO LABOUR NO BREAD.

237. *O*: A man standing holding a shillelagh and a sprig of shamrock within a wreath.

   R: PURE COPPER PREFERABLE TO PAPER in five lines.

238. *O*: A spread eagle, its tail dividing the date 18— 13. HALFPENNY TOKEN.

   R: Britannia seated, holding olive branch and trident, within a wreath.

239. Similar to last, excepting date, which is 1814.

240.   Similar to last, but the eagle is higher on the coin, leaving room under it for the date, which is 1815. The *R* : also is finer work.

241. *O* :   A ship under sail to right. (*See No.* 229.)
      R :   WELLINGTON | WATERLOO | 1815 in 3 lines.

242. *O* :   Laureated bust of Wellington to left within a wreath, no legend.
      R :   Female seated holding scales and wand. TRADE & COMMERCE 1811.

243. *O* :   Laureated bust to right (? Wellington). 1820.
      R :   As No. 241.
              This again, as well as the one preceding, is often *muled* with other obverses and reverses.

244. *O* :   Laureated bust to right, MARQUIS WELLINGTON 1813.
      R :   Female seated resembling Britannia, holding olive branch and wand. COMMERCE.

245. *O* :   Laureated bust to left. THE ILLUSTRIOUS WELLINGTON.
      R :   A harp crowned. WATERLOO HALFPENNY 1816.

246. *O* :   Bust similar to last, with a bow and two ends to the ribbon tying laurel. WELLINGTON HALFPENNY TOKEN.
      R :   Britannia seated, holding olive branch and trident, the date 1814 under, a sprig of oak on either side.

247.   Similar to last but no bow and only one end to ribbon forming tie.

248. *O* :   Bust as before, two sprigs of laurel under it. FIELD MARSHALL WELLINGTON.
      R :   Britannia seated, holding trident and olive branch, two sprigs of laurel under. HALFPENNY TOKEN.

249.   Similar to last, but with date 1813 under Britannia, in place of sprigs of laurel.

250. *O* :   Bust as before. HISPANIAM ET LVSITANIAM RESTITVIT WELLINGTON.

     R :   CUIDAD | RODRIGO | Jan. 19. 1812 | BADAJOZ | April 2.1812 | SALAMANCA | July 22. 1812 | &c. &c. &c. in eight lines within a circle. VIMIERA Aug. 21. 1808. TALAVERA July 28. 1809. ALMEIDA may 5. 1811 ⚓

251. *O* :   As last.

     R :   CUIDAD | RODRIGO | Jan. 19. 1812. | BADAJOZ | April 2. 1812. | SALAMANCA | July 22. 1812. | MADRID | Aug. 12. 1812. in nine lines, the last one being curved, otherwise as last.

252. *O* :   As last.

     R :   SALAMANCA | July 22. 1812. | MADRID | Aug. 12. 1812. | ST SEBASTIAN | Sept. 8. 1813. | PAMPLUNO | oct. 31. 1813. in eight lines, the last one being curved, surrounding this within a circle is CUIDAD RODRIGO jan. 19. 1812. BAJADOZ april 21. 1812. The legend outside circle as before.

253. *O* :   Naked bust of Wellington. FIELD MARSHAL WELLINGTON.

     R :   A harp crowned. HIBERNIA 1805.

254. *O* :   Bust as last. WELLINGTON 1815.

     R :   Somewhat similar bust. BLUCHER.

FARTHING SIZE.

255. *O* :   Ship under sail within a circle. FARTHING TOKEN 1812.

     R :   *R H* in monogram within a wreath of oak leaves and acorns.

256. *O*: ONE FARTHING in two lines within a circle. PURE COPPER PREFERABLE TO PAPER.

R: Female seated on bale holding olive branch and caduceus. TRADE & NAVIGATION 1813.

257. *O*: Ship under sail. COMMERCE.

R: The date 1828 in centre, above it ONE FARTHING—below, TOKEN.

COINS AND TOKENS OF THE WEST INDIES.

THE West India Islands belonging to Great Britain, of which Jamaica is the largest and most important, have an area of nearly 14,000 square miles and a population of 1,250,000. In the early part of the present century slavery existed in all the islands.

Fostered by highly protective duties, they reached a very flourishing condition, and large fortunes were made. This condition was completely artificial; and when slavery was abolished, and the protective duties repealed, an entire collapse took place, and many hitherto wealthy persons were ruined. Up to that time these islands had been regarded as the choicest possessions of the British crown, and a grand outlet for commerce. Since then they have received less attention in every way than they deserve, but are now again resuming their proper position, and it may be hoped that they will once more become prosperous.

With the exception of an attempt in 1822 by striking a quantity of the pieces of Half, Quarter, Eighth and Sixteenth of a Dollar, no provision for the currency of these islands has been made by the mother-country, although later, silver threepences, and threehalfpences, have been issued, and also a special issue of nickel coins for Jamaica. Considerable use has been made of the Spanish dollars, and a number of varieties of cut and countermarked coins will be found in this series. There are also a few tokens issued by private traders. The series, although small, contains pieces of great variety and interest, containing as it does some of the very earliest and rarest of our colonial coins, viz., those of the Somer Islands.

ANTIGUA.

1.   *O*:   A palm-tree dividing the date 18—36 and H—C, ANTIGUA under.

     R: ONE | FARTHING | **stg** (= sterling ?) in three lines within a wreath.

BAHAMA.

2.   *O*:   Bust to right, GEORGIUS III . D . G . REX . 1806. This is similar to the English half-penny.

     R: A ship in full sail, BAHAMA . EXPULSIS PIRATIS RESTITUTA COMMERCIA.

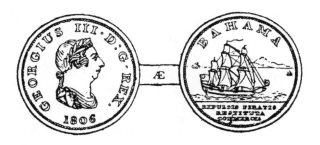

3.   Similar to last, excepting date, which is 1807.

BARBADOES.

Penny size.

4.   *O*:   Negro bust crowned, and a plume of three ostrich feathers, I SERVE . J . MILTON . F . on neck.

     R: A pine apple, BARBADOES PENNY . 1788. This occurs as proof both copper and bronze.

5.   Similar to preceding, but with M. only on truncation of neck.

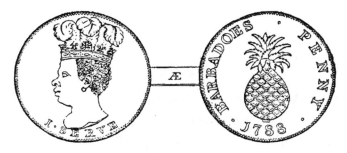

6.   Similar, but with the plume of feathers larger.

7.   Similar, but with the pine apple larger.

8.   Similar, but with the date more expanded.

             All these are found as proofs.

9. *O:*   King seated in a marine car, BARBADOES
             PENNY 1792.

    R: Similar to *O:* of No. 5, but with a larger plume
             of feathers.

10.   Similar to last, but with a dot between BAR-
             BADOES . and PENNY.

11.   Similar to No. 9, but the king's crown comes
             between the N's of PENNY.

Halfpenny.

12.   Similar to No. 9 excepting in size and value.

             Nos. 9 and 12 are found as proofs in silver,
             bronze and copper.

HALFPENNY TOKEN.

13. *O:*   A bale, marked M. T.   MOSES TOLANTO.

     R: A cask, FREEDOM WITHOUT SLAVERY.

Farthing.

14.   Similar, excepting in size and value.

BERMUDAS OR SOMER ISLANDS.

BRASS OR "HOG" MONEY.

Shilling.

15.　*O*:　A hog with XII above it within a beaded circle.
　　　　SOMMER ✿ ISLANDS ✿

　　R:　An antique ship with sails set and flags flying.

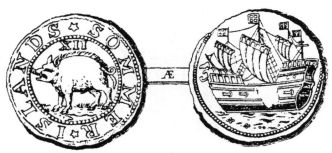

Sixpence.

16.　　　Similar, excepting in size and value.

Threepence.

17.　　　Similar, but without legend on *O*:

Twopence.

18.　　　Similar to last.

COPPER PENNY.

19.　*O*:　Laureated bust to right, GEORGIUS III . D . G .
　　　　REX.

　　R:　A ship in full sail, BERMUDA above, 1793
　　　　below.

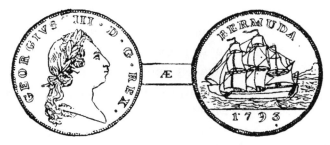

　　　　This occurs as a proof in gold (which is, I
believe, unique), also in silver and bronze.

JAMAICA.
NICKEL.

Penny.

20. *O* :   Coroneted bust to left, within a beaded circle.
             VICTORIA QUEEN ✿ 1869 ✿

    R :   Shield of arms, crest, a crocodile, beneath it a
             ribbon with motto, all within a beaded circle.
             JAMAICA ✿ ONE PENNY ✿

21.   Similar to last, excepting date, which is 1870.
22.   Similar to last, excepting date, which is 1871.
23.   Similar to last, excepting date, which is 1880.
24.   Similar to last, excepting date, which is 1882.
25.   Similar to last, excepting date, which is 1884.
26.   Similar to last, excepting date, which is 1885.

      No 20 occurs as a proof both in copper and
nickel, and all the pennies have L. C. WYON
under bust.

Halfpenny.

27.   Similar to No. 20 excepting in size and value,
             date 1869.
28.   Similar to last, excepting date, which is 1870.
✓ 29.   Similar to last, excepting date, which is 1871.
30.   Similar to last, excepting date, which is 1880.
31.   Similar to last, excepting date, which is 1882,
             and a small H under bust.
32.   Similar to last, excepting date, which is 1884,
             but without the H.
23.   Similar to last, excepting date, which is 1885.

      No. 27 also occurs as a proof both in copper
and nickel.

Farthing.

34.   Similar to No. 20 excepting in size and value, date 1880.

35.   Similar to last, excepting date, which is 1882, and a small н under bust.

36.   Similar to last, excepting date, which is 1884, but without the н.

37.   Similar to last, excepting date, which is 1885.

There are proof sets of 1880 and 1884 in nickel of penny, halfpenny, and farthing.

COPPER TOKENS.

Halfpenny.

38. *O* :   Coach and horses. M. HOWARD FERRY-GRASS.

     R :   Man holding horse. KINGSTON JAMAICA.

Farthing.

39. *O* :   THOMAS LUNDIE & C̥ KINGSTON . 1844.

     R :   A steam-boat . EARL OF ELGIN JAMAICA.

40. *O* :   THOMAS LUNDAY & C̥ IRONMONGERS . WATER STREET 1844.

     R :   As last.

Penny.

41. *O* :   (1ᵈ) | JAMAICA | CURRENCY | BY in four lines in the centre. PAYABLE IN KINGSTON above, and WILLIAM SMITH below incused on a broad rim.

     R :   Arms of Jamaica and supporters. INDUS UTERQUE SERVIAT UNI.

Halfpenny.

42. *O* :   PAYABLE . | IN | KINGSTON | BY | WILLIAM SMITH. displayed in five lines.

     R :   JAMAICA in centre, ONE HALFPENNY. above, and CURRENCY. below.

This also has a broad rim, and part of the legend on each side is incused upon the rim.

43.   *O* :   Bust to left BRITISH COLONIES.
      R :   Female seated on bale, TO FACILITATE
               TRADE.

This last token is generally placed amongst the Jamaica
tokens, although I do not know upon what authority. Sandham, in his "Canadian Coins," classes it as "*doubtful.*"
My own opinion is that it is an English-made nineteenth
century token for general circulation.

ST. KITTS, OR ST. CHRISTOPHER.

44.   A double sous of Louis XVI. for Cayenne coun-
             termarked **S . K .**

ST. LUCIA.

45.   Part of a Spanish dollar countermarked S .
             L u c i e.

46.   Part of a Spanish dollar countermarked S and
             L interlinked.
47.   Part of a Spanish dollar countermarked in three
             places, with S and L as before.

ST. NEVIS.

48.   A thin piece of silver stamped with NEVIS. **6**
             (for sixpence).
49.   A Cayenne sous of Louis XV. countermarked
             NEVIS.

ST. VINCENT.

50.   Part of a Spanish dollar countermarked in three
           places, with S and V interlinked.

TOBAGO.

51.   A double sous of Cayenne countermarked **T**
52.   A double sous of Cayenne countermarked T B.
53.   A double sous of Cayenne countermarked T B
                                                     O
54.   A double sous of Cayenne countermarked   O
                                                     T B
55.   A double sous of Cayenne countermarked |TABAGO.|

TORTOLA.

56.   Part of a Spanish dollar countermarked TORTOLA.

Apropos of this piece there is a striking instance of the
ingenuity of man where the making of money is concerned.
This was supposed to be a quarter of a dollar, and circulated
for 1s 3d, but the makers of it got to be so clever as to
make *five quarters* out of a dollar.

Hence arose a great deal of suspicion and dislike of these
pieces, the result being a great depreciation of their value.

TRINIDAD.

57. *O* : HALF STAMPEE . REDEEMABLE AT H .
            E . RAPSEYS.

     R : Rose, shamrock and thistle. BAKERY &
            GROCERY 9 FREDRICK ST PORT /OF/
            SPAIN.

58. *O* : ONE | FARTHING | TOKEN in three lines,
with an ornament above and below.

R : REDEEMABLE BY J.C.D'ADE & CO.
TRINIDAD.

Ruding says that by a proclamation of the Governor of
Trinidad made June 19th, 1811, a piece of silver was ordered
to be struck from the centre of each Spanish dollar, the
dollar so cut to circulate at the rate or value of nine shillings
(currency), and the piece so cut out to pass current for one
shilling.   Now the question arises, were these pieces triform
or heart-shaped ?   If so, that will satisfactorily account for
Spanish money cut in this shape.   Boyne, in his "Silver
Tokens," mentions these, but although he thought they
might be intended for colonial use, he knew nothing of them.

Another unexplained curiosity is a Spanish dollar of
Ferdinand VII., dated 1811, which is countermarked *G R*
surmounted by a crown.   This may have been intended for
use in the West India Islands at this time as so many
expedients were tried to procure currency, or it may possibly
have been used for Gibraltar.   See a note to a somewhat
similar piece for that place.

There is also a triangular portion of the Spanish dollar
met with which is countermarked W.R. and halfpence
with a similar countermark occur.   These are usually assigned
to the West Indies, and doubtless correctly so.   They are as
follows :—

59.   Triangular portion of Spanish dollar countermarked with W R surmounted with crown in
sunk lines.

60.   An Irish halfpenny of George II. countermarked with W.R surmounted with a crown
in raised lines upon an oblong indent with a
serrated edge.

In addition to the foregoing, there was ordered to be
coined for the West India Islands on the 29th April, 1822,

pieces of *half, quarter, eighth, and sixteenth of a dollar,* similar to those struck for the Mauritius, and an attempt was made about the same time to establish an uniform coinage for the British colonies on the decimal system, and coins, 50 and 100 to the dollar, were struck but never circulated; and again *three-penny and three-halfpenny pieces* were ordered to be issued for the West Indies on September 12th, 1834, which pieces are continued to the present time.

SILVER.

Half Dollar.

61.　*O*:　Ornamental shield of arms, GEORGIUS IV D : G : BRITANNIARUM.

　　R:　An anchor with a crown above it, between II-II　COLONIAR : BRITAN : MONET : 1822.

Quarter Dollar.

62.　　　Similar, but with IV-IV at the sides of shield.

One-eighth Dollar.

63.　　　Similar, but with VIII-VIII at the sides of shield

One-sixteenth Dollar.

64.　　　Similar, but with XVI-XVI at the sides of shield.

COPPER.

Two Cents.

65.　*O*:　Laureated bust to left, GEOR : IV : D : G : BR1 : REX.

　　R:　$\frac{1}{50}$ | DOLLAR in two lines within a wreath of oak leaves, COLONIAL 1823.

One Cent.

66.   O :   Similar to preceding but having $\frac{1}{100}$ DOLLAR.
These pieces are patterns and only found as proofs.

An illustration of No. 66 appears upon the title-page.

Threepenny Piece.

67.   O :   Bust to right, GULIELMUS IIII D : G : BRI-TANNIAR : REX F : D :

R : $\mathbf{3}$ crowned, dividing date 18—34 within a wreath of oak leaves.

68.   Similar to last, excepting date, which is 1835.
69.   Similar to last, excepting date, which is 1836.
70.   Similar to last, excepting date, which is 1837.

Three-halfpenny Piece.

71.   O :   As before.

R : $\mathbf{1\frac{1}{2}}$ with a crown above and the date 1834 below, the whole within a wreath of oak leaves.

72.   Similar to last, excepting date, which is 1835.
73.   Similar to last, excepting date, which is 1836.
74.   Similar to last, excepting date, which is 1837.

Threepenny Piece.

75.   Bust to left, VICTORIA : D : G : BRITAN-NIAR . REGINA F : D :

R : $\mathbf{3}$ crowned, dividing date 18—38 within an oak wreath.

These occur of every date since that year to the present.

Three-halfpenny Piece.

76.   O :   As before.

R : $\mathbf{1\frac{1}{2}}$ crowned, date under 1838 within an oak wreath.

77.	Similar to last, excepting date, which is 1839.
78.	Similar to last, excepting date, which is 1840.
79.	Similar to last, excepting date, which is 1841.
80.	Similar to last, excepting date, which is 1842.
81.	Similar to last, excepting date, which is 1843.
82.	Similar to last, excepting date, which is 1860.
83.	Similar to last, excepting date, which is 1862.

In addition to the pierced and countermarked Spanish Dollars previously mentioned for the various Islands, the following are considered by some collectors as belonging to this series :—

DOMINICA.

84. A Spanish Dollar, from which a circular piece with a crenated edge has been cut.

85. The circular portion cut from the foregoing, stamped with a *𝒟*, radiated. There are fifteen crenations.

These pieces have by some been hitherto assigned to Demerara, but upon insufficient data, the probability being that the pierced Dollar described at Nos. 1 and 2 of British Guiana (*which see*) was the one in use in that Colony, and thus rendering it exceedingly unlikely that another, and that so differently stamped, should be in use for the same place.

GUADALOUPE.

86. A Spanish Dollar, from which a quadrangular piece with a crenated edge has been cut, countermarked ɑ with a small crown over it, on both sides.

87. The piece cut out is stamped with a ɑ radiated. There are twelve crenations.

88. A triangular portion of a Spanish Dollar (? quarter) with G stamped on the angle with a punch; also countermarked ɑ s in a square indent, and with a **2** in a circular indent. Cut portions of Dollars also

21 *

occur somewhat similar, countermarked with a **3**, a **4**, and a **6**, sometimes with a small crown above the figure, and sometimes without.

This island was colonized by the French, in whose possession it has mostly been, but was taken from them by the British in 1779, 1794, and 1810, and again in 1815. It has been supposed that the above pieces were made and used by the English during their time of holding the island in the two latter years.

TOBAGO.

89. A Spanish Dollar with a hexagonal piece cut from the centre.

90. The piece cut from the foregoing is countermarked with a **T**

The similarity of this countermark to that used for No. 51 of this series, gives some foundation for the opinion that these pieces were made for use in Tobago.

TRINIDAD.

I have already hazarded a suggestion that the heart-shaped pieces cut from Dollars, and their divisions, may possibly have been made for this island. In addition to these there is another cut Dollar, thought by some to be the one referred to by Ruding. (*See note following No.* 58 *of this series.*) It is as follows :—

91. A Spanish Dollar, from which a circular piece, with fourteen crenations, has been cut.

92. The piece cut from this Dollar is countermarked with a *J* radiated.

BRITISH HONDURAS.

BRITISH Honduras was taken possession of by English settlers from Jamaica soon after a treaty with Spain in 1667. They were often disturbed by the Spaniards until 1783, since which time we have had comparatively peaceable possession. The only coin specially issued for Honduras is the following Cent:

O: Bust to left crowned VICTORIA QUEEN.

R: **1** in a dotted circle. BRITISH HONDURAS above. ONE CENT 1885 below.

BRITISH GUIANA.

(UNITED COLONY OF DEMERARY AND ESSEQUIBO.)

THIS colony is a section of the northern coast of South America, and includes the settlements of Demerara, Essequibo, and Berbice. It was taken from the Dutch in 1796, but restored to them at the Peace of Amiens, in March, 1802. It again surrendered to the British in September, 1803, and finally became an English colony in 1814.

Ruding, in his Annals, states that a Committee of Privy Council for Trade, for the colonies of Demerara and Essequibo, on May 12th, 1809, recommended a silver coinage of tokens to the amount of £10,000. The monetary system at this period was similar to the old Dutch currency : 16 duits or pfennigs = 1 stiver, which was equal to about two-thirds of an English penny. 23 stivers = 1 guilder; this being equal to $1s\ 1\frac{1}{3}d$ English.

In 1839 the old monetary system was abolished, and dollars and cents introduced after the American model, the 3 guilder piece being made to pass for a dollar. No coins were issued after the change in the system, and English, Spanish, Mexican, South American and United States coins are all now legal tenders at authorized rates.

The only issue of copper was in 1813, when pieces of stivers and half-stivers were struck. There is, however, a copper token for one stiver struck in 1838, which is generally considered to have been made for this colony, although I have not been able to find out anything authentic to justify such an assumption. It has been placed here, as it seems as likely to belong to this series as any other. There is a cut Spanish dollar also, which was most likely in use during the English possession, and as this was the first in order of time, we shall give it priority in description.

SILVER.

1.   A Spanish Dollar, with a circular hole with crenated edge cut in the centre, the upper part of the coin countermarked $\dfrac{E\ \mathcal{v}\ D}{3\ G}.$ within a beaded circle (for 3 Guilders).

This is illustrated from a piece in the cabinet of J. B. Caldecott, Esq.

2.   The circular piece with crenated edge cut from the preceding is countermarked $\dfrac{E\ \mathcal{v}\ D}{3\ B\underline{TS}}$ within a beaded circle (for 3 Bits).

Three Guilders.

3.   *O:*   Laureated and armoured bust to right, GEOR-GIVS III DEI GRATIA.

     R: *3* within an oak wreath, a crown above, and the date, 1809 below, COLONIES OF ESSE-QUEBO & DEMARARY TOKEN.

Two Guilders.

4.   Similar, excepting in size and value.

One Guilder.

5.   Similar, excepting in size and value.

Half Guilder.

6.　　　Similar, excepting in size and value.

Quarter Guilder.

7.　　　Similar, excepting in size and value.

　　　　　The dies for these pieces were engraved by
　　　　Mr. Pingo. They have milled edges, and are
　　　　rarely met with in fine condition.

Three Guilders.

8. *O:*　Bust as before, GEORGIUS III D : G : BRI-
　　　　TANIARUM REX.

　R:　*3* within an oak wreath, a crown above and the
　　　　date, 1816 below, UNITED COLONY OF
　　　　DEMERARY & ESSEQUIBO.

Two Guilders.

9.　　　Similar, excepting in size and value.

One Guilder.

10.　　　Similar, excepting in size and value.

Half Guilder.

11.　　　Similar, excepting in size and value.

Quarter Guilder.

12.　　　Similar, excepting in size and value.

　　　　　The dies for these coins were executed by
　　　　Mr. Wyon. A small T. W is under the bust
　　　　on the three larger pieces, and W. only on the
　　　　two smaller. Nos. 8-12 occur as proofs.

WILLIAM IV.

Three Guilders.

13.   *O*   Bust to right.   GULIELMUS IV D: G: BRI-
TANNIAR. REX F: D:

     R: *3* within an oak wreath, a crown above, the date

         1832 below, UNITED COLONY OF DEME-
RARY & ESSEQUIBO.

Two Guilders.

14.   Similar, excepting in size and value.

One Guilder.

15.   Similar, excepting in size and value.

Half Guilder.

16.   Similar, excepting in size and value.

Quarter Guilder.

17.   Similar, excepting in size and value.

Eighth Guilder.

18.   Similar, excepting in size and value.

One Guilder.

19.   Similar to No. 15, excepting date, which is 1833.

Half Guilder.

20.   Similar to last, excepting in size and value.

Quarter Guilder.

21.   Similar to last, excepting in size and value.

Eighth Guilder.

22.   Similar to last, excepting in size and value.

One Guilder.

23.   Similar to No. 15, excepting date, which is 1835.

Half Guilder.

24.   Similar to last, excepting in size and value.

Quarter Guilder.

25.   Similar to last, excepting in size and value.

Eighth Guilder.

26.   Similar to last, excepting in size and value.

One Guilder.

27.   *O* :   Bust as before, legend also as before.

     R :   ONE GUILDER within a wreath, a crown above, and the date, 1836 below. BRITISH GUIANA.

Half Guilder.

28.   Similar, excepting in size and value.

Quarter Guilder.

29.   Similar, excepting in size and value.

Eighth Guilder.

30.   Similar, excepting in size and value.

      The dies were all engraved by Mr. Wyon, and the larger pieces have w. w. upon the truncation of the neck. There are proofs of Nos. 23-26 with both milled and plain edges, and plain edge proofs of Nos. 27-30.

COPPER.

One Stiver.

31.   *O* :   Laureated bust to right, GEORGIUS III . D : G : REX.

     R :   ONE | STIVER in two lines within a wreath, a crown above, the date 1813 below. COLONIES OF ESSEQUEBO & DEMERARY TOKEN .

Half Stiver.

32.   Similar to preceding, excepting in size and value.

There are proofs of these two tokens in gilt, bronze, and copper. The stiver has w. on the shoulder, and the half-stiver T. W. for Thomas Wyon.

A token for one stiver, apparently used for circulation in this colony, is the last of the series.

33. *O :* A female seated, holding cadeceus and palm branch, TRADE & NAVIGATION 1838.

R : ONE | STIVER in two lines within an inner circle, PURE COPPER PREFERABLE TO PAPER.

COINS AND TOKENS

OF THE BRITISH POSSESSIONS

IN

AUSTRALASIA,

COMPRISING

NEW SOUTH WALES.
VICTORIA.
QUEENSLAND.
SOUTH AUSTRALIA
WESTERN AUSTRALIA.

TASMANIA OR VAN DIE-
MAN'S LAND,
AND
NEW ZEALAND.

COINS AND TOKENS OF AUSTRALIA.

OF coins, strictly so called, our Antipodean Colonies have none. It is true that at Melbourne and Sydney there are mints employed, but as the only coins struck are the sovereign and half-sovereign for general circulation, which are similar to our own, with the exception of a minute initial letter as mint-mark, they can scarcely be styled Colonial coins. At the same time as they differ in this respect it was necessary to mention, although not to describe them. Gold coins were struck at the Sydney mint from 1855 to 1870 from dies sent out from the Royal Mint, London, which in 1867 were declared to be current coin of the realm.

There are a very few gold tokens to describe, and also a few in silver, the majority of the tokens consisting of copper pence and halfpence. In describing the latter they will be arranged alphabetically in their respective provinces, placing the provinces in their chronological order.

GOLD.

1. *O* : A crown within an inner circle, 1852 under. GOVERNMENT ASSAY OFFICE * ADELAIDE *

   R : VALUE | ONE | POUND in three lines within a circle. WEIGHT 5 DWT : 15 GRS : * 22 CARATS *

   There is a variety of this which differs in several minor respects.

2. *O :* A kangaroo, 1853 under. PORT PHILIP
AUSTRALIA incuse on a broad rim.

R : **2** inscribed TWO OUNCES in the centre. PURE
AUSTRALIAN GOLD. TWO OUNCES
incuse as before.

One Ounce.

3. **1** inscribed ONE OUNCE. Similar excepting in
size and value.

Half ounce.

4. $\frac{1}{2}$ Similar.

Quarter ounce.

5. $\frac{1}{4}$ Similar.

These pieces only occur as proofs, and in all
probability were never put in circulation.

Sovereign.

6. *O :* Bust to left, filleted, VICTORIA D : G :
BRITANNIAR : REGINA F : D : 1855.

R : AUSTRALIA surmounted by a crown, within
an olive wreath. SYDNEY MINT above,
ONE SOVEREIGN below.

Half Sovereign.

7. Similar excepting in size and value.

Sovereign.

8. Similar to No. 6 excepting date, which is 1856.

Half Sovereign.

9. Similar to No. 7 excepting date, which is 1856.

There are patterns of this design dated
1853, but no issue took place until 1855.
Proofs occur of all these pieces.

Sovereigns.

10. *O :* Bust to left, laureated. VICTORIA D : G :
BRITANNIAR : REG : F : D : 1857.

R : As No. 6.

11. Similar to No. 10 excepting date, which is 1858.

12.	Similar to No. 10 excepting date, which is 1859.
13.	Similar to No. 10 excepting date, which is 1860.
14.	Similar to No. 10 excepting date, which is 1861.
15.	Similar to No. 10 excepting date, which is 1862.
16.	Similar to No. 10 excepting date, which is 1863.
17.	Similar to No. 10 excepting date, which is 1864.
18.	Similar to No. 10 excepting date, which is 1865.
19.	Similar to No. 10 excepting date, which is 1866.
20.	Similar to No. 10 excepting date, which is 1867.
21.	Similar to No. 10 excepting date, which is 1868.
22.	Similar to No. 10 excepting date, which is 1869.
23.	Similar to No. 10 excepting date, which is 1870.

Half Sovereigns.

24.	Similar to No. 10 excepting in size and value, HALF SOVEREIGN.
25.	Similar to last, excepting date, which is 1858.
26.	Similar to last, excepting date, which is 1859.
27.	Similar to last, excepting date, which is 1860.
28.	Similar to last, excepting date, which is 1861.
29.	Similar to last, excepting date, which is 1863.
30.	Similar to last, excepting date, which is 1865.
31.	Similar to last, excepting date, which is 1867.
32.	Similar to last, excepting date, which is 1869.

There are proofs of Nos. 10, 13, 15, 18, 20, 23, 24, 27, 30 and 31, and possibly of other dates. There was no issue of half-sovereigns in 1862, 1864, 1866, 1868 and 1870, but there are patterns (or proofs) of 1862 and 1866. From the year 1871 sovereigns and half-sovereigns were coined at the mints in Sydney and Melbourne and still continue. These are identical with those struck in England, with the exception that a minute s. for Sydney, and m. for Melbourne distinguishes them, and forms a kind of mint-mark.

SILVER.

English silver coins have always been the authorized currency in the Australian colonies, although from a dearth of supply other expedients have been resorted to, many of the traders of New South Wales having issued notes for sums of sixpence and upwards. In the year 1813 an endeavour was made to meet the great need of a silver currency by cutting the Spanish dollar to make two pieces, of five shillings and of fifteenpence respectively. These are as follows :—

33. *O* : FIVE SHILLINGS and two sprigs of laurel, countermarked upon a Spanish dollar from which a circular portion has been cut in the centre.

    R : NEW SOUTH WALES 1813. Countermarked as before.

34. *O* : A crown in the centre NEW SOUTH WALES 1813.

    R : FIFTEEN | PENCE in two lines in the centre. This is made of the piece cut from the centre of No. 33.

Shillings.

35. *O* : ONE | SHILLING | TOKEN in three lines in the centre. SAWMILLS above, MACINTOSH AND DEGRAVES below.

    R : A kangaroo. TASMANIA 1823.

This is a very rare piece, and is most probably a pattern. It seldom occurs except in proof condition.

22

36.   *O* :   Coroneted bust to left. VICTORIA above,
AUSTRALIA below incused upon a broad
engine-turned rim.

  R :   **1** in the centre.   ONE SHILLING.   This
also is incuse, as before.

Sixpence.
37.   **6** Similar to last excepting in size and value.
These are patterns only, not having been
issued, and are exceedingly rare.   They occur
only as proofs, in gold, silver, and copper.

Threepence.
38.   *O* :   A kangaroo to left and an emu to right, a palm-
tree between them. HOGARTH ERICHSEN
& C<u>O</u> JEWELLERS SYDNEY.

  R :   **3** dividing the date, 18—58, within a wreath
of oak.

39.   *O* :   An emu to left and a kangaroo to right, with
a gum-plant between them.   HOGARTH
ERICHSEN & C<u>O</u> SYDNEY.

  R :   As last.

40.   Similar to No. 38, but legend reads PAYABLE
AT   HOGARTH   ERICHSEN   &   C<u>O</u>
SYDNEY.

41.   *O* :   An emu to left, and a kangaroo to right, with a
gum-plant between them. REMEMBRANCE
OF AUSTRALIA.

  R :   **3** within an olive wreath. HOGARTH &
ERICHSEN SYDNEY 1860.

42.   *O* :   Australian arms, rising sun as crest, supporters
kangaroo and emu. SYDNEY NEW SOUTH
WALES . 1854.

  R :   **3** surmounted by rising sun SILVER
TOKEN . J . G . T.

   There is a silver piece about sixpenny size
which can scarcely be classed as a token, but
which I wish to mention here ; it is as
follows :—

O: Spade and anchor crowned, S . U . at the sides.
SOUTH AUSTRALIA'S PRIDE.
R: Two hands clasped, SAILORS & BROTHERS.

COPPER TOKENS.

These pieces, which constitute the majority of the Australasian currency, are for the most part very uninteresting, having little artistic merit, and, of course, no antiquity to recommend them. They usually have little but the name and address, or business advertisement, together with a Coat of Arms, or some emblem of the trade of their various issues.

Some few, however, are very fine examples of die-sinking and stamping, and one or two of Sydney are quaint specimens of Colonial workmanship. As before stated, the arrangement will be in provinces, first the pence and then the halfpence of each province, arranging the towns alphabetically, and placing the names of the issues in like order.

NEW SOUTH WALES.

Bathurst.

Penny size.

43. O: COLLINS | & CO in two lines in a circle. CHEAP CLOTHING BAZAAR : BATHURST :
R: A kangaroo and emu, T STOKES MELBOURNE under. NEW SOUTH WALES . 1864.

Goulburn.

44. O: A golden fleece in a beaded circle. DAVIES, ALEXANDER & CO . GOULBURN.
R: Australian arms in circle. AUSTRALIAN STORES GOULBURN . ESTABLISHED 1837.

Jamberoo.

45. O: Rose, shamrock and thistle. WILLIAM ALLEN . JAMBEROO . GENERAL STORES.
R: Australian arms. ADVANCE AUSTRALIA above, 1855 beneath.

22 *

Morpeth.

46. *O :*   JAMES CAMPBELL above. GENERAL STORES in centre. . MORPETH . beneath.

    R :   Female standing holding scales and cornucopia, a ship in the distance. AUSTRALIA.

Sydney.

47. *O :*   BATTLE | & | WEIGHT. in three lines in inner circle. 81 & 83 SOUTH HEAD ROAD SYDNEY DRAPERS &c.

    R :   Female standing holding scales and cornucopia.

48. *O :*   ONE | PENNY in two lines in centre. FLAVELLE BROS & Cǫ SYDNEY & BRISBANE.

    R :   Kangaroo and em. W. J. TAYLOR LONDON ̣ in exergue.

49. *O :*   ONE | PENNY in two lines FLAVELLE BROS. & CO. above OPTICIANS & JEWELLERS | . SYDNEY & BRISBANE . below.

    R :   As last.

50. *O :*   HANKS | AND | COMFʸ. in three lines in centre. AUSTRALIAN TEA MART. above, SYDNEY. beneath.

    R :   Australian arms PEACE & PLENTY above, 1857. beneath.

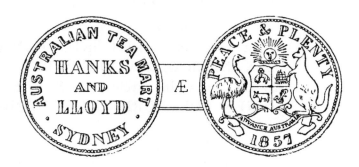

51. *O :*   HANKS | AND | LLOYD in three lines in centre, AUSTRALIAN TEA MART above . SYDNEY . beneath.

R : TO COMMEMORATE THE OPENING OF THE SYDNEY RAILWAY 26TH SEPTR. 1855.

These two tokens are *muled* to form varieties, and there are slight differences in the dies. The token illustrated being one of the *mules* having the *O* : of No. 51, with the *R* : of No. 50.

52. *O* : ESTABLISHED | 1820 | IREDALE & CO | SYDNEY. in four lines—within a circle. IRON MERCHANTS AND GENERAL IRONMONGERS.

R : Britannia seated holding olive branch and trident, a ship in the distance BRITANNIA.

53. *O* : Same as No. 52.

R : Female standing holding scales and cornucopia, water and ship in distance . AUSTRALIA .

There are several varieties of this token differing in the formation of the letters.

54. *O* : J. M. LEICH | TOBACCONIST | 524 GEORGE STREET | SYDNEY . in four lines.

R : Britannia seated similar to No. 52.

55. *O* : J. MACGREGOR | 320 | GEORGE STREET | SYDNEY in four lines. THE CITY TEA WARE- HOUSE * * *

R : Australian arms, ESTABLISHED 1855 in centre. THE SULTANS STEAM COFFEE WORKS * SYDNEY *

56. *O* : METCALFE | & | LLOYD | 478 GEORGE St | SYDNEY in centre. SHIPPING AND FAMILY GROCERS.

R : WINE | AND | SPIRIT | MERCHANTS = PUR- VEYORS OF THE CONCENTRATED FAMILY COFFEE 1863.

57. *O* : B. PALMER | PITT & KING St | SYDNEY = WHOLESALE WINE & SPIRIT DEPOT.

R : A bird holding an olive branch in its mouth. LIVERPOOL ARMS.

58. *O*:   SMITH, PEATE & Co | GROCERS | TEA
           DEALERS | & | WINE MERCHANTS |
           258 & 260 | GEORGE St | SYDNEY.

    R: Female holding scales and cornucopia, water
           and ship in distance ESTABLISHED 1836.

59. *O*:   A view of stores, 424 over door. Another
           building behind, on which is TEA | STORES |
           STEAM | COFFEE | MILLS in five lines. ESTAB-
           LISHED | 1835 | SYDNEY below.   J. C. T. in
           small characters (for J. C. Thornthwaite).

    R: Britannia seated holding trident. BRITANNIA
           1852.

60.   Similar to last except that the arrangement of
           words vary thus TEA | STORES | STEAM | COFFEE
           MILLS in four lines and ESTABLISHED 1835 |
           SYDNEY is in two lines.

61.   Similar to No. 59 excepting date, which is 1853.

62. *O*:   DIE SINKER AND MEDALLIST in centre
           with rose, shamrock, and thistle interspersed
           J. C. THORNTHWAITE. — BOURKE
           STREET SURRY HILLS.

    R: Australian arms.   ADVANCE AUSTRALIA
           1854.

63. *O*:   A. TOOGOOD | MERCHANT | PITT & KING ST. |
           SYDNEY in four lines.

    R: Female seated holding scales and cornucopia.
           AUSTRALIA 1855.

64. *O*:   WEIGHT | AND | JOHNSON | DRAPERS |
           & | OUTFITTERS in six lines in centre.
           LIVERPOOL & LONDON HOUSE. above.
           PITT STREET SYDNEY. beneath.

    R: Female standing holding scales and cornucopia,
           water and ship in distance.

65. *O*:   Bust to left. WHITTY & BROWN MAKERS
           above. SYDNEY beneath.

    R: Female standing as last. NEW SOUTH WALES.

66. *O* :   A ram. . PEACE AND PLENTY . SYDNEY .
          N . S . W .

   R :   As No. 65.

67. *O* :   ONE | PENNY in two lines in an inner circle.
          ADVANCE AUSTRALIA ✤ ✤ ✤

   R :   As No. 65.

Wagga Wagga.

68. *O* :   LOVE & ROBERTS STOREKEEPERS in
          centre. WAGGA WAGGA above. NEW
          SOUTH WALES beneath.

   R :   A plough . T. STOKES MELBOURNE under it. THE
          COMMERCIAL PASTORAL & FARMING
          INTERESTS : 1865.

Wollongong.

69. *O* :   W. F. & D. L. LLOYD | DRAPERS
          GROCERS | WINE | & SPIRIT | MER-
          CHANTS | WOLLONGONG in six lines.

   R :   Australian arms.   COLONIAL PRODUCE
          TAKEN IN EXCHANGE (1859).

Morpeth.

Halfpenny size.

70. *O* :   JAMES CAMPBELL GENERAL STORES
          MORPETH.

   R :   Female standing holding scales and cornucopia,
          a ship in the distance AUSTRALIA.

Sydney.

71.   HANKS AND COMPy.   Similar to No. 50.

72.   HANKS AND LLOYD.   Similar to No. 51.
          These two, like the pennies, are muled to
          make varieties.

73.   J. MACGREGOR.   Similar to No. 55.

74.   METCALFE & LLOYD.   Similar to No. 56.

75.   SMITH PEATE & CO.   Similar to No. 58.

76.   TEA STORES. Similar to No. 59.
77. *O*: F. C. THORNTHWAITE. Similar to No. 62.
    R: Australian arms. SYDNEY . NEW SOUTH
          WALES 1854.
78. *O*: WEIGHT & JOHNSON | DRAPERS | &c |
          LIVERPOOL | & | LONDON HOUSE |
          249 & 251 PITT ST | SYDNEY displayed in
          eight lines.
    R: As No. 64.

Woolongong.

79.'   W. F. & D. L. LLOYD. Similar to No. 69.

VICTORIA.

Ballarat.

Penny size.
80. *O*: Tobacco plant in flower TOBACCO under J. R.
          GRUNDY . MERCHANT, BALLAARAT . 1861.
    R: Australian arms. INDUSTRIA ET FIDES
          OMNIA VINCENT over. VICTORIA
          beneath.
81. *O*: A sprig of tobacco. J. R. GRUNDY MERCHANT
          BALLARAT . 1861.
    R: Female standing holding scales and cornucopia.
          ' Legend as last in raised letters on a broad
          rim.
82. *O*: DAVID JONES | IMPORTER | BALLAARAT | ESTAB:
          1853 in four lines in centre . CRITERION
          DRAPERY ESTABLISHMENT ✳ WHOLESALE AND
          RETAIL ✳
    R: View of the house. CRITERION HOUSE
          STURT ST. BALLAARAT 1862 DAVID JONES
          PROPRIETOR.

83. O: SOUTHWARD | & | SUMPTON | BALLARAT in four lines in inner circle WHOLESALE GROCERS * WINE & SPIRIT MERCHANTS *

R: Australian arms. ADVANCE BALLARAT on scroll. SOUTHWARD & SUMPTON BALLARAT.

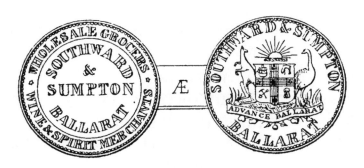

84. O: J. TAYLOR | RED HOUSE | CORNER OF | DANNA & RAGLAN | STREETS | BALLARAT in six lines in centre. BREAD AND BISCUIT BAKER FAMILY GROCER.

R: Australian arms VICTORIA 1862 above. T. STOKES MAKER 100 COLLINS ST. EAST MELBOURNE beneath.

85. O: As last.
R: A wheatsheaf ADVANCE AUSTRALIA 1862.

86. O: As last.
R: A branch of vine with grapes and leaves. VICTORIA 1862 IN VINO VERITAS. T. STOKES MAKER MEL.

87. O: W. R. WATSON & CO. WINE & SPIRIT MERCHANTS TOWN HALL HOTEL ARMSTRONG ST. BALLARAT.

R: As No. 86.

88. Similar to No. 87 except that the vine branch on Rev: is different and the letters of maker's name are larger. For the several varieties of this Rev: see under T. Stokes, Melbourne.

Bendigo.

89. · O : HODGSON BROs. | sailors | gully | & | california | gully | BENDIGO within a circle. WHOLESALE & RETAIL GROCERS & PRODUCE MERCHANTS :

R : An emu, sun's rays at back . ADVANCE VICTORIA on scroll . VICTORIA 1862 . above, T. STOKES MAKER 100 COLLINS S^T EAST MELBOURNE . beneath.

Castlemaine.

90. O : T. BUTTERWORTH & CO. **1** FOREST STREET . CASTLEMAINE.

R : WINE | & | SPIRIT | MERCHANTS in centre. WHOLESALE & RETAIL GROCERS & DRAPERS *

91.   Similar to last excepting that the letters on *Obv* : are bolder.

92. O : As 90.

R : Female seated holding scales and cornucopia . 1859.

93. O : R. CALDER | BARKER ST. | CASTLE-MAINE in three lines in centre . WINE SPIRIT & GENERAL PROVISION MERCHANT : 1862 :

R : Australian arms, &c., as 84.

94. O : W. FROOMES | MARKET SQ^R. | CASTLE-MAINE in three lines in centre. FAMILY DRAPER CLOTHIER & OUTFITTER :

R : As No. 84.

95. O : MURRAY | AND | CHRISTIE | CASTLE-MAINE in four lines.

R : GROCERS | IRONMONGERS | CHINA & GLASS | WARE | MERCHANTS in five lines.

The R : of this token is found *muled* with R : of No. 84.

96. *O*: G. RYLAND | DRAPER | AND | CLOTHIER | MARKET SQ.ᴿᴱ | CASTLEMAINE in six lines.

    R: Similar to No. 84.

Eagle Hawk.

97. *O*: R. GRIEVE EAGLE HAWK in a circle. WHOLESALE & RETAIL GROCER :

    R: Similar to No. 84.

98. *O*: J. W. & G. WILLIAMS | GROCERS | IRON-MONGERS | & | DRAPERS | EAGLE HAWK in six lines.

    R: GOLD OFFICE | WINE. SPIRIT | & | COLONIAL | PRODUCE | MERCHANTS EAGLE HAWK in seven lines.

Geelong.

99. *O*: R. PARKER IRONMONGER in two lines in centre, MOORABOOL STREET GEELONG

    R: Female standing holding scales and cornucopia a ship in the distance. AUSTRALIA.

100. Similar to last except there are two dots after initial R : PARKER and a dot after the word IRONMONGER.

101. Similar to No. 99 excepting that tails of the R'S in the name are turned up.

    There are several other slight varieties of this token.

Melbourne.

102. *O*: Female seated holding scales and cornucopia MELBOURNE VICTORIA 1858.

    R: Australian arms. PEACE & PLENTY.

103. *O:*   ✻ JOHN ANDREW & Co. ✻ IMPORTERS AND GENERAL DRAPERS ✻ in outer circle. 11 LONSDALE STREET WEST ✻ MELBOURNE ✻ within. In the centre a lion with a small crown on his head, and paw resting on a shield.

     R: Female seated holding scales and cornucopia MELBOURNE VICTORIA 1860.

       A similar design to the centre of this token is found on Nos. 109, 118-121, and 146.

104. *O:*   JNO. ANDREW & CO | DRAPERS &c in two lines in the centre. ✻ 11 LONSDALE S.T WEST MELBOURNE.

     R: Kangaroo and emu, VICTORIA 1862.

105. *O:*   I. BOOTH | ✻ DRAPER ✻ | OUTFITTER &c | MELBOURNE | VICTORIA in five lines.

     R: Britannia seated with olive branch and trident BRITANNIA.

106. *O:*   A. DAVIDSON | 112 | COLLINS S.T EAST | CORNER | OF | RUSSELL S.T | MELBOURNE in seven lines within a circle. GROCER WINE & SPIRIT MERCHANT :

     R: As No. 86.

107. *O:*   As last.

     R: As 88.

108. *O:*   EDW.D DE'CARLE & C.O . AUCTIONEERS &c MELBOURNE.

     R: Female seated holding scales and sword. TASMANIA ⚛ ANNO 1855 ⚛

109. *O:*   E. DE CARLE & Co. AUCTIONEERS & LAND AGENTS in outer circle. QUEENS ROYAL ARCADE OFFICE ⚛ within. In the centre a design as No. 103.

     R: Female seated, MELBOURNE VICTORIA 1855.

110. *O* : E. DE CARLE & Co. GROCERS & SPIRIT MERCHANTS . MELBOURNE & PLENTY VICTORIA.

    R : As No. 105.

111. *O* : S. DEEBLE | DRAPER in two lines within a circle LONDON HOUSE BOURKE S^T : MELBOURNE:

    R : Australian arms VICTORIA . 1862 . above, T. STOKES MAKER 100 COLLINS ST. EAST MELBOURNE beneath in two curved lines.

112. *O* : As last.

    R : Similar to last but with ADVANCE AUSTRALIA on scroll under arms.

113. *O* : As last.

    R : An emu with sunrise behind. VICTORIA . 1862 . Maker's name as before.

114. *O* : As last.

    R : Wheatsheaf ADVANCE AUSTRALIA.

115. *O* : EVANS | & | FOSTER | 78 | BOURKE S_T. | EAST in six lines, BOOKSELLERS & STATIONERS : MELBOURNE :

    R : As 113.

116. *O* : A " FLAGSTAFF." FENWICK BROTHERS IMPORTERS & CLOTHIERS 225 KING S_T.

    R : Bust of Queen Victoria, 225 KING STREET MELBOURNE . VICTORIA.

117. *O* : As last.

    R : Similar to last but the bust is smaller and within an inner circle.

118.   *O* :   HIDE & DE CARLE . GROCERS & WINE
              MERCHANTS in outer circle.   ELIZABETH
              STREET . MELBOURNE . within.   In the centre a
              design similar to No. 103.

       R :   Female seated.   MELBOURNE . VICTORIA .
              1857.

119.   Similar to last except date, which is 1858.

120.   Similar to 119 except that the letters and
              figures on *R* : are larger, and that there is
              no dot after the word VICTORIA

                 There are many minor varieties of this
              token.

121.   *O* :   A. G. HODGSON ⚜ OUTFITTER AND
              TAILOR ⚜ in outer circle.   13 LONSDALE
              STREET WEST ⚜ MELBOURNE ⚜ within.   In the
              centre a design similar to No. 103.

       R :   As No. 118, but dated 1860.

122.   *O* :   A. G. HODGSON | OUTFITTER | &c. = 13 LONS-
              DALE St. WEST   MELBOURNE.

       R :   Kangaroo and emu facing.   VICTORIA 1862.

123.   *O* :   J. HOSIE | a thistle with two leaves |
              –10 & 12– | BOURKE St. | EAST in five
              lines within a circle.   THE SCOTCH PIE
              SHOP : MELBOURNE :

       R :   Australian arms.   VICTORIA 1862.

124.   *O* :   As last.

       R :   Similar to last except that there is a rose,
              two thistles, and shamrock between shield of
              arms and scroll.

125.   *O* :   As 122.

       R :   Emu and sunrise, VICTORIA 1862.

126.   Similar to last but with rose, shamrock and
              thistle under emu.

127.   *O* :   As 122.

       R :   Vine branch, J. STOKES MAKER within a circle.
              IN VINO VERITAS : VICTORIA . 1862 :

128.   *O* :   ROBERT HYDE & CO. MELBOURNE | GENERAL | MARINE | STORE | SHIPPERS OF | RAGS GLASS | METALS | &c.

      R :   Australian arms, PEACE & PLENTY 1857.

129.   Similar to last except date, which is 1861.

130.   *O* :   S & S LAZARUS | WHOLESALE | AND RETAIL | FANCY REPOSITORY | 29, 30, 31, 69, 70 & 71 | QUEENS | ARCADE | MELBOURNE in eight lines.

      R :   IMPORTERS | of | BIRMINGHAM | AND | SHEFFIELD | WARE | STATIONERY &c in seven lines.

131.   *O* :   LEVY BROTHERS . ARCADE, MELBOURNE . = IMPORTERS | OF | FANCY | GOODS.

      R :   Female seated holding scales and cornucopia. AUSTRALIA 1855.

132.   *O* :   J. McFARLANE | WHOLESALE AND RETAIL | GROCER in the centre. CORNER OF ELIZABETH & LONSDALE S^{TS.} MELBOURNE.

      R :   Female standing, to the right a lion, to left a lamb. PEACE AND PLENTY.

133.   *O* :   A "buggy." MILLER BROTHERS COACH BUILDERS MELBOURNE.

      R :   Australian arms, VICTORIA . 1862, maker's name under as No. 111.

134.   *O* :   As last.

      R :   Emu and sunrise, VICTORIA . 1862.

135.   *O* :   As last.

      R :   Vine branch, IN VINO VERITAS :

136.   Similar to last excepting that the vine leaves on *R* : are different.

137.   *O* :   MILLER & DISMOOR | DRAPERS | HABER-DASHERS &c | COLLINS . ST | MELBOURNE.

      R :   ONE | PENNY | TOKEN | in three lines SMITH & KEMP BIRM^M under in minute letters.

138.   *O* :   MOUBRAY LUSH | & Co | DRAPERS |
               MELBOURNE in four lines.

       R :   Female standing holding scales and cornucopia,
               ships in distance AUSTRALIA.

139.   *O* :   : GEORGE NICHOLS : opposite CORNER to
               POST OFFICE within a circle.   BOOK-
               SELLER & STATIONER . MELBOURNE.

       R :   Australian arms . VICTORIA . 1862 . Maker's
               name under.

140.   *O* :   HUGH PECK 67 LITTLE COLLINS STREET EAST
               RENTS & DEBTS COLLECTED PROCESS SERVED
               LEVIES FOR RENT ESTABLISHED 1853 MELBOURNE
               Arranged about the coin.

       R :   HUGH PECK 67 LITTLE COLLINS STREET EAST
               ESTATE AGENT & MONEY LENDER HOTEL BROKER
               & VALUATOR ESTABLISHED 1853 MELBOURNE
               Arranged about the coin.

141.   *O* :   As *R* : of last.

       R :   Australian arms, VICTORIA . 1862 Maker's
               name under as No. 111.

142.   *O* :   GEO. PETTY 157 ELIZABETH S^T SMITH-
               FIELD Co MELBOURNE.

       R :   Figure of Justice holding scales and wand.
               VICTORIA.

143.   *O* :   ROBINSON BROs & CO 41 FLINDERS St
               WEST within a circle. VICTORIA COPPER
               WORKS : MELBOURNE :

       R :   Emu and sunrise. VICTORIA . 1862 Maker's
               name and address under.

144.   Similar to last except with rose, shamrock, and
               thistle under emu on *R* :

145.   *O* :   Similar to last.
       R :   Vine branch VICTORIA 1862.

146. *O* : G & W. H. ROCKE . ENGLISH FURNI-
TURE IMPORTERS in outer circle.
18 LONSDALE STREET EAST . MELBOURNE within.
The design in centre similar to No. 103.

R : Female seated, holding scales and cornucopia.
MELBOURNE VICTORIA 1859.

147. *O* : ANNAND SMITH & Co FAMILY GROCERS
. MELBOURNE.

R : Britannia seated, holding olive branch and
trident. BRITANNIA.

148. Similar to last except the olive branch has 11
leaves instead of 14 and there is a minute
H & S at back of shield. (For Heaton &
Sons.)

149. *O* : THOMAS STOKES MAKER 100 COLLINS
ST . EAST ✲ MELBOURNE ✲

R : Australian arms. VICTORIA . 1862. Maker's
name and address under.

150. Similar to last but with a rose, shamrock, and
two thistle leaves between scroll and shield
and maker's name is also smaller.

151. *O* : ´ As 147.

R : Emu and sunrise. VICTORIA . 1862. Maker's
name as before.

152. *O* : T. STOKES | DIE | SINKER | SEAL EN-
GRAVER | LETTER CUTTER | CHECK
& TOKEN | MAKER | MELBOURNE in
eight lines.

R : As last.

153. *O* : T. STOKES | 100 | COLLINS ST | EAST
| MELBOURNE in centre. LETTER
CUTTER BUTTON CHECK & TOKEN
MAKER in outer circle.

R : Vine branch VICTORIA 1862. Maker's name
and address under.

154. *O* :   Centre as last, LETTER CUTTER SEAL EN-
             GRAVER TOKEN MAKER in outer circle.

     R :   Vine branch with eleven large and four small
             leaves and two bunches of grapes VICTORIA
             1862 : IN VINO VERITAS :

155. *O* :   Similar to last except that there are dots after
             CUTTER—ENGRAVER & MAKER.

     R :   Vine branch with nine large and four small
             leaves, two bunches of grapes and tendril.
             T. STOKES MAKER MEL. under.

156. *O* :   As 154.

     R :   Emu and sunrise VICTORIA 1862 rose, sham-
             rock and thistle under emu.

157. *O* :   T. STOKES | 100 | COLLINS ST | EAST in
             four lines within a circle. BUTTON CHECK
             & TOKEN MAKER MELBOURNE.

     R :   Emu and sunrise VICTORIA 1862.

158. *O* :   T. STOKES | 100 | COLLINS ST | EAST |
             MELBOURNE in five lines within a circle.
             MILITARY ORNAMENT BUTTON &
             TOKEN MAKER :

     R :   A wheatsheaf ADVANCE AUSTRALIA 1862.

159. *O* :   As last.

     R :   As 155.

160. *O* :   A wheatsheaf ADVANCE AUSTRALIA 1862.

     R :   Vine branch with eleven large and five small
             leaves, two bunches of grapes and one tendril.

161.   Similar to last, but with eleven large and three
             small leaves.

162.   Similar to last, but with nine large and five
             small leaves, a bunch of grapes beneath the
             fifth and ninth leaf.

163.   Similar to last, a bunch of grapes beneath the
             sixth and ninth leaf.

164. *O* :   Australian arms, VICTORIA . 1862 T. STOKES
             MAKER 100 COLLINS STREET MELBOURNE.

R :   Vine branch with eleven large leaves and five small. Grapes beneath seventh and ninth leaf.

165.   Similar but with ten large and four small leaves. Grapes beneath seventh and tenth leaf.

166.   Similar but with ten large and four small leaves. Grapes beneath fifth and eighth leaf.

It would be difficult to say whether or not some of these are mules, most likely the dies from which they were struck were used as R : dies for other pieces.

167. O :   T. WARBURTON | 11 | LITTLE | BOURKE ST. | WEST in five lines within a circle. IRON & ZINC SPOUTING WORKS : MELBOURNE :

R :   Australian arms . VICTORIA . 1862. Maker's name and address as before.

168. O :   As last.
R :   As No. 153.

169. O :   As last.
R :   As No. 155.

170. O :   As last.
R :   As No. 157.

171. O :   As last.
R :   As No. 158.

172. O :   Female seated, holding scales and cornucopia. WARNOCK BROs MELBOURNE & MALDON.

R :   Australian arms PEACE & PLENTY 1861.

173.   Similar to last, except that there is no & on O : and date on R : is 1863.

Port Albert.

174. O :   PORT | ALBERT | & | SALE | in four lines within a circle. GIPPSLAND : HARD-WARE COMPANY :

R :   Australian arms. VICTORIA . 1862 Maker's name &c. as before.

175. *O*: As last.

    R: A plough TRADE & AGRICULTURE Maker's name &c. as last.

Richmond.

176. *O*: BARROWCLOUGH 100 BRIDGE ROAD within a circle. BOOKSELLER & STATIONER * RICHMOND *

    R: Australian arms VICTORIA 1862. Rose, shamrock, and thistle under shield. Maker's name &c. as No. 174.

177. *O*: R. B. RIDLER | 187 | BRIDGE | ROAD | RICHMOND in five lines within a circle. WHOLESALE & RETAIL BUTCHER :

    R: As No. 174.

178. *O*: As last.

    R: Emu and sunrise, VICTORIA . 1862.

179. *O*: As last.

    R: Wheatsheaf, ADVANCE AUSTRALIA . 1862.

Sale (see also Port Albert).

180. *O*: JAs. DAVEY | & Co. | GIPPS LAND | STORE | FOSTER St. | SALE = WHOLE-SALE & RETAIL DRAPERS GROCERS & IMPORTERS :

    R: As 174.

181. *O* · J. D. LEESON : WATCHMAKER & JEWELLER : FANCY MUSEUM SALE.

    R: As last.

Sandhurst.

182. *O*: STEAD BROTHERS | FRUITERERS | GROCERS | & SEEDSMEN | PALL MALL | SANDHURST.

    R · As No. 174.

183. *O*: As last.

    R: Vine branch, VICTORIA 1862 : IN VINO VERITAS :

Sandridge.

184. *O* : W. C. COOK | BAY ST. | SANDRIDGE
ODDFELLOWS STORE within a circle.
SUGAR COMPANIES TREACLE DE-
LIVERED ORDERS PUNCTUALLY ATTENDED TO.

    R : As No. 174.

South Yarra.

185. *O* : THOs. H. COPE | GENERAL | DRAPER
within a circle. GARDENERS CREEK
ROAD : SOUTH YARRA :

    R : As 174.

Warrnambool.

186. *O* : WILLIAM   BATEMAN   JUN^R   &   C^O
WARRNAMBOOL . around within a circle.
VICTORIA in the centre. IMPORTERS
AND GENERAL MERCHANTS . 1855 .
in outer circle.

    R : Female standing, holding scales and cornucopia.
A ship in the distance. AUSTRALIA.

187. *O* : W. W. JAMESON | & Co | STOREKEEPERS
= LIEBIG STREET WARRNAMBOOL.

    R : As last excepting that the date, 1862, is beneath
the figure.

Williamstown.

188. *O* : MASON | & | CULLEY in three lines in an
inner circle. GENERAL STORES . WIL-
LIAMSTOWN.

    R : Figure of Britannia holding scales and trident.
VICTORIA

Melbourne.

Halfpenny size.

189. *O* : A kangaroo, MELBOURNE. Maker's name
under. W. J. TAYLOR MEDALIST TO THE GREAT
EXHIBITION 1851.

    R : Britannia seated, holding olive branch and
wand. AUSTRALIA.

190.   *O* :   ADAMSON, WATTS, M^CKECHNIE & Co⚜

            WHOLESALE & RETAIL WAREHOUSEMEN

     R :   11 COLLINS S⊤. EAST ✳ MELBOURNE ✳
            MAY 1s⊤ 1855.

191.   *O* :   JOHN ANDREW & Co. IMPORTERS AND
            GENERAL DRAPERS . in outer circle
            11 LONSDALE STREET WEST . MEL-
            BOURNE . in inner circle. In the centre a
            lion with his paw resting on a shield.

     R :   Female seated holding scales and cornucopia,
            a ship in the distance. MELBOURNE
            VICTORIA 1860.

192.   *O* :   J<small>NO</small>. ANDREW & Co. | DRAPERS &c. = 11
            LONSDALE S⊤. WEST MELBOURNE.

     R :   Kangaroo and emu, VICTORIA 1862. Maker's
            name and address under kangaroo. COARD
            LONDON.

193.   *O* :   CROMBIE CLAPPERTON & FINLAY —
            41 WEST LONSDALE STREET ∘ ✿ ∘

     R :   A kangaroo, MELBOURNE. Maker's name and
            address under as *O* : of No. 189.

194.   *O* :   HIDE & DE CARLE . GROCERS & WINE
            MERCHANTS in outer circle ELIZABETH
            STREET | MELBOURNE . within. In the
            centre a design similar to that of No. 191.

     R :   Female seated holding scales and cornucopia
            MELBOURNE . VICTORIA . 1857.

195.   Similar to last, except date, which is 1858.

196.   *O* :   A. G. HODGSON ⚜ OUTFITTER AND
            TAILOR⚜in outer circle 13 LONSDALE STREET
            WEST ⚜ MELBOURNE ⚜ within. In the centre a
            design similar to No. 191.

     R :   As 191.

197.   *O* :   A. G. HODGSON | OUTFITTER | &c in three lines.
            13 LONSDALE S⊤. WEST MELBOURNE.

     R :   Kangaroo and emu, VICTORIA 1862. Maker's
            name and address under COARD LONDON.

198. *O*: THE ORIGINAL ✳ SCOTCH PIE SHOP ✳

    R: 12 BOURKE ST EAST in three lines.

        This token is halfpenny size, but a specimen in the author's cabinet is countermarked 1ˢ

199. *O*: ROBERT HYDE & Co. MELBOURNE GENERAL MARINE STORE SHIPPERS OF RAGS GLASS METALS &C.

    R: Australian arms, PEACE & PLENTY 1857.

200.   Similar to last, except date, which is 1861.

201. *O*: JAMES NOKES GROCER MELBOURNE.

    R: IN COMMEMORATION OF THE LANDING OF ⚜ — SIR CHARLES HOTHAM 22ᴅ JUNE 1854.

202. *O*: As last.

    R: Britannia seated holding palm branch and wand. AUSTRALIA.

203. *O*: T. STOKES | DIE | SINKER | SEAL EN-GRAVER | LETTER CUTTER | CHECK & TOKEN | MAKER | MELBOURNE in eight lines.

    R: MILITARY ORNAMENT AND BUTTON MAKER in outer circle. T. STOKES: 100 COLLINS ST. EAST MELBOURNE within. ELECTRO | PLATING | AND | GILDING in four lines in the centre.

204. *O*: T. W. THOMAS & Co. GROCERS : ⚜ MELBOURNE ⚜

    R: As 201.

205. *O*: THRALE & CROSS . FAMILY GROCER & EGG POWDER STORE HOWARD Sᴛ. NORTH MELBOURNE.

    R: Kangaroo, MELBOURNE. Maker's name and address under as *O*: of No. 189.

206. *O*: As last.

    R: Britannia seated, holding palm branch and wand. AUSTRALIA.

South Yarra.

207. *O:* FISHER | DRAPER | MARLBOROUGH | HOUSE
GARDINERS CREEK ROAD in five lines.

R: Kangaroo and emu, AUSTRALIA 1857.

QUEENSLAND.

Penny size.

208. *O:* MERRY & BUSH . MERCHANTS & GENERAL
IMPORTERS . QUEENSLAND . 1863.

R: Australian arms. PEACE & PLENTY.

Brisbane.

209. *O:* and *R:* alike. BROOKES IRONMONGERS BRIS-
BANE.

210. Similar to last, except that the words "ironmongers" and "Brisbane" are ornamental
instead of plain.

211. *O:* W. & B. BROOKES | IRONMONGERS | BRIS-
BANE, in three lines.

R: Australian arms. QUEENSLAND 1863.

212. *O:* J. W. BUXTON STATIONERY STORES.

R: LADIES   WAREHOUSE   BRISBANE
: QUEENSLAND :

213. *O:* ONE | PENNY in two lines in centre. LAR-
COMBE & COMP^Y ✢ BRISBANE. ✢

R: LARCOMBE & COMP^Y FURNISHING
DRAPERS TAILORS &c. · ✢ ·

214. *O:* As last.

R: As No. 216.
This is most probably a mule.

215. *O:* J. SAWYER | WHOLESALE | & RETAIL |
TOBACCONIST | BRISBANE in five lines.

R: Australian arms. QUEENSLAND 1864.

216. *O*: ONE | PENNY in two lines in centre. STEWART & HEMMANT ✢ DRAPERS ✢

R: An emu. CRITERION . BRISBANE & ROCKHAMPTON . Maker's name and address under W. J. TAYLOR LONDON.

217. *O*: STEWART & HEMMANT CRITERION BRISBANE.

R: DRAPERS in centre. WHOLESALE above, RETAIL beneath.

Ipswich.

218. *O*: T. H. JONES | & Co | IPSWICH | QUEENSLAND | AUSTRALIA in five lines within a circle. IRONMONGERS & GENERAL IMPORTERS ❀

R: Female standing, holding scales and cornucopia. A ship in the distance AUSTRALIA.

219. *O*: JOHN PETTIGREW | & C$^{o.}$ | IPSWICH in three lines in the centre. WHOLESALE AND RETAIL GENERAL MERCHANTS.

R: Australian arms. QUEENSLAND 1865.

This token is of bronze, and rather smaller than the usual penny size.

Rockhampton.

220. *O*: BELL | & | GARDNER in three lines in centre. IRONMONGERS ✡ ROCKHAMPTON ✡

R: PENNY | TOKEN surrounded by a wreath of flowers. The rising sun above.

221. *O*:   QUEENSLAND STORES ROCKHAMPTON
D. T. MULLIGAN.

     R: As No. 219 excepting date, which is 1863.

Toowoomba.

222. *O*:   **T. F. MERRY & Co.** GENERAL MERCHANTS
TOOWOOMBA.

     R: Australian arms. PEACE & PLENTY.

Ipswich.

Halfpenny size.

223.   Similar to No. 219 excepting in size and value.
This token and the penny which it
resembles is of bronze and of the same size
and weight as the English bronze coinage.

Rockhampton.

224.   Similar to No. 221 excepting in size and value.

Toowoomba.

225.   Similar to No. 222 excepting in size and value.

SOUTH AUSTRALIA.

Adelaide.

Penny size.

226. *O*:   CROCKER | & | HAMILTON | **ADELAIDE** |
PORT ADELAIDE in five lines.

     R: CROCKER | & | HAMILTON in three lines in
centre. **DRAPERS CLOTHIERS** &c.

227. *O*:   **HARROLD BROTHERS** | WHOLESALE | & |
RETAIL | IRONMONGERS | HINDLEY
Sᴛ. | **ADELAIDE** in seven lines.

     R: Female seated, holding scales and cornucopia.
A ship in the distance. AUSTRALIA 1858.

228. O : JOHN HOWELL | BOOKSELLER | RUNDLE
St. | ADELAIDE in four lines.

R : A bird (the liver) holding an olive branch in its
mouth LIVERPOOL CHEAP BOOK DEPÔT.

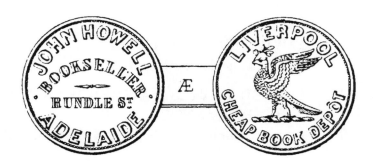

229. O : JOHN HOWELL | BOOKSELLER | HINDLEY
St. | . ADELAIDE . in four lines.

R : As last.

230. O : JOHN   MARTIN | GROCER | AND | TEA
DEALER | 29 | RUNDLE STREET |
ADELAIDE in seven lines.

R : Female standing, holding scales and cornucopia.
AUSTRALIA.

231. O : MARTIN   &   SACH   IRONMONGERS
. ADELAIDE .

R : As last.

232. O : WILLIAM MORGAN | WHOLESALE | & |
RETAIL | GROCER | HINDLEY STREET |
ADELAIDE in seven lines.

R : Female seated, holding scales and cornucopia.
A ship in the distance. AUSTRALIA 1858.

233. O : ALFRED TAYLOR | DRAPER | AND |
CLOTHIER | ADELAIDE | 31 RUNDLE
STREET in six lines.

R : As 230.

Halfpenny size.

234. *O :* CROCKER AND HAMILTON . 1857 .
DRAPERS | SILKMERCERS | AND | CLOTHIERS.

R : View of shop REGENT HOUSE over door. TAILORS
on left window DRAPERS on right. ADELAIDE,
PORT ADELAIDE . AND BURRABURRA.

WESTERN AUSTRALIA.
Freemantle.

Penny size.

235. *O :* ALFRED DAVIES PAWNBROKER HIGH
Sᵀ· FREEMANTLE.

R : A swan swimming WESTERN AUSTRALIA
1865.

236. *O :* Australian arms JOHN HENDERSON
PAWNBROKER.

R : View of shop ONE PENNY TOKEN under. PACK-
ENHAM STREET FREEMANTLE W.A.

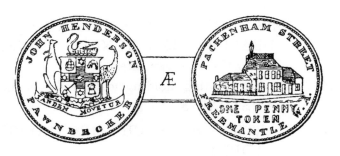

TASMANIA (OR VAN DIEMAN'S LAND).
Campbell Town.

Penny size.

237. *O :* JOSEPH BRICKHILL . DRAPER | AND |
GENERAL IMPORTER . CAMPBELL TOWN.

R : ONE PENNY TOKEN . ADVANCE TASMANIA
1856 . COMMERCIAL HOUSE.

Deloraine.

238. *O :* SAMUEL HENRY DELORAINE EMPORIUM.

R : Kangaroo and emu. TASMANIA 1857.

Hobart Town.

239.   O: LEWIS ABRAHAMS | DRAPER | LIVER-
              POOL STREET | HOBART TOWN.
       R: As last, except date, 1855.

240.   O: J. G. FLEMING . GROCER & TEA DEALER.
              An ornamental wreath in centre within a
              beaded circle.
       R: A sugar-loaf with the letter F upon it, in centre
              within a beaded circle.   SUGAR LOAF
              . HOBART TOWN 1874.

241.   O: I. FRIEDMAN PAWNBROKER ARGYLE
              STREET.
       R: Female seated holding scales and cornucopia.
              A ship in the distance . TASMANIA 1857.

242.   O: O . H | HEDBERG in two lines in the centre,
              OIL & COLOR STORES ❖ ARGYLE
              S̤T HOBART TON ❖
       R: ONE | PENNY in two lines in centre.   O . H .
              HEDBERG ❖ SWEDISH   HOUSE
              HOBART TON ❖

243.   O: As last.
       R: Female seated.   MELBOURNE VICTORIA
              1860.

244.   O: As R: of No. 242.
       R: Britannia seated, holding olive branch and wand.
              AUSTRALIA.
              These two are undoubtedly *mules*.

245.   O: R. HENRY. | WHOLESALE | AND RETAIL |
              IRONMONGER | 94 LIVERPOOL S̤T |
              HOBART TOWN. in five lines.
       R: Three saws and agricultural implements.   ONE
              PENNY   TOKEN . PAYABLE   ON
              DEMAND AT R. HENRY'S.

246.   O: A saw and sickle in centre.   G. HUTTON
              IRONMONGER . HOBART TOWN.
       R: A kangaroo and emu.

247. *O*: WILLIAM ANDREW JARVEY | PAWN-BROKER | AND GENERAL | CLOTHIER | HOBART TOWN in five lines.

R: Three balls suspended by chains from a staff. ONE PENNY TOKEN PAYABLE AT W. A. JARVEY'S . MURRAY STREET.

248. Similar to last, except that the three balls are smaller, and are suspended by rods, not chains, from an ornamental bracket.

249. *O*: A bouquet. H. LIPSCOMBE . MURRAY STREET . HOBART TOWN . ❃ SEEDSMAN & SALESMAN ❃

R: ONE PENNY | TOKEN in two lines in centre. SHIPPING SUPPLIED WITH ALL KINDS OF COLONIAL PRODUCE ✻

250. *O*: H. J. MARSH & BROTHER | IRONMONGERS | MURRY AND | COLLINS ST. | HOBART TOWN in five lines.

R: A scythe head and two knives within a circle, a spade and fork crossed under. ONE SHILLING FOR 12 PENNY TOKENS . PAYABLE AT H. J. MARSH & BROTHER. The scythe and knives are in an inner circle.

251. *O*: Similar to last, excepting name of street is spelt MURRAY, and shape of letters is different.

R: Similar tools to last, but no inner circle.

252. Similar to No. 251 excepting that the tools are differently arranged.

253. *O*: R. ANDREW MATHER . FAMILY DRAPER &c. HOBART TOWN.

R: Female standing, holding scales and cornucopia. A ship in the distance . TASMANIA.

254. *O*: JOSEPH MOIR | WHOLESALE | AND | RETAIL | IRONMONGERY | ESTABLISHMENT | 1850 | HOBART TOWN in eight lines.

R: ONE | PENNY TOKEN | PAYABLE | ON DEMAND | HERE in five lines in centre. ECONOMY HOUSE MURRY STREET.

255. *O*:   A. NICHOLAS | 30 | Liverpool S.^t in three lines in centre. **LIVERPOOL TEA WAREHOUSE** * HOBARTON *

   R: The arms of Liverpool, with supporters, crest, &c.

256. *O*:   ALFRED NICHOLAS | LIVERPOOL | **TEA WAREHOUSE** | LIVERPOOL S.^{T.} | HOBART TOWN in five lines.

   R: Britannia seated, holding palm branch and trident . BRITANNIA.

257. *O*:   R. S. WATERHOUSE | DRAPERY | ESTABLISHMENT | HOBART TOWN | ONE PENNY | TOKEN | MANCHESTER HOUSE in seven lines.

   R: A baby in a "jumper." BABY LINEN — WAREHOUSE — FOR READY MONEY — THE SPIRIT OF TRADE.

258. *O*:   W. D. WOOD | WINE | & | SPIRIT | MERCHANT in five lines in centre. MONT-PELIER RETREAT HOBART TOWN.

   R: A view of the Montpelier Retreat Inn. HOBART TOWN 1855.

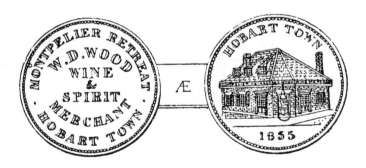

259. *O*:   ONE PENNY TOKEN | PAYABLE | ON DEMAND | HERE | MONTPELIER RETREAT | INN | HOBART TOWN | W. D. WOOD in seven lines.

   R: View of the inn having flagstaff and two trees at back MONTPELIER RETREAT INN W. D. WOOD.

Launceston.

260. *O*: **E. F. DEASE** ONE PENNY in centre. =
WHOLESALE & RETAIL DRAPERY
WAREHOUSE ✣ BRISBANE S͡T ✣

R: A golden fleece. SIC VOS NON VOBIS
VELLERA FERTIS OVES ✣ I place
this token on the authority of *Stainsfield.*
It is placed at Hobart Town by *Neumann*
and *Weyl.*

Newtown.

261. *O*: View of toll-house and gate in centre. NEW
TOWN TOLLGATE ✳ R. JOSEPHS ✳

R: Female seated holding scales and cornucopia.
A ship in the distance. VAN DIEMANS
LAND 1855.

Westbury.

262. *O*: THOMAS WHITE AND SON . WESTBURY .

R: Kangaroo and emu. TASMANIA 1855.

263. Similar to last, except date, which is 1857.

Hobart Town.

Halfpenny size.

264. *O*: LEWIS ABRAHAMS DRAPER LIVER-
POOL STREET HOBART TOWN.

R: As No. 262.

265. *O*: I. FRIEDMAN PAWNBROKER ARGYLE
STREET.

R: Female seated, holding scales and cornucopia.
A ship in the distance. TASMANIA 1857.

266. *O*: O. H. HEDBERG in two lines in the centre,
OIL & COLOR STORES . ARGYLE
S͡T HOBART TON.

R: HALF | PENNY in two lines in the centre.
O. H. HEDBERG . SWEDISH HOUSE
HOBART TON.

267. *O*: As *R*: of last.
     R: As No. 260.
268. *O*: As last.
     R: LIPMAN   LEVY   IMPORTER   AND
          MANUFACTURER   OF   BOOTS   &
          SHOES   WELLINGTON   .   NEW
          ZEALAND

These two are evidently *mules.*

269. *O*: A saw and sickle in centre. G. HUTTON
          IRONMONGER HOBART TOWN.
     R: A kangaroo and emu.
270. *O*: H. J. MARSH & BROTHER . IRONMONGERS HOBART TOWN.
     R: A steamship in centre. HALFPENNY TOKEN TO
          FACILITATE TRADE.   See a very similar token
          for Cape of Good Hope.
271. *O*: ALFRED NICHOLAS | LIVERPOOL | TEA WAREHOUSE |
          LIVERPOOL ST | HOBART TOWN in five lines.
     R: Britannia seated holding palm bush and trident
          BRITANNIA.
272. *O*: R. S. WATERHOUSE | DRAPERY |
          ESTABLISHMENT | HALFPENNY |
          TOKEN | MANCHESTER HOUSE in six
          lines.
     R: A baby in "jumper." BABY LINEN —
          WAREHOUSE   —   FOR   READY
          MONEY — THE SPIRIT OF TRADE.
273. *O*: ONE HALFPENNY TOKEN | PAYABLE | ON DEMAND
          HERE | MONTPELIER   RETREAT | INN | HOBART
          TOWN | W. D. WOOD.
     R: View of the inn.   MONTPELIER RETREAT INN W. D.
          WOOD.

Launceston.

274. *O*: E. F. DEASE HALFPENNY WHOLESALE
          & RETAIL DRAPERY WAREHOUSE
          BRISBANE ST
     R: A golden fleece SIC VOS NON VOBIS
          VELLERA FERTIS OVES. *See* No. 260.

New Town.

275. *O :* View of toll-house and gate in centre. NEW
            TOWN TOLL GATE ✻ R . JOSEPHS ✻

      R : Female seated, holding scales and cornucopia.
            A ship in the distance. VAN DIEMANS
            LAND 1855.

Westbury.

276. *O :* THOMAS WHITE AND SON . WESTBURY.
      R : Kangaroo and emu. TASMANIA 1855.

NEW ZEALAND.

Penny size.

277. *O :* ALLIANCE TEA COMPANY | OPPOSITE |
            BANK OF | NEW ZEALAND | ROBERT
            THOMPSON | MANAGER | 1866.

      R : ITALIAN | WAREHOUSE | FANCY |
            GOODS in four lines in the centre. TEAS
            COFFEES FRUITS & SPICES . 1866.

278. *O :* Bust of Maori chief. ADVANCE NEW
            ZEALAND.

      R : Native standing by palm-tree holding shield
            and spear, mountains behind. NEW
            ZEALAND.

279. *O :* Head of queen laureated. Rose, shamrock and
            thistle under. VICTORIA QUEEN OF
            GREAT BRITAIN.

      R : Britannia seated, holding shield and trident.
            NEW ZEALAND 1879.

            The *O :* and *R :* of No. 278 are used as *R :*
            to two tokens of Christchurch. *See* Nos. 307
            and 308.

Auckland.

280. *R*: **H. ASHTON | IMPORTER | OF | HABER-DASHERY | & | TAILORS | TRIM-MINGS | QUEEN S.T AUCKLAND** in eight lines.

R: Female standing, holding scales and cornucopia. A ship in the distance. NEW ZEALAND 1862.

281. Similar to last except date, which is 1863.

282. *O*: Head of Queen laureated in a beaded circle, VICTORIA . BORN MAY 24 1819.

R: AUCKLAND LICENSED VICTUALLERS ASSOCIATION . ESTABLISHED IN **NEW ZEALAND** APRIL 4 1871.

283. *O*: **CHARLES C. BARLEY WHOLESALE GROCER AUCKLAND NEW ZEALAND.**

R: Female seated, holding scales and cornucopia. GOD SAVE THE QUEEN 1858.

284. *O*: **ARCHIBALD CLARK DRAPER** SHORTLAND STREET AUCKLAND

R: Female seated, holding scales and cornucopia, A ship in the distance. NEW ZEALAND 1857.

285. *O*: Bust full faced. SAMUEL COOMBES MANUFACTURING CLOTHIER QUEEN S.T AUCKLAND.

R: **TAILOR, OUTFITTER | QUEEN STREET | AUCKLAND | S. COOMBES | ALBERT STREET | GRAHAM-TOWN | GENTLEMEN'S MERCER** in seven lines.

286. *O*: **T S. FORSAITH** . WHOLESALE & RETAIL RETAIL DRAPER . MANCHESTER HOUSE . AUCKLAND. The latter within a circle.

R: Similar to 284 excepting date, which is 1858.

24 *

287. *O*:　B. GITTOS | LEATHER | MERCHANT | IM-
PORTER OF | BOOTS & SHOES | &c. &c.
in six lines.

R:　WHOLESALE & RETAIL | LEATHER | &
| GRINDERY | STORES | WYNDHAM
STREET | AUCKLAND | N.Z. | 1864　in
nine lines.

288. *O*:　R. GRATTEN THAMES HOTEL AUCKLAND.

R:　A Maori in a canoe, 1872 beneath, within a
wreath of branches of tree fern.

　　　This piece is smaller than the usual penny
size.

289. *O*:　HOLLAND & BUTLER ✳ 28 & 30 VIC-
TORIA S^T. AUCKLAND ✳ in outer circle.
OIL COLOR & GLASS MERCHANTS on a
painter's palette in centre. STOKES & MARTIN
above the palette, MELBOURNE beneath.

R:　IMPORTERS | OF | PAPERHANGINGS |
GILT MOULDINGS | GLASS SHADES
| & | PAINTERS MATERIALS in seven
lines.

290. *O*:　MORRIS MARKS | PAWNBROKER | AND |
SALESMAN | CORNER OF QUEEN ST. |
WELLESLEY ST | AUCKLAND in seven
lines.

R:　Three balls within a circle.

　　　This again is smaller than the usual penny
size.

291. *O*:　A palm-tree in centre. MORRIN & Co. QUEEN
STREET AUCKLAND GROCERS, WINE &
SPIRIT MERCHANTS.

R:　Female standing, holding scales and cornucopia. Behind a Maori and gold digger
joining hands. ADVANCE AUCKLAND.

292. *O* : S. HAGUE SMITH MERCHANT AUCKLAND WHOLESALE & RETAIL IRONMONGER.

R : Bust of Prince Consort. PRINCE ALBERT BORN AUG^T 26 1819 DIED DEC^R 14 1861.

293. *O* : M. SOMERVILLE | WHOLESALE | FAMILY GROCER | CITY MART | AUCKLAND in five lines.

R : A bouquet of rose, shamrock and thistle. NEW ZEALAND . 1857.

A similar design appears on the *R* : of a token of William Hodgins, Banker, Cloghjordan, with the word IRELAND over, and dated 1858. This, although very similar to the Australasian tokens, is Irish.

294. *O* : Head of Queen filleted. VICTORIA DEI GRATIA 1874.

R : UNITED SERVICE | HOTEL in two lines in centre within a circle. CORNER OF QUEEN & WELLESLEY STREETS . AUCKLAND . N.Z.

295. Similar to last except that the words UNITED SERVICE are in a curved line instead of straight.

296. *O* : EDWARD WATERS QUEEN ST. AUCKLAND WHOLESALE & RETAIL CONFECTIONER.

R : Bust of Maori ONE PENNY TOKEN, STOKES & MARTIN MELBOURNE beneath bust.

297. *O* :   MASON STRUTHERS & CO. WHOLESALE AND
             RETAIL IRONMONGERS STOKE & MARTIN MEL-
             BOURNE.

      R :   Similar to last, but not from the same die and
             with maker's name omitted.

             This token has been placed here from the
             similarity of the reverses, but I have not been
             able to ascertain for what New Zealand town
             it was struck.

Christchurch.

298. *O* :   J. CARO | & CO. | HIGH ST. in three lines
             within a circle. GENERAL IRONMON-
             GERS : CHRISTCHURCH :

      R :   A man ploughing. TRADE AND AGRICULTURE
             STOKES MELB at foot.

299. *O* :   S. CLARKSON | BUILDER | & | IMPORTER |
             CASHEL STREET | CHRIST | CHURCH
             NEW ZEALAND in eight lines.

      R :   Female seated holding scales and cornucopia.
             Ship in distance NEW ZEALAND 1875.

300.   Similar to last, but with two branches crossed
             in place of words BUILDER &.

301. *O* :   A stove in centre. T. W. GOURLAY & Co.
             IMPORTERS OF — AND KITCHENERS CHRIST-
             CHURCH.

      R :   A saw in centre. ECONOMY HOUSE HIGH
             STREET BUILDERS AND FURNISHING IRON-
             MONGERY.

302. *O* :   ONE PENNY between two lines in centre.
             HENRY J. HALL ✿ CHRISTCHURCH
             COFFEE MILLS ✿

      R :   H. J. HALL in centre between two lines.
             FAMILY GROCER ✿ WINE & SPIRIT
             MERCHANT ✿

303. *O* : H. J. HALL in centre between two lines. CHRISTCHURCH ❀ COFFEE MILLS ❀

R : As last.

304. *O* : As last excepting that there are no lines or crosses.

R : H. J. HALL in centre. FAMILY GROCER : WINE & SPIRIT MERCHANT :

305. *O* : As No. 302.

R : Kangaroo and emu. This is evidently a *mule.*

306. *O* : HOBDAY & JOBBERNS DRAPERS WATERLOO HOUSE° CHRISTCHURCH°

R : Arms of the province of Canterbury. AD-VANCE CANTERBURY on a scroll under shield.

307. *O* : A lyre, two trumpets, &c. within a wreath, radiated, a Cupid above, CHRISTCHURCH 1881 below. MILNER & THOMPSON'S CANTERBURY MUSIC DEPÔT & PIANOFORTE WAREHOUSE.

R : Bust of Maori chief. ADVANCE NEW ZEALAND.

308. *O* : SOLE AGENTS | FOR | JOHN BRINS-MEAD | & SONS | PIANOS in five lines in centre. Legend round as last.

R : Maori standing, holding shield, landscape with mountains in distance. NEW ZEALAND.

The *O* : and *R* : of Nos. 307 and 308 have been "muled" and thus three other varieties have been made, all of which appear alike to have been in circulation.

309. *O* : W. PETERSEN : HIGH ST. CHRIST-CHURCH : in outer circle. WATCH-MAKER AND . JEWELLER . in centre.

R : A cup, timepiece, and watch in centre. EVERYTHING SOLD GUARANTEED ALL REPAIRS WELL EXECUTED.

310. *O* : WILLIAM PRATT DIRECT IMPORTER OF EVERY DESCRIPTION OF LINEN DRAPERY AND CLOTHING.

R : ESTABLISHED 1854 in centre. DUNSTABLE HOUSE CASHEL STREET CHRISTCHURCH N.Z.

311. *O* : EDWARD REECE | WHOLESALE | AND RETAIL | BUILDERS | AND FURNISHING | IRONMONGER | BIRMINGHAM | AND SHEFFIELD | WAREHOUSE | CHRISTCHURCH | CANTERBURY | N.Z. in twelve lines.

R : A man shearing a sheep, and a wheatsheaf and sickle. ADVANCE CANTERBURY NEW ZEALAND.

312. *O* : A wheatsheaf, UNION BAKERY COMPANY above it, CHRISTCHURCH beneath.

R : WHOLESALE | AND | RETAIL | BAKERS | CONFECTIONERS | AND | GROCERS displayed in seven lines.

Dunedin.

313. *O* : DAY & MIEVILLE | MERCHANTS | DUNEDIN | OTAGO in four lines.

R : Female seated, holding scales and cornucopia, a ship in the distance. NEW ZEALAND 1857

314. *O* : Royal arms within the garter crowned. " E. DE CARLE & CO MERCHANTS DUNEDIN OTAGO."

R : Female seated, holding scales and cornucopia. VIVANT REGINA 1862.

This is rather smaller than usual penny size.

315. *O* : JONES & WILLIAMSON | WHOLESALE | & | RETAIL | GROCERS | WINE, SPIRIT, | & PROVISION | MERCHANTS | DUNEDIN in nine lines.

R : Similar to No. 313 excepting date, which is 1858.

316. *O*: PERKINS & CO. 𝔇𝔯𝔞𝔭𝔢𝔯𝔰 DUNEDIN.
 R: Female seated, holding scales and cornucopia, a ship in the distance. DUNEDIN NEW ZEALAND.
   This again is a small size penny.

317. *O*: A. S. WILSON | DUNEDIN | OTAGO | MEDICAL HALL in four lines.
 R: As No. 313.

Grahamstown.

318. *O*: 𝔊eorge 𝔐c𝔊aul, COPPERSMITH TINSMITH PLUMBER AND GASFITTER 𝔊raḥamstoⱳn in the centre within a circle . N . E . W . . . . Z . E . A . ·L . A . N . D . . . . extending all round, 18 — 74 at the sides.
 R: Engine house and shaft. ADVANCE THAMES GOLDFIELDS under, in an inner circle.

Invercargill.

319. *O*: S. BEAVEN IRONMONGER & MERCHANT INVERCARGILL N.Z.
 R: Australian Arms PEACE & PLENTY 1863.

Nelson.

320. *O*: J. M. MERRINGTON & Co. | WHOLESALE | & | RETAIL | DRAPERS | & | OUTFIT-TERS | NELSON in eight lines.
 R: Female standing, holding scales and cornucopia. ADVANCE NEW ZEALAND.

New Plymouth.

321. *O*: JOHN GILMOUR NEW PLYMOUTH . NEW ZEALAND .
 R: A New Zealand landscape.

Taranaki.

322. *O :* BROWN AND DUTHIE WHOLESALE &
RETAIL IRONMONGERS BROUGHAM
STREET.

R : View of Mount Egmont, TARANAKI 1866.

Timaru.

323. *O :* CLARKSON AND TURNBULL . 1865 .
GENERAL | IMPORTERS | DRAPERS | CLOTHIERS | &c.
the latter in five lines within a beaded circle.

R : View of harbour, a steamship and lighthouse.
NEW ZEALAND above, TIMARU below.

Wanganui.

324. *O :* J. HURLEY & CO. SHIPPING | SUPPLIED
WANGANUI | NEW ZEALAND in centre, with-
in a circle. CONFECTIONERS, BAKERS, & GROCERS ·
ESTABLISHED 1853 in outer circle.

R : Female seated holding anchor, by her side
a beehive and cornucopia, two wheatsheafs
and a bale in the background, a ship on the
sea in the distance.

Wellington.

325. *O :* D. ANDERSON'S GENERAL STORES .
WELLINGTON.

R : Female standing, holding scales and cornucopia,
a ship in the distance.

326. *O :* KIRCALDIE & STAINS GENERAL DRAPERS AND
OUTFITTERS . WELLINGTON.

R : Shield of Arms, Crest, and Motto (FORTISSIMA
VERITAS) KIRKCALDIE & STAINS .
WELLINGTON .

This is another small sized penny.

327. *O*: LIPMAN LEVY IMPORTER AND MANU-
FACTURER OF BOOTS & SHOES . WEL-
LINGTON . NEW ZEALAND.

R: LEATHER | & GRINDERY | OF ALL | DE-
SCRIPTION | THE TRADE | SUPPLIED
in six lines in the centre. ONE PENNY
TOKEN . PAYABLE AT L. LEVY'S LAMBTON
QUAY . around the token.

328. *O*: As last.

R: Draped and laureated bust of Wellington
WELLINGTON & ERIN GO BRAGH.

329. *O*: As last.

R: Britannia seated, holding olive branch and
wand. AUSTRALIA.

These two tokens are suspiciously like
mules, and are always in fine condition.

330. *O*: JAMES WALLACE GROCER &c. . WEL-
LINGTON .

R: Female sitting, holding scales and cornucopia,
a ship in the distance 1859.

Auckland.

Halfpenny size.

331. *O*: H. ASHTON | IMPORTER | OF | HABER-
DASHERY | & | TAILORS | TRIMMINGS
QUEEN Sᵀ AUCKLAND in eight lines.

R: Female seated, holding scales and cornucopia,
a ship in the distance. NEW ZEALAND
1858.

332. Similar to last excepting date, which is 1859.

333. *O*: T. S. FORSAITH . WHOLESALE & RETAIL
DRAPER . MANCHESTER | HOUSE |.
AUCKLAND . The latter within a circle.

R: As No. 331.

Christchurch.

334. *O* :   HALF | PENNY between two lines in centre.
             HENRY J. HALL . CHRISTCHURCH
             COFFEE MILLS .

      R :   H. J. HALL between two lines in centre.
             FAMILY GROCER . WINE & SPIRIT
             MERCHANT .

335. *O* :   As last.

      R :   LIPMAN LEVY. *See* No. 327.

336. *O* :   As *R* : of 334.

      R :   A golden fleece. *See* No. 260.
                     These two are evidently *mules*.

337. *O* :   EDWARD REECE. Similar to No. 311,
             excepting in size and value.

Wanganui.

338.   T. HURLET & CO. Similar to No. 324,
             excepting in size and value.

Wellington.

339.   D. ANDERSON. Similar to No. 325, excepting
             in size and value.

340.   KIRKCALDIE & STAINS. Similar to No.
             326, excepting in size and value.

341.   LIPMAN LEVY. Similar to No. 327, except-
             ing that HALFPENNY is substituted for
             ONE PENNY on reverse.

342. *O* :   A saddle and stirrup in centre. J. W. MEARS
             SADLER . LAMBTON QUAY WELLING-
             TON .

      R :   ONE HALFPENNY TOKEN . PAYABLE
             AT J. W. MEARS COLLAR AND HAR-
             NESS MAKER . NEW ZEALAND.

343.   JAMES WALLACE. Similar to No. 330
             except in size and value.

MISCELLANEOUS.

Penny size.

344. O: ONE PENNY in two lines within an inner
circle. ADVANCE AUSTRALIA ⚜ ⚜ ⚜

   R: Kangaroo and emu. Maker's name and
address under, W. J. TAYLOR LONDON.

345. O: Australian Arms. PEACE & PLENTY 1859.

   R: Female seated, holding scales and cornucopia,
ship in distance, 1859 beneath.

      These are most likely *mules,* as each of
the sides have been used for other tokens.

346. O: THE AUSTRALIAN | TOKENS | MANUFACTURED BY
| T. POPE & CO. | (COIN & PRESS MAKERS |
ST. PAUL'S SQR. | BIRMINGHAM,) | ARE VERY
PROFITABLE | TO EXPORT in nine lines.

   R: Britannia seated, holding olive branch and
trident, ship in distance. BRITANNIA.

      This token, in more senses than one,
" speaks for itself."

347. O: Head of Professor Holloway, J. MOORE incused
on the neck. PROFESSOR HOLLOWAY
LONDON.

   R: Hygeia seated. HOLLOWAY'S PILLS AND
OINTMENT 1857.

348.   Similar to last, excepting date, which is 1858.

Halfpenny size.

349.   Similar to No. 347, except in size and value.

350.   Similar to No. 348, except in size and value.

      These four pieces were used in the Austra-
lian Colonies as small change. There is a
specimen of No. 347 in the Author's cabinet
countermarked as follows—THOMAS AGENT
GEELONG.

351. O: Head of Queen filleted, VICTORIA 5TH
OCTOBER 1857.

   R: View of Church, 1851 beneath.

INDEX.

—————•┼•—————

₊ The legends upon the various pieces will be found in
the index printed in Italics.

A.

C.

D.

N.

U.

V.

NUMISMATIC WORKS

on sale by

BERNARD QUARITCH, 15 Piccadilly, LONDON.

————————⊰⋈⊱————————

HAWKINS' SILVER COINS OF ENGLAND, THIRD EDITION, revised and enlarged by R. LL. KENYON, Esq., thick 8vo., 508 *pp. and 55 plates containing figures of about 520 Coins, by F. W. Fairholt and F. J. Lees, Roxburghe, gilt top*, £1. 16*s* 1887

" A third edition having been called for, the text has been carefully revised, and the coins found and published during the last ten years have been described in their proper places. Several additions have been made to the lists of the mints before the Conquest, and some additions and alterations have been made throughout the work. But the most important alteration has been in the reign of Edward III, where it is shown that all of the coins hitherto attributed to him were struck subsequently to 1351, and that those struck before, during, and after the Treaty of Bretigny, may be distinguished by the titles inscribed on them ; in accordance with the arrangement adopted by the editor in his book on English Gold Coins This will clear the way for a more satisfactory arrangement than has hitherto been possible of the coins which have been attributed to Edward I and II, but some of which must now be given to the first half of Edward III's reign ; but such a redistribution can only be made after careful examination of a very large number of these coins, and for such examination the editor has lately had neither time nor opportunity."—*Preface to the Third Edition.*

The Companion to Hawkins' SILVER *Coins of England:*

KENYON'S HISTORY OF THE GOLD COINAGE OF ENGLAND, by R. LL. KENYON, *Editor of the third edition of Hawkins' Silver Coins of England,* 1 vol. demy 8vo., (*uniform with the work of Hawkins*), 24 *plates, engraved by* F. J. LEES, *Member of the Numismatic Society, Roxburghe, gilt top*, 24*s* 1883

This work contains a complete account of the English current gold coins, from the earliest Saxon times to the present reign, with 200 illustrations, and includes a description of gold coins attributed to the first half of the seventh century. It is hoped that the light which an examination of the gold coins throws upon the proper appropriation of the silver, as for instance in the reigns of Henry V and VI and of Edward V, together with the information about the history of the coinage which this volume contains, may make it acceptable to collectors, even though their cabinets may not contain a great number of gold coins.

MONTAGU'S COPPER COINAGE OF ENGLAND: The Copper, Tin and Bronze Coinage and Patterns for Coins of England, from the Reign of Elizabeth to that of Her present Majesty, royal 8vo. *numerous woodcuts of Groats, Pennies, Half-pennies and Farthings, Roxburghe, gilt top,* 10s 6d   1885

> The standard work on the Copper Coinage of this Country.

AKERMAN'S COINS OF THE ROMANS relating to Britain, described and illustrated, second edition, greatly enlarged, 8vo. *7 plates and many woodcuts, cloth,* 10s 6d   1844

> The object of this little work is to bring under one view the coins of the Romans which relate to the province of Britain. It is hoped that it will not only find favour with the antiquary and the numismatist, but will also interest all who are curious in the early history of our island; some of the principal events in which, during a long period of the Roman occupation, are recorded on the coins of the conquerors.

*** BERNARD QUARITCH is the Agent of the

NUMISMATIC SOCIETY OF LONDON,

and supplies recent and back numbers of their
CHRONICLE.

CPSIA information can be obtained
at www.ICGtesting.com
Printed in the USA
BVHW01*1545190218
508513BV00008B/107/P

9 780260 284761